"Practical and easy to use. You'll come back to this resource over and over again in your work with couples and families."

Gary Chapman, Marriage & Family Life Consultants, Inc. and author of *The 5 Love Languages*

"If you work with couples or families, this book is an indispensable resource! The authors address real issues and give practical steps to financial and relational health."

Les Parrott, author of *You're Stronger Than You Think*

"Tim Clinton and Scott and Bethany Palmer have tackled a critical topic with *The Quick-Reference Guide to Counseling on Money, Finances & Relationships*. In a day when so many marriages are negatively impacted by financial conflicts, this book will be an invaluable resource to Christian therapists seeking to help couples resolve their 'money issues.'"

Bill Maier, clinical psychologist and radio host

"I've had the privilege, over almost 40 years, of answering thousands of financial questions and have come to the firm conclusion that almost every financial problem is symptomatic of a spiritual or emotional issue. In many cases the real need is not a financial counselor, but a professional counselor. I am delighted to see this book as a tool for the counseling world."

Ron Blue, president, Kingdom Advisors

The Quick-Reference Guide to

COUNSELING ON MONEY, FINANCES & RELATIONSHIPS

DR. TIM CLINTON
and
BETHANY and SCOTT PALMER

BakerBooks
a division of Baker Publishing Group
Grand Rapids, Michigan

© 2012 by Tim Clinton

Published by Baker Books
a division of Baker Publishing Group
P.O. Box 6287, Grand Rapids, MI 49516-6287
www.bakerbooks.com

Printed in the United States of America

Library of Congress Cataloging-in-Publication Data
Clinton, Timothy E., 1960–
    The quick-reference guide to counseling on money, finances & relationships /
Tim Clinton and Bethany and Scott Palmer.
        p.   cm.
    ISBN 978–0–8010–7233–8 (pbk.)
    1. Money—Religious aspects—Christianity. 2. Wealth—Religious aspects—
Christianity. 3. Interpersonal relations—Religious aspects—Christianity. I. Palmer,
Bethany, 1965– II. Palmer, Scott, 1971– III. Title.
BR115.W4C58 2012
253.5—dc23   2012022181

To protect the privacy of those who have shared their stories with the authors, details and names have been changed.

The internet addresses, email addresses, and phone numbers in this book are accurate at the time of publication. They are provided as a resource. Baker Publishing Group does not endorse them or vouch for their content or permanence.

12   13   14   15   16   17   18   7   6   5   4   3   2   1

Contents

Introduction

Because money is both a universal blessing and concern, *The Quick-Reference Guide to Counseling on Money, Finances & Relationships* is designed to equip professional counselors, pastors, and lay counselors to help those who are struggling with many and varied financial issues in relationships. Many (if not most) people who come for help with relational and emotional problems struggle also with their finances. Money may not be the main reason they came for help, but it's a significant contributing factor—due to the fact that money affects just about every aspect of life. If we scratch below the surface, we may realize many of their personal stresses relate to money, and many of the relational difficulties they face are directly related to conflict over money. Studies show that disagreements about money were a major contributing factor in 70 percent of divorces *(First Comes Love, Then Comes Money)*. Often financial struggles complicate the emotional and relational difficulties in the lives of those who come for counseling, but relatively few counselors address this important topic.

In this guide we focus on three important areas:

1. Defining a financial relationship
2. The five Money Personalities
3. Forty financial relationship topics

The purpose of this guide is to address the needs of people under emotional and relational strain because of financial problems, no matter how these problems have occurred—through debt or any other factor. People whose financial struggles have produced anxiety, depression, and family conflict need understanding, support, and direction.

Each of the forty topics includes insights about how to approach clients across the financial spectrum. The issue isn't how much money an individual or a couple has, but how they are handling stress and communication related to their finances.

If you are a professional counselor, this guide can help you:

- accurately determine a client's problems by using the assessments in each section
- see a client's problem and solutions from a biblical perspective

- give clear guidance to your clients so they can take steps forward to resolve pressing financial-communication problems
- create a network of financial professionals and other resources for your clients

If you are a pastor or lay counselor, we recommend that you take time to read through the entire book, marking key points in each section that stand out to you. As you become familiar with the topics, problems, approaches, and resources, you can make a list of referral resources in your community. The guide will help you:

- gain information about the nature of money challenges
- assist you in compiling a list of competent referral resources
- assess the nature and severity of the person's problem
- remind you that there are limits to a lay caregiver's role

ESTABLISH A NETWORK OF FINANCIAL PROFESSIONALS

Financial stresses complicate the lives of many of the people who come for emotional, relational, and spiritual counseling. Often those who are struggling in marriage or raising teenagers argue about money. People who are depressed may have gone "over the edge" because of financial trouble or they may experience the strains of low income and debt because they are so depressed they can't work. Some people use spending like a drug, hoping the next new purchase will give them relief and a moment of happiness.

Many counselors avoid addressing financial issues because they don't feel competent in this area—and perhaps because they struggle with their own finances. The purpose of this book is not to urge you to become an expert in financial management, but instead, to provide insights to help you address this crucial issue when it arises in the lives of your clients.

In many (if not most) cases, your clients will need more help with financial matters than you can offer, so it's important for you to find and vet a few financial professionals you can trust. Some specialize in helping people who are buried in debt, and others can help with mortgages, insurance, or legal matters. In your church and your community, look for insurance agents, financial planners, and attorneys who have a sterling reputation for compassion and excellence in their field. Creating this network takes time, but it will be a valuable resource for many of your clients—and when these professionals have clients with emotional problems, they'll probably refer them to you.

HOW TO USE THIS GUIDE

This Quick-Reference Guide provides insights and resources to help you assess problems and offer effective solutions. The elements in each section are:

1. **Portraits.** The Portraits show how a specific issue (for example, setting goals, debt, budgeting, compulsive shopping) surfaces in individual lives and relationships. We provide several portraits for each topic because one issue can present itself in different ways in different individuals' lives.

2. **Definitions and Key Thoughts.** This section will help you understand the nuances of the problem and provide direction for your conversations with the person.

3. **Assessment Interview.** For each topic this section provides important, probing questions you can use to assess the person's needs and situation.

4. **Wise Counsel.** Here there are additional insights into the problem, the biblical perspective, the path forward, or another issue related to your care for people.

5. **Action Steps.** This is one of the most important sections in the guide because it helps your conversation move from assessment to creating a map and a workable plan for financial health.

6. **Biblical Insights.** Here we provide passages of Scripture that relate to the topic and several important points that help to explain the significance of the passage. You may want to share these passages with clients or you may choose to study them yourself to enrich your understanding of how God works to change lives. Many of the Scriptures can be used for several topics. For example, passages about financial discipline, hope, and patience relate very broadly. Take some time to look over the passages related to each topic to find ones that apply to the people who come to you for help.

7. **Prayer Starter.** Many Christians welcome—and even expect—prayer as an integral part of the counseling process, but prayer is not appropriate with everyone. If a person isn't a believer or has shown resistance to God, you can pray silently during the session or after the appointment is over and the person has left. We realize individual preferences about prayer and the needs of those we help differ greatly, but we didn't want to overlook prayer as an essential element in biblical counseling. The Prayer Starter sections provide a few simple lines to begin lifting up a prayer out loud or silently, during the appointment or at other times.

8. **Recommended Resources.** This guide is not meant to provide you with an exhaustive look at any of the topics. For each topic, we suggest resources that give an overview and provide a brief template for addressing the needs. Continuing education is very important, so each Recommended Resources section lists at least a few books or multimedia programs we have found to be useful and trustworthy.

ADDITIONAL RESOURCES

The American Association of Christian Counselors (AACC) provides training, curricula, books, workshops, and other resources to equip people to care for others. At the end of each topic in this guide, you'll find specific resources for that issue, but we recommend additional materials and online help for those who want broader input on counseling topics and skills. These include:

The Bible for Hope: Caring for People God's Way by Dr. Tim Clinton (Thomas Nelson).

Caring for People God's Way: Personal and Emotional Issues, Addictions, Grief, and Trauma by Tim Clinton, Archibald Hart, and George Ohlschlager (Thomas Nelson).

Other valuable training resources are offered through Light University Online (www.lightuonline.com). Programs include:

Biblical Counseling

Professional Life Coaching

Crisis Response and Trauma Care

In addition, the AACC offers many more resources and training on three websites:

www.ecounseling.com

www.aacc.net

Continue to sharpen your skills and deepen your understanding of issues that affect the people God puts in your path. These resources can help:

www.crown.org

www.themoneycouple.com

. . . .

The American Association of Christian Counselors has nearly fifty thousand members throughout the country and around the world. The AACC is dedicated to providing the finest resources to help professional counselors, pastors, and lay counselors care for hurting people. Outstanding training, books, and events augment membership benefits that include the magazine, *Christian Counseling Today*. For more information about the AACC, go to www.aacc.net.

Defining a Financial Relationship

Researchers have found that 75 percent of divorces in the US involve financial conflict. We are finding that it isn't the broken financial plan that is tearing relationships apart; it is the bickering, the fighting, and the grating on each other's nerves that is. How can people stop fighting, learn to understand each other in a whole new way, and actually want to have discussions about money? How can they have a healthy Money Relationship?

After all, doesn't money affect nearly every decision a couple makes and doesn't money affect every couple you work with? Think about these questions:

- Doesn't money affect where they go on vacation?
- Doesn't money affect the kind of wedding a couple pulls together?
- Doesn't money affect where a couple works?
- Doesn't money affect where a couple buys their groceries?
- Doesn't money affect where a couple gets their coffee?
- Doesn't money affect what grade of gasoline a couple puts in their car?

So the challenge is, how can a couple have a Money Relationship (not a financial plan) that will allow passion to return to their interactions and provide the sense that they are both being heard?

While helping couples, it is absolutely imperative that you understand that couples have a Money Relationship. It is crucial to remember that the success of a couple's Money Relationship is measured by their having fewer and fewer thoughts like:

- Why doesn't my spouse take our finances seriously?
- Why do I feel like my spouse wants to control our finances?
- Why can't I take some risks with our money?
- Why can't we ever get ahead?
- Why do I always feel that I am under a magnifying glass when I spend money?

As counselors we need to assess how a couple views money and quickly get an understanding of their money differences. Our goals must be to help them understand their individuality and to work at bringing them back together. When we understand the Money Personality of our clients, we have a whole new way to assess and diagnosis their problems and to understand their Money Relationship. If we agree that money affects just about every discussion, every day, then having this tool will prove to be the key that opens the door to more harmony for the couples we serve.

Identifying the Five Money Personalities

As you read through these Money Personalities, remember that everyone has two of the five Money Personalities—a primary and a secondary personality.

The five Money Personalities are:

- **Saver**. Savers rarely spend impulsively. They will scour the internet for deals, figure out how to save money on a vacation, and make sure they have the money in hand before making a purchase. They avoid credit card debt like head lice. Savers hate paying interest and accruing debt. They want to pay off every bill, in full, right away.
- **Spender.** Spenders are carefree with their money. They aren't concerned about how much they spend or on whom they spend money. They aren't necessarily rich—we know Spenders who can do some serious shopping at the dollar store. Spenders just like spending.
- **Risk Taker**. For the Risk Taker the thrill of jumping into a financial challenge doesn't come just from a huge payout on an investment. It comes from taking the risk in the first place. Even if they never hit it big, Risk Takers never give up on following the rush they get from trying out a new idea, even if it costs them everything. It's just how they're wired.
- **Security Seeker**. Security Seekers like to know the financial future is settled and safe. They are all about low-risk investments, hefty life and property insurance, and secure retirement funds. When it comes to money, the Security Seeker's motto is "The safer, the better."
- **Flyer**. The Flyer is perhaps the most unusual Money Personality in that the personality has very little to do with money. Flyers don't think about money—at all. They're not anxious about it, they're not consumed by it. They have absolutely no emotional response to money.

Adolescent Children and Allowances

1 PORTRAITS

- Susan and her husband got a divorce a year ago. Their son, Alex, is fifteen years old and lives with her. Everyone has been deeply hurt by the breakup of the family. Alex masks his hurt with plenty of anger and he has begun hanging out with kids who smoke weed. He's become emotionally withdrawn from Susan. To try to win him back, she has offered him a car when he turns sixteen in a few months. In addition, she gives him lots of money for clothes, games, and electronics—an expense she can't afford. But no matter how much she gives him, it's never enough to get him out of his seething depression.

- Jack is only thirteen but he's following in his father's footsteps as the ultimate bargain shopper. He loves to shop but he hates spending money. When he wants to buy something, he spends days (even weeks) trying to find the best deal. His father is so proud of him, but he's driving his sister and mother nuts. When they argue, his dad always takes his side. What began as idiosyncrasies among the men in the family have become divisive.

- Emily is fourteen. She receives a generous allowance from her parents each week, but when they remind her that she needs to clean up her room as part of the deal, she shrugs and ignores them. Her room is a perpetual pigsty. When they confront her and threaten to withhold her allowance, she flippantly says, "I'm sorry," and complains that her life will be ruined if they don't give her the money. She has trained her parents well. No matter how irresponsible she acts, they keep giving in to her whines.

- Since Rob was a baby, his dad has started several businesses. Some of these companies did well, and the family enjoyed prosperity, but some failed. Rob is seventeen but he seems to be very unsure about himself and how to handle money. During some periods of time, he acts like his father—spending freely without a care in the world. But at other times, he becomes insecure and saves every penny he can put his hands on. His mother knows there's something wrong, but she can't put her finger on it.

2 DEFINITIONS AND KEY THOUGHTS

- Psychologists observe that *adolescence* is a pivotal time in human development. Healthy children who are twelve years old have developed a sense of competence,

14

especially by doing their work in school and around the house. As they become adolescents, these kids enter a time when they gain the insights and skills to become successful young adults. From twelve to eighteen years old (and some experts would say into their twenties), children must answer the question of *identity*: Who am I? To be able to navigate these waters, they have to integrate the lessons they learned earlier in life—trust, independence, competence, and self-control.

- Typically during adolescence, children push against authority. In fact, often they take positions that are the opposite of those held by their parents. They may not hold these beliefs long because they're just seeing if their parents will continue to love them if they show a rebellious spirit. Many parents are upset when their "sweet little" boy or girl becomes defiant in these years. They need to understand that it's the child's job to *become an individual*, a separate, healthy young adult. If teenagers continue to act and think like a child, they will be developmentally stunted for life.

- Adolescent years are full of *trial and error*. In school, relationships, hobbies, sports, games, handling money, and every other aspect of life, kids try new things to see if they work. They need room to experiment with new ideas and values, but not so much that they harm themselves or others. Parents, especially *insecure parents*, may feel deeply threatened by their child's new behaviors. In an attempt to control their kids, these parents may prevent them from growing up.

- Parents of adolescents may make one of two opposite *mistakes regarding money*: they overindulge their kids with money and things or they are too rigid and controlling. For children to become strong young adults, they have to internalize *values* and see how those values work out in real life. Overindulgence prevents them from suffering the consequences of poor choices, but rigid control limits their creativity and short-circuits learning.

- In every aspect of their lives, kids need parents to give them "roots and wings," a *solid foundation* of love, respect, and security, and enough freedom to try new things and learn important lessons for the future.

ASSESSMENT INTERVIEW 3

In most cases, parents come for help when they feel their adolescent children are out of control—usually in many areas of life, not just financially. Explain the five Money Personalities and then ask:

1. What is your Money Personality?
2. What is your child's Money Personality?
3. How do your Money Personalities complement and conflict?
4. How would you describe the problem your child is having?
5. How might this problem reflect some insecurity in the family dynamics? What's the connection?
6. How can you avoid the opposite problems of overindulgence and rigid control? What might the "golden mean" of love, respect, and natural consequences look like in your family?

7. Are you afraid to let your child experience the consequences of his poor choices? Where might this fear come from? How does it affect your child?

8. A Money Huddle is designed to facilitate good communication for a couple or a family. It is a time where you set aside all distractions and work on your Money Relationship: evaluate debt and savings, discuss priorities, reflect on successes, and set goals. You need to have this meeting once a month and it should not take more than one hour. How would it help you and your child?

9. What are some steps you need to take to help your child become more mature and responsible with money (and every other part of his life)?

10. How can I help?

4 WISE COUNSEL

The goal of parenting adolescents isn't to control their behavior but to give them a strong foundation and confidence as they take steps in becoming mature young adults. There's a big difference between the maturity of a twelve-year-old and a twenty-year-old, and there's not a button to push to cause instant change. The parent's job is to provide plenty of support while gradually turning more responsibility over to the child to make his own decisions. Some of these choices will be wrong, but the parent needs to be very careful not to bail out the child and prevent him from learning from natural consequences.

Quite often current or past pain in a parent's life causes poor parenting. When parents are wracked by guilt because of past failures, divorce, or financial problems, they may try to buy the love of a child with money and gifts. They may feel out of control and overcorrect by being demanding and rigid, or conversely, they may withdraw and become emotionally distant from the child. The primary problem in these cases is the parent, not the child.

In some families, children learn to play one parent against the other to get their way. These triangles are destructive, based on secret alliances and manipulation. When the adolescent whines and demands his way, one parent supports him against the wishes of the other. This painful dynamic isn't resolved easily. It must be exposed and addressed so that new patterns of respect and honesty become normal. The Money Huddle is a valuable tool to facilitate this process.

Here are some money management principles to impart to adolescents.

- *Start saving early.* If children have a goal to buy something, they'll be motivated to save for it. Parents who give children whatever they want prevent them from learning important principles of discipline and delayed gratification.

- *Allowances come with responsibilities.* Young children and adolescents need to know that money doesn't drop from trees. Experts have different opinions about allowances, but allowances have a more positive impact if children realize they have to do chores to receive them.

- *Natural consequences.* In most cases parents shouldn't just bail out a child who has spent his money and can't buy something he wants—or even needs. It doesn't hurt for a child to do without, feel the pinch, and learn a valuable lesson about budgeting. If the child whines and begs for more, the parent can simply say, "You had complete control over your money and you made a choice. I love you too much to short-circuit the lesson you're going to learn. You'll do better next time, but only if you learn this lesson."

- *How matching funds work*. For large purchases, parents may want to offer to match money the child saves as an encouragement for fiscal discipline. The parent, of course, needs to approve of the item to be purchased—or at least tolerate it. The important issue here isn't the thing that will be bought, but instead, it's the development of prudence and the discipline of saving.
- *Using bank accounts and credit cards*. Checking accounts and credit cards may be appropriate as the child becomes an older adolescent, but parents should put limits on spending and credit. As the child proves to be responsible, these limits can gradually be raised.
- *Money discussions*. Regular, honest discussions about money clear up misconceptions and build relationships in the family, but parents need to make their disclosures and stories age appropriate.

ACTION STEPS : 5

1. Explain the five Money Personalities and help the parent identify himself and his adolescent children. Discuss the way their Money Personalities complement each other and how they may conflict with each other's and with their child's.
2. Discuss principles of active listening, good communication, and conflict resolution, and answer any questions.
3. Go over the principles of money management in the Wise Counsel section and answer any questions. Help the parent determine his priorities and processes in moving forward with his kids.

BIBLICAL INSIGHTS : 6

Hear, O Israel: The LORD our God, the LORD is one. Love the LORD your God with all your heart and with all your soul and with all your strength. These commandments that I give you today are to be on your hearts. Impress them on your children. Talk about them when you sit at home and when you walk along the road, when you lie down and when you get up. Tie them as symbols on your hands and bind them on your foreheads. Write them on the doorframes of your houses and on your gates.

Deuteronomy 6:4–9

Children, including adolescents, are sponges soaking in the atmosphere of their surroundings, and especially the attitudes of their parents. In one of the most important directives given to God's people, Moses tells them to teach, model, and discuss sound principles of godly living with their kids.

Fathers, do not embitter your children, or they will become discouraged.

Colossians 3:21

Dads (and moms too) can exasperate their children in many different ways: by spoiling them, controlling them too tightly, or being too disengaged from them. Our task as parents is to provide plenty of love and affirmation, but gradually give them more freedom to make their own choices, even if some of those choices are poor.

Don't let anyone look down on you because you are young, but set an example for the believers in speech, in conduct, in love, in faith and in purity.

1 Timothy 4:12

Paul encouraged Timothy to be mature and strong. In the same way, the parents' job is to equip their kids to become healthy young adults who can face the world's challenges with confidence and skill.

You then, my son, be strong in the grace that is in Christ Jesus. And the things you have heard me say in the presence of many witnesses entrust to reliable people who will also be qualified to teach others.

2 Timothy 2:1–2

Principles are passed down from generation to generation. Paul reminded Timothy that he was going to relate Paul's heart and purpose to others who would then pass them on to still more people. As we equip our kids with biblical values and behaviors, we can be sure they'll pass them down to their kids and grandkids. It's a legacy of truth, honor, and love.

7 PRAYER STARTER

Father, this parent wants to equip his child for a successful future. He needs your help. Give him wisdom about himself, his child, and his family. Help him trust you for wisdom and strength as he makes changes in the way he handles money, talks about money, and faces the challenges of money. Thank you for your grace . . .

8 RECOMMENDED RESOURCES

Munchbach, Jim. *Make Your Money Count: Connecting Your Resources to What Matters Most*. Baxter Press, 2007.

Palmer, Bethany, and Scott Palmer. *First Comes Love, Then Comes Money: A Couple's Guide to Financial Communication*. HarperOne, 2009.

Ramsey, Dave. *The Total Money Makeover: A Proven Plan for Financial Success*. Thomas Nelson, 2009.

Adult Children

PORTRAITS : 1

- After Barry graduated from college, he moved back home to look for a job. After a few months he found one but he enjoyed eating his mother's cooking—and he really liked not having to pay rent each month. Now he's thirty-four, still single, and working in a job with little promise for the future. At times he seems to be discouraged but he's not motivated to get out and create an independent life for himself. His parents, Bob and Janie, don't know what to do. They love him and are committed to supporting him but they're afraid he's wasting his life. Janie wants Barry to leave and get an apartment, but Bob argues with her. He wants to keep their son around the house so he can keep an eye on him. They are all frustrated, but nothing ever changes.

- Charlotte and her husband, Bryan, live about two hundred miles from her parents. They want to buy a new house because they just had their second child and their apartment seems a little crowded, but they don't have enough money. They have never complained and they didn't ask for any help for a down payment. Her parents want to help them by giving them (or maybe loaning them) $15,000. They can afford it but they're not sure it's the right thing to do.

- Amanda is forty-one. She's been a drug addict since high school. Her parents, Mark and Amy, have tried to help her as much as they can, but her addiction has shredded family relationships. Mark works for a major oil company and makes a good salary with a significant annual bonus. For the past twenty-two years, however, he and Amy have lived in the same little house and have taken few vacations because virtually all their extra money has gone to rehab clinics. There have been a few glimmers of hope over the years, but always within a few months, Amanda has reverted to using cocaine and meth. Her health is a wreck, she has three children by three different men, and she lives with her parents because she can't hold a job. Mark and Amy's other two kids are furious with them—not because of the money, but because Amanda is taking advantage of her parents' kindness and they have no boundaries on their handouts. Family gatherings are few and fierce. Mark and Amy have so much invested in their wayward daughter that they can't imagine pushing her out on her own.

- Joanne got a divorce from Paul a year ago, and she's struggling to make life work for herself and her two young sons. Her parents live nearby. They are glad to come over and help with the kids but they realize Joanne needs more than babysitting. Joanne doesn't want her parents' financial assistance, but her

19

job and child support don't bring in enough. Her dad told her, "Let us give you some money every month for a year until you can get on your feet. Then we'll see how you're doing." Joanne wept. She felt a strange mixture of shame, relief, and love.

2 DEFINITIONS AND KEY THOUGHTS

- We don't sound the debt alarm very often, but when it comes to young adult children asking their parents for help with debt, well, the alarm bells start ringing!

- These days, even nineteen-year-olds can be riddled with *debt*. Student loans, car loans, and credit card debt can add up quickly, leaving young people buried in debt before they've even cashed their first paycheck. And debt follows young people for a long time. Take a look at these sobering statistics:

  — Sallie Mae reports that the average amount of credit card debt held by college graduates is $3,173 (*USA Today*).
  — The average student loan after graduation is $23,000 (projectonstudentdebt.org).
  — 10 percent of college students graduate with a minimum of $39,300 in debt (accepted.com).
  — One out of every five students default on their student loans (projectonstudentdebt.org).

- Parents have to make some tough decisions about how much help to give their child when she ends up deep in debt. Before they write a check, they should ask these questions:

  1. *Where did this debt come from?* Is your child spending money on clothes, Starbucks, and nights out with friends, or is her debt the result of something less predictable, such as medical expenses, a change in her housing situation, the loss of a job, an added college class? If your child has ended up in debt because of unforeseen circumstances and you're able to help her out, do it. If the debt is the result of careless spending, this would be a great time to help her learn how to live within her means.
  2. *Have we bailed our child out before?* Every young adult will run into money problems sooner or later—it's part of growing up. But if your child has chronic money problems and can't seem to work them out on her own, it's time for you to consider seriously how much longer you will help her out of jams. If this is a pattern, your child needs a financial education, not a handout.
  3. *How can we help our child think differently about spending, saving, and debt?* If you don't know your child's Money Personality, this is a great time to figure it out. If your child is a Spender, help her understand her natural propensity toward debt and work out a plan to help her spend within her

means. If she is a Risk Taker, explain how saving more now can help her make smarter investments later. Once you and your child understand how she approaches financial issues, you can find ways to help her deal with her current debt and avoid getting stuck in it again.

4. *When should reality hit?* If your child is spending like crazy, it might be tempting to cut her off and leave her to deal with the consequences. But not every young adult is ready for total financial independence. Most will need to take on a little bit of responsibility at a time. Start your child on the road to independence by going over any credit card statements with her. If you haven't already, explain how credit card companies make money and how much the interest really costs. Help her prioritize her spending and even make a budget and figure out how to pay off her debt. And be transparent. If you have had challenges with debt, share your experiences.

5. *How can we use this conversation to strengthen our relationship with our child?* Your attitude will speak volumes to your child. Make sure you stay calm as you talk about your child's debt. If you decide to bail her out, explain your decision and what you expect in return for your help. If you say no, explain that decision as well and offer your help in working out a plan for paying off the debt. Make sure you and your spouse are both involved in these conversations—a united front tells your child that you care about her and want to work together as a family to find a way forward.

- Young adults are returning home at an increasing rate, but that doesn't mean they have to return to *financial dependence*. Helping your child manage her debt by showing her how to pay it down will be one of the best life skills you can give her.

ASSESSMENT INTERVIEW 3

1. Describe your relationship with your adult child.
2. How strong or unhealthy is your son or daughter emotionally, relationally, vocationally, and financially?
3. Have you helped financially in the past? What were the circumstances? When you stopped, what happened?
4. If you help financially, what do you expect to happen—to your child, to your marriage, to you?
5. If you don't help, what do you expect to happen?
6. How might natural consequences be a good teacher for your son or daughter?
7. Beyond solving the immediate financial problem, what are your hopes for your son or daughter?
8. What part of how you treat your adult child do you and your spouse agree on? What do you disagree about? How does giving so much attention to your child affect you personally and your relationship with each other?
9. How can I help?

4 WISE COUNSEL

Every parent knows that our care and concern for our children doesn't stop when they hit adulthood. But most of us are a little unclear on how that care should play out financially. Trying to figure out when and how to help adult children with money problems can lead parents into all kinds of financial miscommunication and conflict. It doesn't have to be that way. While the best approach for a parent will, of course, depend on the situation, parents need to keep in mind six guidelines as they make financial decisions about their adult children.

1. *Know your child's Money Personality.* You know better than anyone that each of your children is unique. That means they will each deal with money in unique ways. So base your decisions about helping your child on her Money Personality (see http://www.themoneycouple.com/money-personalities.htm) and her history with money. We know a couple whose son has a long history of money problems. He's a Flyer and doesn't think about money or worry too much about whether he has any. But when he needs to repair his car, guess who he calls? Helping him out only perpetuates this cycle. That's very different from a child who handles her money well but needs a one-time loan to cover an unexpected expense.

2. *It's okay not to play fair.* We also see a lot of couples who feel that they need to give all of their children the same things—if one gets money, they all get money. But it really is okay to help one child financially and not another, as long as you have good reasons for doing so. Naturally, you don't want to give or withhold money to manipulate or punish your children, but it can be perfectly fine to say no to one child and yes to another. You can offer equal amounts of love without offering equal amounts of financial assistance.

3. *Respect each other.* We're parents too and we know someone's always a softy when it comes to the kids. If one of you is more inclined to help your child than the other, work to find a compromise—consider giving a smaller loan or offering other kinds of emotional support. Recognize that you both want the best for your child and you need to figure out how to give her just that. And if your spouse says no, don't slip your child a hundred dollars the next time she comes over for dinner. Keep working with your partner to come to a position on which you can both agree. Don't let this decision undermine your relationship with each other.

4. *Don't hurt yourselves to take care of your kids.* We see so many parents who would rather decimate their own resources than see their kids struggle. But giving away money when you can't afford it doesn't help anyone in the long run. Protect yourselves—for your sake and the sake of your children.

5. *Decide if there will be strings.* Most financial transactions, especially those between family members, have some kind of strings attached. If you are giving money to your adult children, be as clear as humanly possible about what you expect in return. If you want to be paid back, talk about a time line and possible interest. If you think helping pay for a car means you get to use it now and then, work out an arrangement that everyone can agree to. If you hope for more visits

or phone calls or meals together, say so. Lay out all the expectations on the front end and avoid the strife that comes with poor financial communication.

6. *If there are strings, get them in writing.* Save everyone the drama of miscommunication and hurt feelings and write down every nuance of your agreement. No expectation is too small. Sign it, have your child sign it, and make copies for both of you. If you are expecting the loan to be repaid, you might want to consider filling out a promissory note (you can find a template at lawdepot. com) that serves as a legally binding agreement.

With a little thought and clear communication, parents can protect their family from the kind of relational damage only money conflicts can cause.

ACTION STEPS : 5

1. Help the parent determine why she wants to help her child. If there is any compulsive behavior or guilt motivation, address these in counseling. If these things aren't discussed, the parent will revert to old habits fairly quickly.
2. Explain the importance of natural consequences as life's best teachers. One of the jobs as parents is to avoid getting in the way of these lessons.
3. Discuss the particular financial needs of the adult child, and help the parent come up with a plan to encourage the child to grow in maturity as well as to provide any financial assistance.
4. Continue to coach and counsel the parent as she implements the principles you've imparted to her.

BIBLICAL INSIGHTS : 6

If your brother or sister sins against you, rebuke them; and if they repent, forgive them. Even if they sin against you seven times in a day and seven times come back to you saying "I repent," you must forgive them.

Luke 17:3–4

Far too often parents confuse loving their adult children with enabling them. When people are sinning by being irresponsible and selfish, we need to rebuke them and forgive them. We do them harm by always bailing them out of their self-inflicted problems.

Then the righteous will answer him, "Lord, when did we see you hungry and feed you, or thirsty and give you something to drink? When did we see you a stranger and invite you in, or needing clothes and clothe you? When did we see you sick or in prison and go to visit you?" The King will reply, "Truly I tell you, whatever you did for one of the least of these brothers and sisters of mine, you did for me."

Matthew 25:37–40

There are times when adult children need their parents' help. With wisdom, love, and patience, we can step in to provide financial assistance (as well as time and energy) to care for a child experiencing health problems or the impact of a natural disaster, or we can offer short-term, targeted support to overcome irresponsible behavior.

Love must be sincere. Hate what is evil; cling to what is good. Be devoted to one another in love. Honor one another above yourselves. Never be lacking in zeal, but keep your spiritual fervor, serving the Lord. Be joyful in hope, patient in affliction, faithful in prayer.

Romans 12:9–12

Parents need to examine their own hearts to determine their motives for financially assisting their adult children. If they are doing it for selfish reasons, they need to stop, repent, and choose a different path. The problem, of course, is that our hearts are full of self-deception. We can convince ourselves that we're pure and noble even if our motives are very selfish.

Live in peace with each other. And we urge you, brothers and sisters, warn those who are idle and disruptive, encourage the disheartened, help the weak, be patient with everyone. Make sure that nobody pays back wrong for wrong, but always strive to do what is good for each other and for everyone else.

1 Thessalonians 5:13–15

Parents need God's wisdom to know when to encourage, when to offer tangible assistance, when to step back and be patient, and when to rebuke a wayward child.

7 PRAYER STARTER

Lord Jesus, we need your help. An adult child is in need, but the parent is not sure what to do. Help her sort out her motives, communicate clearly and wisely, and develop a plan that is best for all concerned. Most of all, Lord, give her a desire to honor you in these decisions . . .

8 RECOMMENDED RESOURCES

Munchbach, Jim. *Make Your Money Count: Connecting Your Resources to What Matters Most.* Baxter Press, 2007.

Palmer, Bethany, and Scott Palmer. *First Comes Love, Then Comes Money: A Couple's Guide to Financial Communication.* HarperOne, 2009.

http://www.ronblue.com/

http://www.mvelopes.com/focusonthefamily/

Aging Parents

- Kate had been happy and independent all her life, even after her husband, Will, died a few years ago. Recently, however, her daughter Marge has been concerned. Kate's chronic health problems have gotten worse, and she's beginning to show signs of dementia. Marge has tried to talk to her mom about moving into an assisted living facility, but her mother adamantly refuses. And besides, Marge isn't sure Social Security and her dad's small pension would be enough to pay the bills there. "I'm afraid I'm going to go over to her house one day and find her dead," Marge told a friend.

- Jerry and Julia both retired fifteen years ago. They thought they had plenty of money in their retirement accounts, but health expenses and a downturn in the market are depleting their savings. Now they worry a lot about what they'll do when the money runs out. They've owned their home for more than forty years, and their son Jonathan has talked to them about the benefits of a reverse mortgage. "Sounds like voodoo to me," Jerry growled. "It might be the best thing for you and Mom," Jonathan said patiently as he explained for the fifth time how it works.

- Lisa has been concerned about her mother for the last several years. When she drives over for her weekly visits, she notices that often her mother has several boxes of things she has bought when she watched shopping channels on television. She doesn't need any of it. When Lisa sneaks a look at her mother's checkbook, she sees large expenses for things that don't make sense—to companies that she has a hard time finding, even online. She's afraid her mother is being scammed. When she asks her mother about the checks, she complains, "Can't I make my own decisions? I'm an adult, you know." Lisa checks with a lawyer about a power of attorney. "It seems like the only option at this point," she explains to him.

- Larry's mother has been living like a hermit for the past few years. She gets out only to go to the doctor, and her home is stacked with old magazines, newspapers, and dirty clothes. From time to time, Larry's wife, Jan, tries to sneak in to clean up when Larry is taking his mother to the doctor, but when they return, his mother becomes furious with both of them. Larry has asked several times to see her checkbook and savings statements, but she always has an excuse to avoid his "snooping around." Larry is finally ready to confront his mother about her lifestyle, her deteriorating health, and her finances, but he's not looking forward to it at all.

2 DEFINITIONS AND KEY THOUGHTS

- Often, as parents age and lose physical and mental capabilities, the *roles of parent and child* reverse because the parents need to be cared for instead of being the caregivers. The adjustment may be painful and difficult for both parties, but especially for the parents, who are losing their sense of identity and independence.
- To complicate matters, some adults find they are part of "the *sandwich generation*," caring for their parents and their adolescent or young adult kids at the same time. The emotional and financial strain of this burden can cause problems for the marriage of a sandwich generation couple.
- As parents' health or mental status deteriorates, their medical expenses escalate, and a budget that seemed reasonable at retirement ceases to work. Hard choices must be made, but it's not unusual when the parents don't even want to talk about the reality of their situation. They may be depressed and passive or they may be fiercely resistant or they may alternate between the two. In these difficult situations, emotional and relational tensions greatly complicate the financial dilemma.
- As elderly people become more isolated and think less clearly, they are more vulnerable to *scams*. A lady who was taken for thousands of dollars lamented, "But he seemed like such a nice young man."
- Sons and daughters may not feel comfortable asking to see their parents' checkbook and other financial statements, but they can't determine how to help if they don't have a good grasp of reality.
- The most common *financial issues* in helping elderly parents involve housing, transportation, health, shopping, and overall financial management. Each of these can easily get out of control and wreck a person's financial status.
- *Reverse mortgages* may be valid sources of income for elderly people who have substantial equity in their homes, but the risks involved must be addressed.

3 ASSESSMENT INTERVIEW

When an individual or couple comes for counseling regarding an elderly parent, they typically need help sorting out the complexities of the changing relationship, as well as specific direction about the finances.

1. What are your chief concerns about your parent's physical, mental, and financial health?
2. How have you seen your parent's condition change in the past few years or few months?
3. What is your parent's financial status? Is there enough money to pay the current bills?
4. Does your parent need additional care, such as home health care or an assisted living facility?

5. As you consider your parent's future needs for housing, transportation, health, and other necessities, is there enough money in savings?
6. What options have you considered to pay your parent's anticipated expenses in the future?
7. Do you have access to your parent's doctor? Do you have a competent, trusted financial counselor who can help? Have you considered talking to a lawyer about a power of attorney?
8. How are others in the family responding to the needs you see in your parent's life? How is their help (or lack of help) affecting you?
9. How can I help?

WISE COUNSEL : 4

When the sons and daughters of the elderly come for counseling, they may express concern for their parents but they also may feel considerable tension about their ability to step into a caregiving role for them. The reversal of roles may be more traumatic and difficult than finding the money to pay the bills.

Sons and daughters need to base their plans and decisions on objective reality, not conjecture or hearsay. If they haven't visited their parent, they need to go there to observe how things really are. They need access to the checkbook and other financial statements if they are going to assume responsibility to help or even to give advice.

Children of the elderly need to recognize genuine emergencies. It's not unusual for the condition of the elderly to deteriorate very quickly. They may lose one or several of their abilities: mental, emotional, physical, financial, and relational.

As children talk to their parents, they need to speak calmly and patiently, expecting resistance, especially if the parents have not appreciated offers of help before. Instead of beginning with demands for compliance, sons and daughters can express their love and their hope for their parent's future; then they can engage in conversation about viable options, considering multiple choices for housing, transportation, health care, weekly shopping, additional income, and other expenses. Adult children who are gaining experience in the Money Huddle and the principles of active listening and communication can use those skills in conversations with their parents.

It may be wise to hire a financial counselor to help sort out the finances and come up with a workable budget. In fact, this may be part of the adult children's preparation for the first conversation with the parent.

The stress of caring for an elderly parent can take its toll on a marriage. Encourage the adult children to take care of themselves as they care for their parents.

ACTION STEPS : 5

1. In the assessment, determine the level of stress the adult child feels in attempting to care for his parent. Quite often the strain of this care becomes a significant factor in causing harm to a marriage and health.

2. Explain the principles of good communication and conflict resolution. Help the client learn how to communicate clearly and frequently with a spouse before attempting to have a difficult conversation with a parent.

3. Explain that usually the adult child's role isn't to force the parent to do anything. It's important to maintain a good relationship, so the child needs to communicate with love and respect, being willing to compromise instead of control. He needs to stay calm and gracious, expecting resistance, and patiently letting the parent process ideas and options.

4. Suggest that the adult child get a handle on the parent's finances, asking, not demanding. In addition, he needs to consider alternatives, such as a power of attorney, when a parent can't take care of himself.

5. Suggest that the client find a financial manager or an attorney if needed.

6. Remain engaged with the client to offer support and encouragement during the long months and years of trying to care for an elderly parent.

6 BIBLICAL INSIGHTS

Do not rebuke an older man harshly, but exhort him as if he were your father. Treat younger men as brothers, older women as mothers, and younger women as sisters, with absolute purity.

1 Timothy 5:1–2

We may feel exasperated and be tempted to be impatient when we relate to our elderly parents, but God will give us grace to treat them with the utmost respect—even when they don't treat us that way.

Anyone who does not provide for their relatives, and especially for their own household, has denied the faith and is worse than an unbeliever.

1 Timothy 5:8

Patiently and persistently caring for our parents in their old age is a sign to others of our true faith in God.

Rejoice in the Lord always. I will say it again: Rejoice! Let your gentleness be evident to all. The Lord is near. Do not be anxious about anything, but in every situation, by prayer and petition, with thanksgiving, present your requests to God. And the peace of God, which transcends all understanding, will guard your hearts and your minds in Christ Jesus.

Philippians 4:4–7

Caring for an elderly parent is sometimes rewarding and wonderful but often painful and difficult. We need to remember that we're never alone. God is near. As we pray and thank God, his Spirit will give us peace, joy, and love for our parents.

"Honor your father and mother"—which is the first commandment with a promise—"so that it may go well with you and that you may enjoy long life on the earth."

Ephesians 6:2–3

Our parents aren't projects to be managed; they are the people who gave us life. No matter how old and infirm they are, we can honor them with love, patience, and respect. God promises to bless us as we bless them.

PRAYER STARTER : 7

Father, you love our parents even more than we do, and your heart breaks when you see them suffering in old age. Give us wisdom and patience as we try to help. Sometimes we get so tired, but we remember how you care for us so persistently. Thank you for the honor of caring for those who gave us life . . .

RECOMMENDED RESOURCES : 8

Munchbach, Jim. *Make Your Money Count: Connecting Your Resources to What Matters Most.* Baxter Press, 2007.

Palmer, Bethany, and Scott Palmer. *First Comes Love, Then Comes Money: A Couple's Guide to Financial Communication.* HarperOne, 2009.

http://www.ronblue.com/

http://www.mvelopes.com/focusonthefamily/

http://www.daveramsey.com/home/

http://www.crown.org/

Alimony, Divorce, and Child Support

1 PORTRAITS

- Two years after Barbara and Chris were divorced, she's still overwhelmed by the pain. All she can think about each day is how he betrayed her, and now, how he's taking advantage of her and her two children. He has a new girlfriend, and they're talking about getting married, but Barbara is still living in the bitter past. For more than a year, she felt paralyzed as she watched her bank balance dwindle. Recently she got a new job, but she still doesn't earn enough to make it. Though she got the house in the settlement, she can't make the monthly payments, even with the child support payments. She doesn't know what to do.

- Connie and Rob saw a counselor for about five months, but Rob quit going. This was Connie's last hope for their marriage, and now she doesn't see how they can continue to live together. She has forgiven him as much as she knows how, but his drug addiction has made her life very hard. And besides, she's pretty sure he's found someone else. For years she has put off making the decision but now she has set up appointments with her pastor, her counselor, an attorney, and a financial planner. She wants to take care of herself and her daughter.

- While a junior in high school, Jaime got pregnant. Her boyfriend wasn't interested in marrying her, and she wasn't too sure she wanted to marry him anyway. Her parents went for counseling to figure out how to help her. First, they told the counselor about Jaime's being verbally, emotionally, and physically abused by her boyfriend. Jaime filed for a protective order, and it was granted. Her parents promised to provide any money she needed, but the court demanded that the father of the child pay child support. In fifteen months he's made one payment. "If I could get him out of my life," Jaime explained, "I wouldn't want another dime from him."

- Martha has been married four times. The last time, she was married to a man who owned a trucking company, and her settlement was very handsome. This was, though, her fourth failed marriage. She needs help managing the money, but even more, she needs help managing her life.

2 DEFINITIONS AND KEY THOUGHTS

- According to Webster's, *alimony* is "an allowance made to one spouse by the other for support pending or after legal separation or divorce."

- *Child support* is "money paid for the care of one's minor child, especially payments to a divorced spouse or a guardian under a decree of divorce" (Dictionary.com).

- A failed marriage is one of the most devastating events in a person's life. Marriage offers the promise of love, companionship, and intimacy. When it fails, people's hearts are shattered. The emotions generated by a divorce are intense and prolonged but they can shift from day to day. People experience hurt, anger, bitterness, confusion, loneliness, anxiety, depression, and every other painful feeling known to mankind. In addition, many people cling to a sense of hope that the spouse will come back. This hope is often coupled with intense shame for not being able to make the marriage work and guilt for particular acts that contributed to the demise of the relationship. Many people are paralyzed by all these feelings and perceptions, so they make very few choices about their money—and the ones they make tend to be poor.

- For a divorce, financial agreements are essentially a *business deal*. As much as possible, those who are going through a divorce and those who have recently experienced this separation need to be dispassionate and clearheaded. If they can avoid emotional explosions and implosions, they can think more clearly and chart a course for the future, including their financial future.

- Communicate the *principles of conflict resolution*. Instead of making recriminations, the couple can show respect for each other in the negotiations before the divorce and in the implementation after it.

- People who are getting a divorce need to step back and consider what life will be like after the divorce is final. They need to take steps to set up separate accounts and protect their assets. Some of the particulars they can address are:

  — review their personal credit report

  — open bank accounts and credit card accounts

  — make sure retirement accounts are in their name

  — review health care coverage or the need for a new policy

  — create a workable budget of anticipated income and expenses

- Frequently people who are already divorced get into financial trouble when the spouse fails to make payments for child support or alimony. In these cases the offended party doesn't make much headway by either exploding in anger or becoming passive and compliant. Instead, a clear mind and cool action are necessary. An attorney/mediator may be required to force the former spouse to follow the terms of the settlement.

- Many divorcing couples think the *divorce decree* is supreme, but if they don't change the beneficiaries listed in wills, IRAs, and other financial documents, the ex-spouse may remain the *primary beneficiary*. It doesn't take much to make these changes, and they are necessary.

- A *COBRA plan* will provide medical insurance for up to eighteen months after a policy ends. Medical expenses can wreck a budget, so the divorcing couple must be sure their coverage doesn't lapse.

3 ASSESSMENT INTERVIEW

1. What is your current financial status?
2. As you consider a divorce (or deal with a divorce), what are reasonable expectations about your finances?
3. How might an explosion of emotions get in the way of a workable settlement? How might depression and passivity prevent you from getting the settlement you need?
4. Have you talked to an attorney/mediator about the settlement? If not, why not? If so, what was the attorney's advice?
5. Have you talked to a financial manager? If not, why not? If so, what was this person's advice?
6. Do you have a list of items related to your finances that you need to take care of, such as setting up a separate bank account, going back to your maiden name, protecting your retirement account?
7. How can I help?

4 WISE COUNSEL

Divorce inflicts some of the deepest wounds in a person's life, and these feelings come when we are most in need of a clear mind and good command of negotiation skills. Many people in this position—before or after the divorce is final—need someone to walk them through the process of financial management step-by-step.

Women who have been full-time homemakers can be at considerable risk at this pivotal time in their lives. They've been out of the workforce for many years, their skills have atrophied, new technologies have passed them by, and they've lost confidence in their ability to make life work.

One of the hardest things divorcing (or recently divorced) people will ever do is treat their divorce settlement as a business deal. They may be tempted to use it to inflict punishment and take revenge on the spouse. Instead, they need to think of that person as a vendor and the settlement as a business arrangement in which both people need to win.

People need to understand their state laws regarding divorce settlements. Laws differ from state to state. For example, find out if assets brought into the marriage are taken out by the same person. Similarly, debts brought into the marriage, such as college loans, are not joint property. The initial debtor still owns it when the marriage dissolves.

For emotional stability, many women try to keep the house and forgo an equitable division of savings and retirement accounts. In many cases this proves to be a disaster if the wife doesn't have sufficient regular income to continue to make house payments, so she loses the house, probably selling it for less than she owes in a distress sale.

ACTION STEPS ⦙ 5

1. In the assessment, observe the emotional and mental status of the client. No doubt, severe emotional distress will be present, but big decisions are imminent and they require sound thinking.
2. As much as possible, help the client see the negotiations of the divorce settlement as a business deal. If the divorce is already final and the client is upset about the terms or payments, help her think in concrete terms, establish a checklist of things to do, and then help her prioritize them so she will get them done.
3. Teach the client the principles of conflict resolution, but adapt them to a strained and broken relationship. The goal, then, isn't intimacy and trust, but respect for another party in a business deal. If the client insists on revenge, a settlement may require the expense of an attorney and the implementation may always be contentious.
4. Many people who are going through (or have recently gone through) a divorce need the help of a financial manager to make good decisions about the future. In many cases, deeply hurt people have difficulty thinking clearly. A professional can offer assistance.
5. Continue to help the client process the painful emotions, grieve the losses, and find hope for a meaningful future.

BIBLICAL INSIGHTS ⦙ 6

Be sure you know the condition of your flocks, give careful attention to your herds.

Proverbs 27:23

In times of crisis and transition, we need to be diligent to take care of the people and things that matter to us. We may be tempted to give up or get even, but instead, we need to think clearly and act decisively to make good financial decisions.

A gentle answer turns away wrath, but a harsh word stirs up anger.

Proverbs 15:1

When we fight fair, we look for a workable solution everyone can live with. A divorcing couple is no longer trying to build an intimate relationship, but they can still treat each other with respect.

Like a city whose walls are broken through is a person who lacks self-control.

Proverbs 25:28

Self-control is necessary in any interaction, but when explosive feelings are aroused through divorce, we have to choose to be in control instead of giving in to our natural desires for vengeance or self-pity. Maintaining our sanity, lowering our voice, and looking for reasonable solutions make us strong—like living in a fortified city.

Do not repay anyone evil for evil. Be careful to do what is right in the eyes of everyone. If it is possible, as far as it depends on you, live at peace with everyone. Do not take revenge, my dear friends, but leave room for God's wrath, for it is written: "It is mine to avenge; I will repay," says the Lord.

Romans 12:17–19

We can't control how the other person acts, but we can choose to offer a path of peace and reason for the future. As we reflect on our deep hurt and disappointment, we may want to pay back the offender. Instead, we need to take her off our hook and put her on God's. He can deal with her in his time and in his way. We can trust him for justice.

7 PRAYER STARTER

Father, you are sovereign and good. In our hurt, the last thing we want to do is think clearly and act nobly, but that's what you want us to do. This person needs your help. Thank you for your Spirit's love and power. We trust you to give her a clear mind so she can make good choices about the future . . .

8 RECOMMENDED RESOURCES

Munchbach, Jim. *Make Your Money Count: Connecting Your Resources to What Matters Most.* Baxter Press, 2007.

Palmer, Bethany, and Scott Palmer. *First Comes Love, Then Comes Money: A Couple's Guide to Financial Communication.* HarperOne, 2009.

Ramsey, Dave. *The Money Answer Book.* Thomas Nelson, 2009.

http://www.ronblue.com/

http://www.mvelopes.com/focusonthefamily/

http://www.daveramsey.com/home/

http://www.crown.org/

Back-to-School Spending

PORTRAITS : 1

- When Rod got a promotion, he and Cindy moved to a new city. They wanted the best for their twins, so they enrolled them in a private school. Swallowing hard and digging deep, they paid the tuition but they were shocked to find out how much they'd have to shell out on uniforms, musical instruments, books, and athletic fees. They hadn't planned on all those expenses.

- Marilyn is a single mom trying to make ends meet on a limited income. She works two jobs to earn a little extra money. When her three children prepared for the next year in school, she carefully planned for her daughter to wear her older sister's hand-me-down clothes and shoes. This arrangement had worked well when the younger one was in grammar school, but now she's entering junior high. She pitched a fit! Marilyn had to find a way to make peace and stay within her budget.

- Mark and Sandra often fought about money. Mark is a Spender, and Sandra is a Security Seeker. When their two kids were getting ready for the next year of school, Mark wanted to take them shopping. When they returned from their shopping trip, they had spent $1,500. Sandra insisted they take at least half of the things back, but Mark and the kids were outraged.

- Rich and Anna stared at the list of things their kids' schools suggested they buy for the new year. "We can't afford all this," Rich moaned. Anna answered, "But we don't want Bethany and Allen to be the laughingstocks of the school. We *have* to get these things." Rich dug in his heels, but Anna prevailed in insisting on getting everything on the lists. Months later, Rich was still bitter.

DEFINITIONS AND KEY THOUGHTS : 2

- In recent years stores have started back-to-school sales in July. But even with sales, each year people with school-age kids are staring down a major outlay of money for school supplies, new clothes, activity fees, and other *school-related expenses*. On top of the notebooks, shoes, jeans, and backpacks that make up the shopping lists, more and more parents are being asked to support their schools by helping stock classrooms with art materials and cleaning supplies. And those folders and pencils and paper towels can add up to real budget breakers.

- In 2010, according to the National Retail Federation, the average American family would spend more than $600 on clothes, shoes, supplies, and electronics during the back-to-school season, making it the second biggest consumer "event" of the year. (You can probably guess what the first is!)
- Back-to-school shopping sounds innocent enough but often a limited budget clashes with parental pride and a child's high expectations. And when there is poor communication—if the parents don't communicate clearly and well with each other and the kids—the family can suffer a major blowup.

3 ASSESSMENT INTERVIEW

In many cases, the reason a client brings up back-to-school spending in counseling is because it has caused significant conflict in the family. To understand the dynamics of the problem, explain the Money Personalities and ask these questions:

1. Describe the nature of the conflict you and your family experienced. Was it primarily between spouses, primarily with the kids, or throughout the family?
2. What is your Money Personality? What is the Money Personality of each person in the family? What are some possible points of misunderstanding and conflict based on these profiles?
3. Did you see any triangles develop, with two family members pairing off as allies against another? This dynamic is typical in conflicts, no matter what the cause may be.
4. Describe the normal communication styles of each member of the family. How did this situation bring out the worst in some of you?
5. Are you teaching your kids to be good money managers? How are you imparting these skills to them?
6. What are realistic expectations and expenditures for back-to-school spending?
7. What are some creative alternatives that would lower expenses or provide some money for extra expenses?
8. How is this communication problem affecting you, your marriage, and your relationship with your kids?
9. How can I help?

4 WISE COUNSEL

Unlike Christmas, the expenses involved in back-to-school spending may catch people unaware. How many parents plan for back-to-school spending in their annual budgets? Not us! Even if parents haven't been saving their pennies for the annual trip to the school supply aisle, they can still plan for these expenses and make sure they don't end up with a battered budget. These tips for parents can help:

- *Decide who will do the school shopping.* Clear communication will prevent doubling up on items, or worse, spending more than you need to. Once you decide who will do the shopping, talk through what you expect to spend and make a list of items you need, to prevent overbuying. This is particularly helpful if one of you is a Saver and the other is a Spender. The Saver needs to understand that, yes, your child really does need a fresh box of crayons and not a bag of broken stubs from under the couch. And the Spender needs to understand that the 24-pack on sale for a quarter will work just as well as the 150-count tower of rainbow colors that costs twenty bucks.

- *Involve your kids.* Shopping for school supplies with the kids in tow can be less fun than a root canal. But getting the kids to help with the shopping can teach them some valuable lessons. When kids choose their supplies and clothes, they are likely to take better care of them. Shopping with you also teaches them how to spend wisely. Talk them through the decisions—would it be better to buy a pack of six small erasers for $2 or a pack of two large erasers for $1? Do they need new tennis shoes for the first day of school or can their current pair get them through the first couple of months? Getting kids involved makes you think through your purchases more carefully and that can only help your bottom line.

- *Start early.* You don't have to wait until the last week before school starts to gather supplies. Starting early gives you the advantage of spreading the expense out over a few months. And many retailers hold their first big back-to-school sales in July, giving early shoppers a little more bang for their buck.

- *Talk about it.* Very few couples ever talk about back-to-school spending. One person does the shopping and doesn't think twice about it. But when $600 shows up on the credit card bill, there's bound to be some discussion! So avoid the potential conflict this change in your monthly spending can bring and talk about it now, before a single pencil is purchased.

ACTION STEPS 5

1. Encourage the client to identify his Money Personality, as well as the Money Personality of each member of the family. Discuss the way their perceptions, desires, and needs have affected their communication about back-to-school spending.
2. Teach the principles of good communication and conflict resolution. Make specific applications in the context of the current difficulties in the family.
3. The spouses need to clear up any misunderstandings between them, forgive hurts, and find common ground before they involve their children in the discussion.
4. When past hurts are being mended and forgiven, the parents can have an honest conversation about their budget, realistic expectations, and creative solutions to spending needs.

6 BIBLICAL INSIGHTS

The prudent see danger and take refuge, but the simple keep going and pay the penalty.

Proverbs 27:12

The reason a client brings up a problem related to back-to-school spending isn't about backpacks and pencils. It's much bigger and deeper than that. In most cases, this issue has surfaced tensions in the family between spouses and with the kids. If they don't address the underlying expectations, assumptions, and disputes, the seemingly small problem can escalate and poison family communication.

Love must be sincere. Hate what is evil; cling to what is good. Be devoted to one another in love. Honor one another above yourselves.

Romans 12:9–10

In all family conflicts, between parents and with kids, the default positions are fight and flight. Both are means to attempt to control others for personal gain. Genuine love, on the other hand, doesn't run away from difficulties. It addresses them and looks for a resolution that works for everybody. And it doesn't clamp down and demand its way. It listens carefully, appreciates different opinions, and communicates clearly and with grace.

Do not let any unwholesome talk come out of your mouths, but only what is helpful for building others up according to their needs, that it may benefit those who listen. And do not grieve the Holy Spirit of God, with whom you were sealed for the day of redemption. Get rid of all bitterness, rage and anger, brawling and slander, along with every form of malice. Be kind and compassionate to one another, forgiving each other, just as in Christ God forgave you.

Ephesians 4:29–32

Instead of blowing up or running away from a disagreement, people (especially parents) can make a commitment to build up and affirm each person involved. At every point, they choose kindness over angry domination and they forgive those who have hurt them, always looking at the forgiveness Christ has given them as the motivation and source of their own ability to forgive.

I am not saying this because I am in need, for I have learned to be content whatever the circumstances. I know what it is to be in need, and I know what it is to have plenty. I have learned the secret of being content in any and every situation, whether well fed or hungry, whether living in plenty or in want. I can do all this through him who gives me strength.

Philippians 4:11–13

In back-to-school spending, one of the biggest problems is comparison. Parents want their kids to have the best of everything, and the kids don't want to look dorky in front of their friends. Comparison promises prestige but it doesn't lead to genuine contentment. We find that only in the unconditional love, forgiveness, and acceptance of Christ. When our hearts are flooded with him, we find peace in every circumstance.

PRAYER STARTER : 7

Lord, this parent wants to be a good provider for his child but he's realizing that buying a lot of nice things isn't the most important contribution he can make. Help him model and teach your values of love, contentment, and joy. Give his family wisdom about spending, but even more, help them learn to communicate with each other in grace and love . . .

RECOMMENDED RESOURCES : 8

Munchbach, Jim. *Make Your Money Count: Connecting Your Resources to What Matters Most*. Baxter Press, 2007.

Palmer, Bethany, and Scott Palmer. *First Comes Love, Then Comes Money: A Couple's Guide to Financial Communication*. HarperOne, 2009.

http://www.ronblue.com/

http://www.mvelopes.com/focusonthefamily/

http://www.daveramsey.com/home/

http://www.crown.org/

Bankruptcy

1 PORTRAITS

- Evan opened a DVD rental store when times were very good. For several years, he raked in the money. He and his wife, Amanda, bought a vacation home at the beach and one in the mountains, two new luxury cars, and a big house in the nicest neighborhood in town. When the first online DVD rental and download site opened, Evan thought it would be no big deal. He was wrong. For two years he saw his profits decline. He let some of his employees go and, finally, he closed his store. By that time he was deeply in debt. He needed to sell his houses and cars, but the recession caused their value to fall to less than he owed. He was under water everywhere he looked. For a year he tried to dig his way out of the hole. By then he was deeply depressed. His attorney and financial advisor told him to declare bankruptcy.

- Stephen was sure his hot stock tip would pan out. He was so sure that he borrowed against his home equity and his 401(k) to buy as much as possible on margin. At first the stock soared, but after two months it crashed. Stephen's broker called to tell him he needed to pay $1.5 million within the week. He dreaded telling his wife, Marcy. He calculated that all his assets were worth $1.1 million. After meeting with an attorney, he decided to declare bankruptcy. When he finally told Marcy, she was furious. She had no idea his investments had put their future at risk. "You told me it was safe!" she screamed. "How can I ever trust you again?"

- Greg and Tricia were having a hard time making it on her salary after he lost his job. They decided to hope for the best, so they stayed in their nice home and used their credit card for cash advances each month to make ends meet. "It'll work out," Tricia assured Greg. But as the months dragged on, after almost a year, they owed $40,000 on three cards. By then Greg's perpetual discouragement and Tricia's resentment had compounded their financial trouble. His solution was to declare bankruptcy. Outraged, Tricia left with their twin boys to live with her parents. "Your name is on those cards too," he reminded her as she backed out of the driveway.

- Charles had been a successful real estate developer. He loved the game of playing the cycles of boom and bust. Sometimes he played them really well and made millions, but three times in his career, the market cycle had clobbered him. Each time, he declared bankruptcy. His wife, Gail, was much more cautious. When things were going well, she wanted to put a lot of the money in savings, but Charles insisted on living it up. When things went bad, she took it personally. "How can I face our friends?" she lamented. Charles shrugged. "This is the third time we've hit rock bottom," he said, "and each time before, we've gotten back on our feet. It's no big deal."

DEFINITIONS AND KEY THOUGHTS 2

- *Bankruptcy* is the legal status of an organization or individual that cannot repay debts to creditors. A *voluntary bankruptcy* is initiated by the debtor; an *involuntary bankruptcy* is the creditors' attempt to recoup a portion owed to them or initiate the restructuring of the debt for future repayment.

- In essence, bankruptcy is a personal or organizational failure. In previous generations it created a socially negative stigma that could stick with the person and family for generations. Today it has become more common so it doesn't have the same negative connotation. Still, financial failure can cause severe stress, creating psychological, physical, and relational problems for the individual and the family.

- In the United States, the *federal jurisdiction for bankruptcy* is found in the United States Constitution (in Article 1, Section 8, Clause 4), which allows Congress to enact "uniform laws on the subject of bankruptcies throughout the United States." In addition, Congress has enacted statute law, primarily in the Bankruptcy Code, located at Title 11 of the United States Code. Federal law is further amplified by state law.

- In the Bankruptcy Code, there are *six types of bankruptcy*. The following are the three most commonly used.

  — Chapter 7 provides for the liquidation of assets for individuals and organizations.
  — Chapter 11 allows companies (and sometimes individuals) to continue to operate during a restructuring and/or reorganization.
  — Chapter 13, also known as the Wage Earner Bankruptcy, is designed for individuals with a regular source of income to develop a plan to repay all or part of their debt.

ASSESSMENT INTERVIEW 3

1. Are you considering bankruptcy or have you already filed for bankruptcy?
2. What led to this consideration or decision?
3. How has the financial strain affected you and your most important relationships?
4. Do you have an attorney and a financial advisor who are helping you through these decisions?
5. What are your next steps—financially, personally, and relationally?
6. What do you expect will happen as a result of the bankruptcy? What are your hopes for the future?
7. How can I help?

4 WISE COUNSEL

Financial ruin seldom happens in an instant. Usually the dissolution of a financial structure occurs over a period of time due to several (or many) poor choices or unforeseen circumstances. Invariably, the prospect of bankruptcy causes enormous emotional stress, with corollary physical problems and relational conflict.

The different Money Personalities handle risk and adversity in very different ways. For example, bankruptcy for Risk Takers is only an inconvenience. They see it as part of the business cycle of boom and bust, and they have confidence they'll come out of it and land on their feet. On the other hand, Security Seekers see bankruptcy as a catastrophe! They take it very personally, and they are often devastated by the way it destroys their sense of stability.

Depression, heart problems, and somatic health complaints are common when people face financial ruin. In many cases their most cherished hopes for themselves and their family have been shattered, but they feel helpless to do anything about it. In counseling, one of the goals is to help the person begin to take steps toward health—emotional, spiritual, relational, and financial.

If she hasn't already found competent counsel, explain to the client the need to hire an attorney and a financial advisor, both of whom should specialize in bankruptcy.

The individual may have come to counseling for depression, or a couple may have come because they are experiencing conflict as a result of a financial collapse. At an appropriate time in the counseling process, explain the five Money Personalities and relate the personality to how each individual is handling the situation. With a couple, discuss the principles of good communication and conflict resolution.

5 ACTION STEPS

1. Determine the severity of the presenting needs in the life of the individual or couple. The first glimpse may reveal the effects of stress or relational conflict. As you dig deeper into the cause of the problem, you may discover more significant financial distress.
2. If bankruptcy is being considered, refer the client to an attorney and a financial advisor who are skilled in bankruptcy proceedings.
3. Address the symptoms, thinking patterns, and powerful emotions related to any depression, anxiety, and resentment.
4. Explain the five Money Personalities and help her identify herself and her spouse.
5. Monitor the individual or couple's progress and help them take steps forward in dealing with stress and conflict. They will need assurance that God can use this setback for good in their lives.

BIBLICAL INSIGHTS : 6

But Joseph said to them, "Don't be afraid. Am I in the place of God? You intended to harm me, but God intended it for good to accomplish what is now being done, the saving of many lives."

Genesis 50:19–20

No matter who has committed a sin or made dumb mistakes, God wants to use everything in our lives to accomplish something good and right and beautiful—if we'll trust him.

Why, my soul, are you downcast? Why so disturbed within me? Put your hope in God, for I will yet praise him, my Savior and my God.

Psalm 42:5

When we experience financial ruin, we naturally become deeply discouraged. We may ask lots of questions and be tempted to try to assign blame. The Lord wants us to do something much more constructive but against human nature. He wants us to rivet our attention on his goodness and greatness, praise and thank him, and look for his way forward.

Therefore, since we have been justified through faith, we have peace with God through our Lord Jesus Christ, through whom we have gained access by faith into this grace in which we now stand. And we boast in the hope of the glory of God. Not only so, but we also glory in our sufferings, because we know that suffering produces perseverance; perseverance, character; and character, hope. And hope does not put us to shame, because God's love has been poured out into our hearts through the Holy Spirit, who has been given to us.

Romans 5:1–5

No matter what the cause might be, God will use difficulties in our lives as classrooms to teach us life's most important lessons, to carve a good character, and to clarify our sense of hope in God's love and purpose for us.

Humble yourselves, therefore, under God's mighty hand, that he may lift you up in due time. Cast all your anxiety on him because he cares for you.

1 Peter 5:6–7

Financial problems make us feel helpless and inferior. In reaction we may spend our energies blaming others or finding fault with ourselves. Instead, God wants us to look to him, to put our past, present, and future in his hands, and trust him to lead us—because he cares for us.

7 PRAYER STARTER

Father, this woman is in trouble. In some ways, it doesn't matter how she got here but now she needs to trust you for her future. Your Word says you never leave us or forsake us. Thank you for that assurance. She needs it when she feels alone and helpless. Use this situation to teach her the lessons she needs to learn. At least one of those is to trust that you are good and your purposes for her aren't stopped by this situation. She is yours, Lord . . .

8 RECOMMENDED RESOURCES

Munchbach, Jim. *Make Your Money Count: Connecting Your Resources to What Matters Most*. Baxter Press, 2007.

Palmer, Bethany, and Scott Palmer. *First Comes Love, Then Comes Money: A Couple's Guide to Financial Communication*. HarperOne, 2009.

http://www.ronblue.com/

http://www.mvelopes.com/focusonthefamily/

http://www.daveramsey.com/home/

http://www.crown.org/

Before Marriage

- Edwardo and Thalia have been engaged for six months, but their wedding is still a year away. They love each other very much and they've helped each other financially at different times in their relationship. When Edwardo was out of work for a couple of months, Thalia paid his rent. And when Thalia wrecked her car and didn't have enough to cover the deductible, Edwardo gladly paid it for her. Now they're thinking about putting their finances together in a joint checking account and joint credit cards.

- Hank and Maria are getting married in a month, but their disagreements about money have intensified as their wedding day approaches. She wants to have a lavish wedding and a grand honeymoon. He keeps looking at the dollar amounts and cringing. He has said several times, "How in the world are we ever going to pay all this off?" She laughs. "But we only get married once, honey. We'll find a way."

- Ellen has gradually been putting the squeeze on Don about all his expenses. "We can't afford all those things when we get married," she scolded. "So why don't we save some money now by canceling some of those magazine subscriptions, gym memberships, and extras on your cable bill?" Every time Ellen makes her demands, Don withdraws a little more. He's secretly thinking about calling off the wedding. He's not sure he can stand a lifetime of financial bickering.

- Cliff is a Flyer. He rarely thinks about how much money he's spending. But he's marrying Alicia, who is a very tight Saver. She puts away money in a personal savings account every month and she matches funds for her 401(k). Cliff has told her, "I can't wait to get my hands on all that dough!" She wonders if he's serious. She suspects he is but she doesn't know what to do about it.

DEFINITIONS AND KEY THOUGHTS : 2

- A couple's engagement is a truly special time in their relationship. They are filled with hope and excitement as they plan their wedding and think about their future together. This is also the time when they start dreaming about the life they're going to build: where they'll live, what kind of family they might have, what kind of adventures they'll enjoy, and how they'll handle their money as a couple.

- In all the fun and emotion of being engaged, money conversations often get left out. Talking about finances doesn't seem very romantic and is probably not a subject of conversation an engaged couple would choose. But it is essential for a couple who plans to marry and spend their lives together to talk about how they will handle their money. This is as important as talking about kids or sex or where they will live.

3 ASSESSMENT INTERVIEW

If you're conducting premarriage counseling, the issue of finances will be an important part of your discussion. Describe the Money Personalities and ask the individual or couple to identify themselves and each other. If an individual or couple has come for help because of conflicts related to finances, use these questions.

1. Tell me about your relationship. How long have you been engaged?
2. What drew you together? What do you enjoy about each other?
3. What is your Money Personality? What is your fiancé(e)'s Money Personality?
4. What are some areas of common ground concerning money that the two of you share, such as spending, saving, investing?
5. What are some areas that have caused friction?
6. What are your hopes and dreams related to your relationship and money?
7. What are your fears?
8. What processes need to be put in place to facilitate good communication between you so that you both have realistic expectations about your relationship and money?
9. How can I help?

4 WISE COUNSEL

When a couple marries, they meld every part of their lives, including their finances. They need to build a solid foundation for their financial relationship by being completely honest about how each of them thinks about and deals with money.

There are resources online for an engaged couple, including twenty questions to help them talk about what makes them unique. You may want to encourage the couple to discuss these questions to help them understand any differences they may have in their thinking about money. Encourage the couple to feel free to bring any problems that are discovered through their discussion to a counseling session. The resources are at the following websites:

http://www.themoneycouple.com/should-we-marry-our-money-before-we-say-I-do-mcm.htm

http://www.themoneycouple.com/20-questions.htm

http://www.themoneycouple.com/money-personalities.htm

Should a couple combine their finances before the wedding day? We say absolutely not. A couple's money should not be married before *they* are legally married. We have seen too many engagements end, leaving couples who have combined their money with the painful task of sorting it all out during an already difficult time. The couple probably already shares money with each other, but things like savings accounts, credit cards, retirement funds, and checkbooks should not be shared until marriage. Combining these finances before they've created a legal union can create headaches they don't need.

However, as we've said, the fact that a couple does not share all their money doesn't mean they shouldn't be talking about it. We believe that strong financial communication has to start *before* marriage—hopefully before they even get engaged. Encourage the couple to plan a Money Huddle and talk about the six topics that will save their marriage before it has begun:

1. *Money Personalities.* Help the couple understand Money Personalities and then encourage them to discuss their differences. Understanding how each other thinks about and deals with money is the foundation of healthy financial communication. If a couple doesn't learn how to communicate about money, they have a long, painful future ahead of them. Encourage them to think about how they will compromise when the inevitable conflicts come up. Impress on them the importance of this.

2. *Debt.* There is no substitute for an honest conversation about debt. Encourage the couple to tell each other about any debt they may have. They should also figure out how they will pay it off. How will the debt impact their finances for the next few years? How can they work together to manage the debt?

3. *Income.* The couple can get a realistic picture of the present and the future by talking about how much money each of them makes. It's amazing how many people don't really know what their spouse is paid. Not only will knowing this help the couple make plans for the first few years of their life together, it helps prevent financial secrets from creeping into the marriage. (You may want to refer to http://www.themoneycouple.com/five-categories-financial-infidelity-mcm.htm.)

4. *Expenses.* If the couple does not have a good idea of their monthly expenses, encourage them to spend some time figuring it out. Besides the normal expenses of rent and food, they may have a car payment, a gym membership, medical expenses, and loan payments. Each partner should write down all their monthly expenses, then combine the totals to get an idea of how much they'll spend as a couple. Then they should compare it to their joint income. If they find they have some wiggle room, great. If they are spending way more than they're earning, they will have some budget decisions to make once they start their life together.

5. *Savings.* The couple should talk about how much each of them has saved, whether it's $100 or $100,000. They should discuss the process they used to save as well as the following questions: How important is it to you to have money in savings? What kind of sacrifices have you made to put money away? What investments do you have—or hope to have? Help them recognize that

as they plan for their financial future—vacations, emergency money, college funds, retirement—they will need to have an ongoing conversation that might as well begin now.

6. *Expectations.* Eventually couples who are headed toward a lifelong commitment need to talk realistically about their vision for their future and the implications that vision has for their finances. They should cover everything in their discussion. Do you want to own a house? How soon? Do you see yourselves living in a specific part of the country? What will that mean for your finances? How do you think children will change your financial picture? Will one of you want to stay home when the children are young? Do you see yourself changing careers or going back to school? Again, an honest conversation now can save you tons of heartache later.

5 : ACTION STEPS

1. Explain the Money Personalities and ask the individual or couple to identify themselves and each other. Take time to discuss the areas of common perceptions and potential conflicts in how they perceive and handle money.
2. Take time to discuss each of these important topics: debt, income, expenses, and savings. Talk about where they are now, their expectations of how they want to work together on financial issues, and how to communicate clearly to overcome potential sources of conflict.
3. Look for any pressure applied by parents, including financial strings attached, that might be used to control the couple as they get married. For instance, some parents talk privately to their child to complain about the fiancée's financial perceptions or spending. Describe the danger of listening to this kind of input, and help the couple set appropriate boundaries to protect their relationship.

6 : BIBLICAL INSIGHTS

The plans of the diligent lead to profit as surely as haste leads to poverty.

Proverbs 21:5

Dreams are powerful things; they can propel us to excellence or they can distract us from God's plan for our lives. Without good plans, dreams are just ideas that seldom go anywhere.

Humility is the fear of the LORD; its wages are riches and honor and life.

Proverbs 22:4

Many people don't give a thought to God when they are handling their money, but every aspect of life—including money, sex, work, leisure, and everything else—needs to be under the mighty hand of God. When we follow him with all our heart, we can expect many blessings, including strength and wisdom when we're tested.

In the paths of the wicked are snares and pitfalls, but those who would preserve their life stay far from them.

Proverbs 22:5

As we uncover our dreams, we may realize that a lot of our time has been spent in thinking about having as much or more than someone else. When we become aware of the damage inflicted by envy and jealousy, we learn to stay far away from them and cling to the Lord.

But I am afraid that just as Eve was deceived by the serpent's cunning, your minds may somehow be led astray from your sincere and pure devotion to Christ.

2 Corinthians 11:3

We are engaged in a spiritual fight for our hearts and minds. Advertising deceives us, and comparison drives us to focus our attention in the wrong places. As we learn to follow Christ with a "sincere and pure devotion," we still fight against temptation but we have God's armor and weapons in the fight.

PRAYER STARTER 7

Lord Jesus, this couple belongs to you, and you are worthy of their deepest devotion. They want to put you in the center of their relationship. Guide them in every area, including their finances . . .

RECOMMENDED RESOURCES 8

Munchbach, Jim. *Make Your Money Count: Connecting Your Resources to What Matters Most*. Baxter Press, 2007.

Palmer, Bethany, and Scott Palmer. *First Comes Love, Then Comes Money: A Couple's Guide to Financial Communication*. HarperOne, 2009.

http://www.ronblue.com/

http://www.mvelopes.com/focusonthefamily/

http://www.daveramsey.com/home/

http://www.crown.org/

Budgeting and Cash Flow

1 PORTRAITS

- Maria and her husband divorced about a year ago. She kept the house, living there with her three children. In the past few months, however, she has had a hard time making the mortgage payment. She needs a job but she wants to find something that lets her be at home when the kids come home from school. As her financial situation has deteriorated, she hasn't had the emotional strength to face the reality that she doesn't have enough money to make it each month. But now something has to change, or she's going to lose her home.

- Josh and Rebecca have been married for twenty years, but when it comes to money, they might as well be from two different planets. He's a free spender; she's a tightwad who watches every dime. She's tried to impose a budget on Josh, but he just shrugs and buys whatever he wants. At this point the problem isn't each line item on Rebecca's budget spreadsheet; it's the distance between them caused by his unwillingness to change and her resentment.

- Colleen and Ben have twin girls in high school. One is in band and the other is in musicals. Both of them spend a lot of money on trips, costumes, and events. This is their junior year, and Colleen and Ben are taking the girls all over the state to visit universities where they might be accepted. Late at night on one of the trips, Colleen asked Ben, "We don't have a nickel left every month now. What's going to happen when they're in school and we have more bills to pay?"

- Jay is single and in his thirties. He has a good job but he spends every penny he makes every month—and often a little bit more. "I don't know what happens," he told a friend. "When I got my job, I splurged a little. I got some new furniture (really needed it too) and a new television. The credit terms looked pretty good. And since then, I got a new smart phone with lots of apps, joined a health club, and became partner in a hunting lease. All of those things looked perfectly reasonable at the time, but now I'm in big trouble. I can make the minimum payments on my credit cards but I'm not making any headway in paying them off."

2 DEFINITIONS AND KEY THOUGHTS

- A *budget* is simply a plan to manage monthly expenses and income. It's not scary and it's not rocket science. For it to work, however, it requires honesty, common sense, and a measure of discipline. To make a budget, make a list of the major categories of expenses. Beside each item write, in one column, the average expense for that item in the last three months (or year) and, in the next column, the amount you plan to spend on that item next month. In another list write down the sources and amounts of income and compare the totals. If you are planning to spend more than you will have in income, you will need to adjust your spending plans.

- The categories of expenses on a budget often include:

  — savings
  — giving
  — housing
  — food
  — utilities
  — entertainment
  — transportation
  — clothes
  — medical/dental/fitness
  — recreation
  — debts/credit card payments
  — personal expenses

  Expenses that don't fit in these categories can be called "other" or listed separately.

- All expenses should be included in the budget. It's tempting to assume that an expense is minor and doesn't really matter, but those things add up and can wreck a budget.
- Many people who come to counseling have presenting problems of anxiety, depression, or relational difficulties, and in many cases, these problems are compounded by financial distress. A sound, reasonable, workable budget is a foundation tool that will lower levels of stress, so getting money under control can have benefits in every other area of life.
- In a family, everyone needs to buy into the budget process. Each person may have different financial personalities, but each can make a significant contribution and play an important role in making it work for everybody. Good communication needs equal parts grace and truth, and good communication is important in the planning phase and in implementation. The benefits need to be clearly articulated and reinforced at each step, and progress should be celebrated (in a cost effective way, of course).
- A few families create a budget to fine-tune their spending habits, but most of those who come to counseling need much more dramatic change in how they handle finances. As they write down their usual monthly expenses and compare the figure to their income, they realize they need to make some hard choices to cut back in some areas. Parents need to be good models of courage and prudence for their kids, but everyone in the family probably needs to make a cut or two. (In some families, however, a family member has tried to fix the problem for

years by being a martyr, sacrificing and saving when no one else was spending responsibly. These people should understand that they don't need to play the role of hero any longer, but they may actually feel awkward when they aren't playing this role.)

- Creating and living by a budget are skills to be developed, not pills to swallow. Most couples and families need about three months to work out the kinks in a budget and make necessary adjustments so that it works really well. The first month is the most awkward because that's when the most dramatic changes are implemented.

3 ASSESSMENT INTERVIEW

Explain the Money Personalities, and then ask these questions:

1. What is your Money Personality? What is your spouse's Money Personality? After considering these profiles, what are some points where you complement each other? Where might there be points of misunderstanding or differences in perception and potential conflict?
2. How do debt and other money troubles affect your mood and relationships?
3. Are you and your family on a budget?
4. Have you ever tried to create and live on a budget? If so, what happened? How was it sabotaged, rejected, or abandoned?
5. What difference would it make for you and your family to live on a reasonable budget? What benefits would you experience?
6. Which members of your family would resist? How will you address this resistance?
7. Do you have a template for a budget? When will you prepare it?
8. What significant changes do you think your family needs to make to lower expenses?
9. How can I help?

4 WISE COUNSEL

Though any reasonable person could look at a family's debt and the corresponding conflict caused by money trouble and offer concrete solutions for substantive progress, many families resist needed changes. As many philosophers and theologians have observed, "People have an almost limitless capacity for self-deception." We feel completely justified in our foolish patterns of behavior, and when we realize there's a problem, it's always someone else's fault. Creating a budget is very simple and easy, but many who come to counseling simply won't do it. They feel more comfortable living with the heartache and chaos of debt than making a few simple, courageous choices to live within their means. Don't be surprised by any number of tactics of resistance.

Quite often the best way to approach this issue is communication. As you talk with a couple or family about the tension in their relationships, along with the miscommunication, demands, and manipulation, you can use the problem of spending as one of the items they can learn to talk about. Use their working together to create and live on a budget as an example of how they can take steps forward in other areas of communication and understanding. Individuals and couples who come for counseling will benefit from the insights about the Money Personalities.

Some people will be tenacious in working out a budget over the course of months, but others want to quit at the first bump in the road. Again, use this as a process tool to talk about perceptions, expectations, and communication. Giving up too soon on a budget may be a symptom of a much deeper psychological problem of insecurity and the fear of failure.

ACTION STEPS 5

1. In the assessment interview, discover the link between the presenting problem and trouble with money. When money is a factor, it's almost always a symptom of a relational problem, and it can occur even in the wealthiest families. Greed, fear, and jealousy know no economic bounds.
2. Explain the five Money Personalities and help them identify themselves and each other. Discuss the potential sources of conflict between their personalities. Communicate principles of active listening, good communication, and conflict resolution, and answer any questions.
3. If an individual, couple, or family is spending too much money, offer a template for a simple budget and walk them through the process of creating it. Let them do their homework to determine their existing monthly expenses. If they can agree on spending goals and limits, have them do that at home and give a report when they see you. If, however, they experience too much conflict over setting these targets, ask them to discuss them with you in the room. Then use their conversation as a tool to help them with their relationships as well as with their finances.
4. Focus on the benefits of living within their means. Explain that they'll have lower levels of stress, more peace and security, and fewer arguments—at least about money.
5. Monitor progress over the first weeks and months to help them make adjustments and communicate appropriately about any disagreements.
6. If they need more help than you can give them about financial matters, especially about severe debt problems, foreclosure of a home, and other major problems, refer them to a competent financial professional who can assist them.

BIBLICAL INSIGHTS 6

Desire without knowledge is not good—how much more will hasty feet miss the way!

Proverbs 19:2

Perhaps the biggest problem with money is that we don't even think about how we're spending it. If we wait to consider our budget until the moment we want something, we'll often make impulsive—and poor—choices about what we buy.

The wise store up choice food and olive oil, but fools gulp theirs down.

Proverbs 21:20

Wise people consider their choices, often well ahead of the moment when the decision is actually made. But fools rush to consume anything that promises to make them happy at the moment.

So whether you eat or drink or whatever you do, do it all for the glory of God. Do not cause anyone to stumble, whether Jews, Greeks or the church of God— even as I try to please everyone in every way. For I am not seeking my own good but the good of many, so that they may be saved.

1 Corinthians 10:31–33

Every choice about money, relationships, entertainment, friends, career, and everything else in life is a reflection of our deepest desires and values. And people are watching. As we live for Christ and make choices that honor him, we build credibility with those around us—family, friends, and neighbors.

What causes fights and quarrels among you? Don't they come from your desires that battle within you? You desire but do not have, so you kill. You covet but you cannot get what you want, so you quarrel and fight. You do not have because you do not ask God. When you ask, you do not receive, because you ask with wrong motives, that you may spend what you get on your pleasures.

James 4:1–3

In families, some of the biggest fights are about money. (Other major points of conflict for couples are sex, children, and in-laws.) People are, by nature, selfish. James's point is that unregulated selfishness creates demands, which ultimately ruin our most cherished relationships. His letter encourages us to be honest about the selfishness in our hearts, experience the grace of Christ in his forgiveness, and make better choices. Selfishness is the deep root of why we make a budget and stick to it.

7 PRAYER STARTER

Father, this couple has allowed money, or the lack of it, to rule their lives and hurt their relationship. They want to change and are making a commitment to create a workable budget, make necessary adjustments to make it better, and stick to it so that they live within their means. Lord, they need your wisdom and encouragement as they work together to make this happen . . .

RECOMMENDED RESOURCES 8

Munchbach, Jim. *Make Your Money Count: Connecting Your Resources to What Matters Most*. Baxter Press, 2007.

Palmer, Bethany, and Scott Palmer. *First Comes Love, Then Comes Money: A Couple's Guide to Financial Communication*. HarperOne, 2009.

http://www.ronblue.com/

http://www.mvelopes.com/focusonthefamily/

http://www.daveramsey.com/home/

http://www.crown.org/

College Planning

1 PORTRAITS

- For twenty years Harold had a great job in a growing industry. As his son and daughter grew up, he felt sure he could pay for their college expenses out of his savings and current earnings. When the kids were in high school, a senior and a sophomore, his company was bought out, and he lost his job in the merger. After a year, having burned through a lot of his savings, he finally got another job, but at about half his previous salary. He doesn't know what he's going to do about paying for the kids' college education now.

- Beth and Peter heard about a "529" educational savings plan, and when they checked it out, it seemed a perfect way for them to begin saving for their three children's education. They got a good jump on it. They began putting money into the fund when their kids were six, four, and three.

- Warren saved enough money for his son to go to college, but after the divorce, he didn't have a dime to spare. His plan was for his son to attend a state school, but his son's heart was set on an Ivy League education. Secretly, Warren hoped his son wouldn't be accepted, but the young man was thrilled to get an acceptance letter. Warren was proud of his son, but his mind raced with worries about how he could pay for the quadrupled costs. He began researching scholarships, grants, and school loans. He was determined to make something work for his son.

- Stewart and Maria had hardly come home from the hospital with their baby girl when Stewart put his first check into a tax-free education account through his broker. "This isn't just about getting into a good school and getting a good education," he told his beaming wife. "It's about her future long after she graduates. I want her to be prepared for anything."

2 DEFINITIONS AND KEY THOUGHTS

- As anyone who has researched college costs knows, college education is expensive and the cost is rising. Children grow up fast and are ready to go off to school before parents can blink, so the sooner the parents start saving the better.

- Many different types of savings accounts are useful for college costs, including *traditional savings accounts, tax-free accounts, annuities, U.S. savings bonds, Section 529 college savings plans, and Coverdell education savings accounts.*

- The average *annual tuition and fees* for *public four-year colleges* is $7,605 for in-state students and $11,990 for out-of-state. *Private nonprofit schools* average $27,293. By far, the least expensive type of school is the *public two-year college* that averages $2,713 a year in tuition and fees.

- Of course, tuition and fees are only part of the expense. Other costs include *room and board* (often $1,000 per month), *books and supplies* (averaging $1,137 a year), *personal expenses* (averaging $1,989 a year), and *transportation* (averaging $1,071 for on-campus students at four-year public colleges).

- Parents and prospective students can consider and pursue several different sources of funding, including *parents' savings, grants, scholarships, student loans, work-study programs, and student employment* while in school. In a recent year, 48 percent of *federal financial aid* was for scholarships and grants, 47 percent went to loans, and 5 percent was for federal work-study programs and *educational tax benefits*. (Statistics in this section are from www.collegeboard.com.)

- How to pay for college education has become a national obsession. For those who want advice or assistance, plenty of articles, books, and websites are available. An underutilized resource is the colleges themselves. They are eager to assist parents because they want students to attend.

ASSESSMENT INTERVIEW 3

Explain the Money Personalities and use the insights to stimulate the discussion about this important topic.

1. What is your Money Personality? What is your spouse's Money Personality? What is your child's? What are areas from these profiles that complement each other? What differences in your personalities might encourage differing perceptions and cause misunderstandings and conflict?
2. Is paying for college a concern for you?
3. How is the stress affecting you and your relationships?
4. What are your current plans to pay tuition and expenses?
5. What options have you considered?
6. Which ones seem best for you and your child?
7. How can I help?

WISE COUNSEL 4

Financial stresses contribute to many of the problems in people's lives, but they probably will not go to a therapist, pastor, or lay counselor with college education expenses as the presenting problem.

As you assess the reason the person or couple has come to you, you may discover that they have a child preparing to go to college or already attending. Ask if this is putting any financial strain on the family. They may realize that this cost is contributing to their conflict and raising stress levels.

Probably you don't have the expertise to give professional guidance on education funding, but you can offer some commonsense suggestions and remind the client that God will lead and provide. Most individuals and couples who come for counseling will benefit from the insights of the five Money Personalities.

Refer clients to a professional financial counselor who can help them with specific questions and investment instruments they can use to save for their children's education.

5 ACTION STEPS

1. In the assessment interview, determine the presence and nature of any financial stress, in this case related to paying for a child's college education. Specifically, note how this strain is affecting the individual and the communication in the family.
2. Often, in addition to looking at any financial strain, a child leaving for college can create separation anxiety for the parents, especially the mother, and sometimes also for the child. This sense of impending loss (or actual loss if the child has already left) may be a more critical issue than the funding.
3. Explain the five Money Personalities and help the client identify herself and her spouse. Discuss how she may perceive financial issues, including college funding, differently than her spouse. Discuss any tensions and talk about the principles of good communication and conflict resolution.
4. Offer some suggestions for funding sources but don't get too detailed in this discussion, unless you have expertise in this area.
5. Refer the person or couple to a financial professional, financial aid office at the college, or the government agency FAFSA (Free Application for Federal Student Aid).
6. As counseling continues, monitor progress on finding the right financial strategy for college funding and continue to help the individual or couple cling to hope for the future.

6 BIBLICAL INSIGHTS

Dishonest money dwindles away, but whoever gathers money little by little makes it grow.

Proverbs 13:11

Some parents fail to plan and save for a child's college education until it's too late. Wise parents begin early and stay with it. The costs are almost always more than they first anticipated.

The plans of the diligent lead to profit as surely as haste leads to poverty.

Proverbs 21:5

Good financial planning takes wisdom and discipline. Finding the right blend of funding (such as savings, scholarships, and grants) requires research and good advice from people who have traveled this road before.

By wisdom a house is built, and through understanding it is established; through knowledge its rooms are filled with rare and beautiful treasures.

Proverbs 24:3–4

Wisdom is much more than book knowledge, and it's more than a college education. Real wisdom is the ability to apply that knowledge. A college education prepares a child for a lifetime of success, but she needs to learn to trust God and follow him as she applies what she's learned.

PRAYER STARTER 7

Father, you have wonderful plans for this child who wants to go to college, and you want to give the parents wisdom so they can find the right funding sources. Thank you, Lord, that you own all things and you want to teach valuable lessons even in the search for these funds. Help them trust you in every step . . .

RECOMMENDED RESOURCES 8

Munchbach, Jim. *Make Your Money Count: Connecting Your Resources to What Matters Most.* Baxter Press, 2007.

Palmer, Bethany, and Scott Palmer. *First Comes Love, Then Comes Money: A Couple's Guide to Financial Communication.* HarperOne, 2009.

http://www.ronblue.com/

http://www.mvelopes.com/focusonthefamily/

http://www.daveramsey.com/home/

http://www.crown.org/

Compulsive Gambling

1 PORTRAITS

- Rod started betting on college football games with his buddies in college. Every Saturday, they sat at one of their apartments to watch the scores and see how much they won or lost. His new bride was amused by Rod and his friends. She didn't seem to mind at all. After Rod graduated and got a job, a new friend introduced him to a group of guys who bet on pro football. The amount bet was bigger, but Rod enjoyed the thrill of it all. Before long he began using a bookie to place his bets. Some Sundays he won thousands and some weekends he lost thousands. After a string of bad weeks, he couldn't pay for his losses. When a man showed up at his door demanding cash, Rod's wife asked him what was going on. He had told her about the times he had won but not the times he had lost.

- Brandon enjoyed playing Texas hold 'em with his friends on Saturday nights. Each week, they started after his kids had gone to bed. His wife, Betty, served them snacks and then she headed off to bed too. The thrill of the game captured Brandon's thoughts. Then a guy at work told him about an online poker site he used, and soon Brandon was hooked. Gradually he spent more time on the site. He'd play in his study late into the night with the door closed and became increasingly withdrawn from Betty and the kids. She thought he was concerned about stress at work—at least that's what he told her when she asked why he was so tense all the time. After several months, he had lost more than $10,000.

- April and her husband, Paul, drove one hundred miles to a casino to play blackjack every few months, but she didn't tell him that she made the trip alone much more often. She loved to gamble. She began going once a month, then once a week, and now she goes twice a week. She's been getting money as loans on their credit card, and she's hiding the statements from Paul. After several months without a payment, the credit card company has been calling. Usually she's able to grab the phone before Paul does, but one day, she wasn't at home and Paul took the call. At first, he tried to tell the caller it was all a mistake, but after some time, he realized something was very wrong. When he confronted April, she tried to deny it but soon she broke down and showed him the box of receipts for cash advances from their card. He was devastated. He exploded, "How can I ever trust you again?"

- Glen enjoyed the dog races. He thought he had a knack for picking winners because there were streaks when he brought home a lot of cash. But the law of averages caught up with him, and he found himself deeply in debt. He had sold his wife's jewelry, but since he seldom took her out to nice places anymore, she didn't even notice. But when she came home one day and found that her laptop was gone, she realized something was wrong. She asked Glen about it, and he mumbled that she must have misplaced it. She knew that wasn't true, but it took her three months to uncover the truth about her husband's lies, stealing, and secret life.

DEFINITIONS AND KEY THOUGHTS 2

- *Compulsive gambling* is a process addiction, which means that a behavior releases chemicals in the brain, producing excitement. Like other addictions, the effect of tolerance demands increasing amounts of the behavior to produce the desired feelings, so the addictive gambling escalates over time.
- Often compulsive gambling begins innocently, but gradually over time the person becomes obsessed with winning and loses control over time, money, and responsible behavior. The stages of addiction include:

  — *Use.* The person enjoys the behavior with no adverse effects.
  — *Misuse.* The behavior begins to affect family relationships and job performance. Thoughts about playing or using begin to dominate the person's thinking. Secrets and lies are first used to keep others from knowing about the problem.
  — *Abuse.* Increasingly the person is obsessed with the behavior or substance. A person addicted to gambling will fantasize about winning and plan his day around the behavior. In this stage, the person chooses gambling over spouse, kids, friends, health, career, and God.
  — *Addiction.* The person is consumed by thoughts of the substance or behavior and lives for it. For the gambler, every decision is analyzed to determine how he can gamble, win, and avoid painful consequences. Lies have become a pervasive relational habit.

- The spouse and children are deeply affected by a person's decline into addictive gambling. Like the gambler, their denial may begin innocently as they give him the benefit of the doubt, but after a while, they may avoid the painful reality as a survival mechanism. If they try to face the hard truth, it may elicit explosions of denial and blame from the gambler, or it may just be too difficult to admit that life is out of control.
- Like most addicts, many compulsive gamblers have to hit bottom before they are willing to change. Their bottom may come in the form of a financial collapse, the threat of a spouse leaving them, physical problems, or the loss of their job.

3 ASSESSMENT INTERVIEW

In most cases, the person who comes for counseling is the spouse of the compulsive gambler. If the addict comes, it is often after the spouse has come for weeks or months and has grown strong enough to confront the addict and demand change. These questions are designed for the spouse of a compulsive gambler.

1. How did you discover your spouse's problem with gambling?
2. Are you being hounded by bill collectors?
3. How is the behavior affecting your relationship? Your children? Your spouse's career?
4. Has your spouse ever promised to quit gambling? If so, what happened? How have repeated but broken promises affected your willingness to trust him?
5. Have you uncovered lies and secrets related to this behavior? How did he respond when you confronted him with these facts?
6. How does he act when he wins? When he loses?
7. How have you tried to control his mood or his behavior? How well have your attempts worked?
8. What consequences have you set (if any) if he continues the behavior?
9. How can I help?

4 WISE COUNSEL

Certainly not everyone who gambles has an addiction, but many people don't notice the problem until it's far down the road. Many of the behaviors, including obsessive thoughts and secret acts, remain hidden for a long time. And when the person is confronted, he is usually defensive and makes plenty of excuses, and perhaps convincingly so.

Compulsive gambling is a personal and spiritual problem in which the addict is out of control and dominated by the behavior. It is a family and relational problem that destroys trust with the spouse and children. And it is a financial problem that drives the person into debt and threatens the financial future of the family.

Everyone in the family needs help to face reality and take steps toward healing and responsibility. The addict needs to go through a process of repentance and develop a new, healthy set of beliefs and habits. But the spouse may have enabled the behavior for a long time. She needs to experience healing, find hope, and be committed to the truth. She will learn to set consequences, not out of spite, but because she loves her husband and wants the best for him.

Compulsive gamblers may hit bottom when they run out of money and run out of people to lend them any more. At that point they are deeply in debt, and the family is in crisis—financially and relationally. In addition to therapy, addiction recovery, and professional financial counseling, the couple will benefit from understanding the five Money Personalities and principles of good communication.

ACTION STEPS : 5

1. In dealing with any addictive behavior, a careful intervention may be required. Consider setting up a formal, professional intervention with appropriate and immediate steps into therapy or recovery, along with significant mutually agreed upon consequences for refusal to take these steps.

2. Help the spouse of the compulsive gambler sort out the deep and conflicting feelings and thoughts about the person. Quite often love is mixed with rage, and too much trust is blended with feelings of betrayal. The spouse needs as much help as the addict.

3. At an appropriate time in the recovery process when both people are making progress, explain the five Money Personalities to help them understand themselves and each other.

4. Discuss the principles of good communication and conflict resolution, and answer any questions about how to apply these principles.

5. If needed, refer the couple (or spouse) to a competent financial professional to create a budget and take steps toward solvency.

BIBLICAL INSIGHTS : 6

Whoever loves money never has enough; whoever loves wealth is never satisfied with their income. This too is meaningless.

Ecclesiastes 5:10

The thirst for more is the opposite of contentment. Compulsive gambling thrives on comparison as the addict, who is never satisfied, looks at others who have more things or more winnings.

No one can serve two masters. Either you will hate the one and love the other, or you will be devoted to the one and despise the other. You cannot serve both God and money.

Luke 16:13

With any addiction, the substance or behavior effectively pushes God out of the center of our lives. When we prefer anything other than him, we are actually showing that we are devoted to it and that we despise him. This may sound harsh, but Jesus is making the point that we always put whatever we treasure in the highest place in our affections.

"I have the right to do anything," you say—but not everything is beneficial. "I have the right to do anything"—but I will not be mastered by anything.

1 Corinthians 6:12

The Bible doesn't say that gambling is a sin, but anything, even good things like food, sex, and leisure, can become sinful if we let those things become our master.

Do not lie to each other, since you have taken off your old self with its practices and have put on the new self, which is being renewed in knowledge in the image of its Creator.

Colossians 3:9–10

As we walk with Christ and experience his love, forgiveness, and purpose, we have the courage to be honest with each other, overcome any type of infidelity, and build relationships based on renewed trust.

7 PRAYER STARTER

Father, this couple has let their lives become dominated by destructive habits, secrets, and lies. They are turning to you for help. Thank you for your kindness and power. We trust your Spirit to guide them as they take hard steps toward truth, toward you, and toward each other. They have a long way to go, but we know that you are with them . . .

8 RECOMMENDED RESOURCES

Munchbach, Jim. *Make Your Money Count: Connecting Your Resources to What Matters Most*. Baxter Press, 2007.

Palmer, Bethany, and Scott Palmer. *First Comes Love, Then Comes Money: A Couple's Guide to Financial Communication*. HarperOne, 2009.

http://www.ronblue.com/

http://www.mvelopes.com/focusonthefamily/

http://www.daveramsey.com/home/

http://www.crown.org/

Compulsive Saving

- Samantha has run out of money before and she's determined that it will never happen again. She treasures every dollar she earns, agonizes over every one she spends, and knows to the penny how much her expenses are each month. She reviews every bill, spending hours each month poring over them to see if there are any charges she can contest. When she finds one, she gets on the phone and protests until she gets the charge reversed.

- Craig's friends laugh when they spend time with him because they can't go anywhere without his angling for a better deal. He tries to bargain at restaurants, the theater, and everywhere else to see if he can save a dime. He scours the ads in the paper and online to be sure he gets the very best possible price on anything he buys—and then he still asks for a lower price.

- Jayne is driving her husband crazy. Both of them make a good salary, but she refuses to spend any of what she makes. She grew up in a very poor family and she's afraid she may end up with no money again. She constantly worries about every expense, no matter how reasonable and necessary, and she argues with her husband when he spends more than she thinks he should, which happens regularly.

- Steven drives a car with two hundred thousand miles on it. A few years ago a friend suggested he get a new car, or at least a newer used car. Steven replied, "No way. I'm going to drive this thing until it's stone cold dead! No need to waste money when I have a perfectly good car." But it's not a perfectly good car. He's spent enough money on repairs in the past two years to buy a new one. Still, he's sure each repair is the last one his car will need.

DEFINITIONS AND KEY THOUGHTS 2

- Often *compulsive saving* is associated with hoarding, but the focus is on conserving money, not things.
- Usually the issues that drive compulsive saving are insecurity and the fear of being poor. The person feels driven to save as much money as possible, and the money provides a security blanket.
- Strategies to save money may prove to be counterproductive. The person keeps cars, appliances, computers, and other devices long past their prime, spending

an inordinate amount of money on repairs. And after the items are repaired with expensive parts and service, they're still out of date and vulnerable to other parts breaking.

- Many compulsive savers are preoccupied with their bills. They develop a "me against them" mentality with the electric company, landlord, cable company, and everyone else who sends them a bill each month. Occasionally they find a genuine error and then they feel completely justified in challenging every line on each bill each month.

- The behaviors and attitudes associated with compulsive saving cause conflicts in relationships with a spouse, children, and friends. These relational difficulties make the compulsive saver feel more isolated and insecure, which may in turn drive more pathological behavior.

3 : ASSESSMENT INTERVIEW

It won't be hard for this person to identify her Money Personality, but it will be helpful to determine the Money Personality of others in the family. This process can shed some light on the causes of disagreement and conflict.

1. What is your Money Personality? What is the Money Personality of each person close to you in your family and circle of friends?
2. How do you feel about spending money? What kind of spending makes you feel anxious?
3. What are some ways you try to save money?
4. How well do they work? How do they affect the people around you?
5. Do you have any outdated items that are costing more in repairs than they're worth? Why do you keep them?
6. Have you ever been poor? If so, how did the experience affect you?
7. How would your life be different if you were free from the fear of being poor?
8. How can I help?

4 : WISE COUNSEL

Compulsive saving is associated with deep feelings of insecurity and an inordinate preoccupation with controlling expenses. The problem may be related to obsessive compulsive disorder (OCD). This disorder isn't grounded in logic, so a rational pursuit of an explanation of the behavior may not be helpful. It is the result of powerful, consuming perceptions and fears that drive the person's actions.

People who struggle with this problem need to find peace and security at the deepest level in their lives. In addition, they can develop realistic perceptions about the nature of bills and the life expectancy of products. For instance, they can learn to trust that major companies aren't out to gouge them by overcharging. There may occasionally be a mistake on their bill, but this is rare. They will be much healthier if they take the risk of overpaying on rare occasions instead of being consumed with finding errors.

And every product—including cars, clothes, appliances, and computers—has a life expectancy. If we keep them too long, they begin to cost more than they're worth.

People who struggle with compulsive saving can learn new skills and practices, such as paying bills without scrutinizing them, throwing away items that are past their prime, and adequately maintaining equipment but replacing it when it no longer works as it should.

ACTION STEPS 5

1. Determine the severity of the problem with compulsive saving by analyzing how it is affecting normal activity and relationships.
2. Explore the underlying insecurities. In the initial assessment, discuss the potential of a family history of poverty or cycles of wealth and poverty.
3. Discuss the Money Personalities and ask the person to identify her personality and that of others close to her.
4. Provide specific, tangible behavioral goals to correct the most common problems with compulsive saving, such as scrutinizing bills for errors, analyzing bank statements, or spending too much on repairing items that should be discarded and replaced.
5. Changing ingrained patterns of thinking and behavior is a long-term process. Stay in touch with the client to provide support to facilitate steps forward.

BIBLICAL INSIGHTS 6

The Lord is my shepherd, I lack nothing. He makes me lie down in green pastures, he leads me beside quiet waters, he refreshes my soul. He guides me along the right paths for his name's sake. Even though I walk through the darkest valley, I will fear no evil, for you are with me; your rod and your staff, they comfort me.

Psalm 23:1–4

Our sense of security doesn't come from analyzing and controlling every detail of our lives. In fact, doing that enflames feelings of insecurity because we're never convinced we've done enough. In this beautiful psalm, David describes the deep trust we can have in God's goodness, his attention to every need, and his ability to provide for us. We rest in him.

Therefore I tell you, do not worry about your life, what you will eat or drink; or about your body, what you will wear. Is not life more than food, and the body more than clothes? Look at the birds of the air; they do not sow or reap or store away in barns, and yet your heavenly Father feeds them. Are you not much more valuable than they? Can any one of you by worrying add a single hour to your life? . . . But seek first his kingdom and his righteousness, and all these things will be given to you as well. Therefore do not worry about tomorrow, for tomorrow will worry about itself. Each day has enough trouble of its own.

Matthew 6:25–27, 33–34

Jesus told his followers that worry is the opposite of trust. When we fail to trust his goodness and greatness, we become preoccupied with all kinds of things that consume our thoughts, cloud our hearts, and poison our relationships. Christ is worth putting first in our lives.

Therefore, I urge you, brothers and sisters, in view of God's mercy, to offer your bodies as a living sacrifice, holy and pleasing to God—this is your true and proper worship. Do not conform to the pattern of this world, but be transformed by the renewing of your mind. Then you will be able to test and approve what God's will is—his good, pleasing and perfect will.

Romans 12:1–2

Our lives aren't changed by magic. We change bit by bit as we present ourselves to God, dive deep into his Word, and let it transform our minds from fear to trust. When that happens, we'll be able to interpret the events of life more fully from his perspective.

Not that I have already obtained all this, or have already arrived at my goal, but I press on to take hold of that for which Christ Jesus took hold of me. Brothers and sisters, I do not consider myself yet to have taken hold of it. But one thing I do: Forgetting what is behind and straining toward what is ahead, I press on toward the goal to win the prize for which God has called me heavenward in Christ Jesus.

Philippians 3:12–14

Until we see Jesus face-to-face, we're going to experience struggles with temptations, difficulties, and our fallen nature. Our task is to rivet our minds on the character of Christ and keep moving forward to follow him even in the most painful times. When we do that, we'll experience more joy and freedom than ever before.

7 PRAYER STARTER

Father, this woman is your child. May she be convinced of your wonderful love and acceptance and may she find in you a new sense of stability and security. Help her make better choices about money so she will become free from fear and the compulsion to save. Thank you . . .

RECOMMENDED RESOURCES 8

Munchbach, Jim. *Make Your Money Count: Connecting Your Resources to What Matters Most.* Baxter Press, 2007.

Palmer, Bethany, and Scott Palmer. *First Comes Love, Then Comes Money: A Couple's Guide to Financial Communication.* HarperOne, 2009.

http://www.ronblue.com/

http://www.mvelopes.com/focusonthefamily/

http://www.daveramsey.com/home/

http://www.crown.org/

Compulsive Spending

1 PORTRAITS

- Kim couldn't stop thinking about going to the mall. Every day, she spent hours going over flyers and ads to check the best prices. She would drive to the mall even if she didn't need anything, just to watch people shop. Many times she couldn't help herself; she had to buy something. When she did, she felt energized and alive. Her whole life revolved around thinking about shopping, planning to shop, shopping, and then planning her next trip the next day.

- Jake never met a deal he didn't like. He checked prices of televisions on dozens of online sites, even if he had just bought one. He checked the prices of running shoes, even though he had four pairs in his closet. When he and Phyllis first married, she laughed and thought his obsession with shopping was cute, but after three years it was long past cute. It was consuming his life and ruining hers. She pleaded with him to realize how it was controlling his life, but he blew her off. "I'm just trying to save a few dollars. You don't want us to waste money, do you?" Phyllis was afraid she had wasted her life being married to Jake.

- Car salesmen love to see people like Maria walk in the door. Maria lives by her emotions, and her feelings drive her purchases—especially big purchases like cars. She's had a string of new cars, and each time, she's been upside down when she got a new one. Each time, though, she "loved the color," "loved the smell," "loved the look," or loved something else about the car, so she bought it.

- Georgia and Chris came to counseling because they can't stop fighting. Among the many issues that are problems in their marriage is money. Georgia loves to go to the mall and buy new clothes. Every month she spends a small fortune. When Chris complains, she insists, "I take most of the things back. It's no big deal!" When they first got married, their disagreements about spending were minor but soon they escalated into a power struggle, with hurt feelings and blame. "He doesn't understand," she complains. "She spends way too much on nothing," he grouses.

2 DEFINITIONS AND KEY THOUGHTS

- Dr. James Mitchell, chairman of the department of neuroscience at the University of North Dakota School of Medicine and Health Sciences and lead author of a study on cognitive behavior therapy for *compulsive-buying disorder*, says that compulsive shopping can be just as addictive and destructive as alcohol or drugs. Much more common among women than men, compulsive shopping often coexists with other mental health problems, such as depression, alcoholism, and eating disorders. Women may shop for clothes or shoes, but men go for electronics or books. Many of the items compulsive shoppers acquire are never used. It's the thrill of the hunt that's important to them, not the items themselves. Of course credit card debt is prevalent among compulsive shoppers.

- Different Money Personalities have very different perceptions about spending. At the extremes, some of them can develop the pathological behavior of compulsive spending.

  — *Savers* get a kick out of saving money. They look for bargains and feel exhilarated when they get something for less. To them, a good deal isn't good enough. They're looking for a steal! They are at risk of becoming *hoarders* who never get rid of things or even use them.

  — *Spenders* get just as much of a rush out of buying for others as for themselves. They feel joy in the hunt for something new and they're not concerned about the price. "It's all about cash flow," they insist. They are at risk of becoming *compulsive spenders*, out of control and deeply in debt.

  — *Risk Takers* shop for things that have an upside potential, some danger, or at least some flash. Investments are more interesting to them than shoes, but if they have to shop for clothes, either they want something that is loud and proud or they want shopping to end quickly because it's so boring. A few of them may become *compulsive spenders*.

  — *Security Seekers* aren't as interested in the things they can buy as what the things mean. They investigate thoroughly, from something as small as where to eat to as large as the purchase of a house. They may look like *Savers*, but there's a difference. *Savers* are interested in the here and now, but *Security Seekers* are focused on the future. They may develop a habit of *hoarding* things as a security blanket.

  — *Flyers* are laid back, easygoing, and highly relational. Money and things don't really matter that much to them. Shopping and spending are entirely functional. They don't care that much about saving money or getting a great deal. They don't get a thrill from taking financial risks and see no need to analyze their spending. They just want to have fun with their friends.

ASSESSMENT INTERVIEW 3

1. What are your spending habits? How would those who love you describe your spending habits?
2. How do these habits contribute to the problems you want to talk about today?
3. Which Money Personality best represents you? How does it reflect your spending behavior?
4. What about your spending patterns is good and normal? What is problematic?

5. Have you tried to change your behavior? If so, what happened?
6. What are your goals for counseling related to spending?
7. How will making progress in this area affect you and your relationships?
8. How can I help?

4 WISE COUNSEL

The Money Personalities give clients a baseline to talk about their perceptions, feelings, and behaviors about money and particularly about spending. Go over the five different personalities to help your client identify his personality and that of his partner.

In the assessment interview, examine the client's personal history and look for significant emotional wounds and resulting compulsive and obsessive patterns. These will probably show up in many areas of life, not just finances. Clients who express problems with shopping may actually be involved in compulsive behavior but are very reluctant to discuss it. Quite often their behavior causes conflict in marriage or other relationships, but like others with personality disorders, they seldom see the problem.

Determine the severity of the spending problem. If it's a mild disagreement between partners, address it as a communication issue. But if you determine the problem is compulsive shopping, use appropriate interventions to correct misbeliefs and impart liberating truth.

5 ACTION STEPS

1. Describe the Money Personalities and help the client self-identify. Talk about the client's spending pattern.
2. Identify triggers that propel the person to inordinate and destructive behaviors, including compulsive spending.
3. Address the underlying addictive behavior with appropriate therapies. Be sure to refer the client if unfamiliar with appropriate therapies.
4. Help the client formulate a reasonable, workable budget, with clear benefits for meeting target goals at every step.
5. Foster good communication and the support of spouse, children, church members, and others in a supportive community.
6. Follow-up is essential. Habits of a lifetime aren't changed quickly. It takes concerted effort, discipline, and reinforcement for the person to create new patterns of thinking and acting.

6 BIBLICAL INSIGHTS

By wisdom a house is built, and through understanding it is established;
through knowledge its rooms are filled with rare and beautiful treasures.

Proverbs 24:3–4

God's wisdom addresses our deepest motivations, not just our behavior. As we search God's Word, we find that we fall short in many ways, but God's grace forgives and restores. With this assurance, we can experience his power and seek his will in every area of our lives.

Like a city whose walls are broken through is a person who lacks self-control.

Proverbs 25:28

Many people are out of control in their spending habits. Their lack of self-control leaves them vulnerable to compulsions, shame, and conflict with others.

The prudent see danger and take refuge, but the simple keep going and pay the penalty.

Proverbs 27:12

There is real danger in foolish spending habits, but many people don't see any need to change. We are wise to open our eyes and see how foolish spending and hoarding affect people—maybe even us.

This day is holy to our Lord. Do not grieve, for the joy of the LORD is your strength.

Nehemiah 8:10

In every area of our lives, we need to let the love, joy, power, and forgiveness of God soak into every fiber of our being. As we delight in him, our hearts are filled with his love and we become less demanding of people and things to make us happy.

PRAYER STARTER : 7

Father, help this person see the damage caused by poor spending habits, realizing that it's about a lot more than buying new stuff; it's about his heart. Please fill him, Lord. Cause him to know you and delight in you so that things are crowded out of his heart. May you be honored by every dime he spends and every dime he doesn't spend . . .

RECOMMENDED RESOURCES : 8

Munchbach, Jim. *Make Your Money Count: Connecting Your Resources to What Matters Most*. Baxter Press, 2007.

Palmer, Bethany, and Scott Palmer. *First Comes Love, Then Comes Money: A Couple's Guide to Financial Communication*. HarperOne, 2009.

http://www.ronblue.com/

http://www.mvelopes.com/focusonthefamily/

Control and Compromise

1 PORTRAITS

- Sharon's solution to the painful arguments with her husband, Phil, is to avoid talking about money at all. "He gets so angry so quickly," she laments. "There's just no use in trying to talk about it. I know we should be able to talk about our finances—and plenty of other things couples talk about—but it's safer just to let it go." As the years have gone by, they have talked less and less about important things in their relationship and their family.

- Beth was attracted to James because he was the strong, silent type. He never seemed to be confused and he always knew what he wanted in life. After they were married, she realized his self-control bled over into his relationship with her. Only a week after they returned from their honeymoon, James barked at her for buying a hairbrush. "You need to check with me before you buy anything. Do you understand?" he growled. She hoped he was just having a bad day, but it was much more than that. The romance of their engagement quickly evaporated as James's true colors came through. He was cold, calculating, and demanding. Beth felt she was only as valuable as one of the tools in his toolbox, and sometimes she thought she was at the bottom of the toolbox. James kept the checkbook, paid the bills, and gave Beth a weekly allowance. She knew she couldn't spend any more than he gave her or she'd be in big trouble. All day every day, her thoughts went from thinking she must be the most despicable wife on the planet to daydreaming about finding a man who would really love her.

- "Why is Eric so passive?" Monica complained to a friend who was trying to help her. Monica and Eric's relationship had begun well, but four long years of clinical depression had crushed his spirits. Even after Eric began working again, he didn't seem to have enough energy and confidence to fully engage Monica—sexually, emotionally, or in any other way. Whenever she asked him for his ideas about a major purchase, he just shrugged. "Whatever you want to do is fine with me." Monica was certainly capable of making the decisions, but she wasn't happy with the status of the relationship.

- Nicki and Michael are intense about everything. They both built successful companies and have strong personalities. When they talk about money—or anything else for that matter—they fight like cats and dogs. Both of them have to win, and they pull out the big guns to attack each other. Sometimes one of them gets the upper hand with a better reason for a decision, but even then both of them lose. Their relationship is an armed truce occasionally punctuated by all-out warfare.

DEFINITIONS AND KEY THOUGHTS : 2

- People may try to control others in many different ways. Often people use *anger and intimidation*, but *self-pity, running away, lies,* and *using knowledge to intimidate* are also means of control. Some people try to *dominate* others to get their way, while other people try to avoid conflict by giving in to demands or getting away from the dominating person—and it's not unusual for these people to be married to each other.

- Early in a relationship, two people may develop certain behaviors to cope with conflict, and these behaviors can become normal and habitual in the relationship. For example, one person dominates and the other gives in or both dig in their heels and insist on their own way or both avoid a difficult topic at all costs.

- Those who try to dominate see the relationship as "one up/one down." They have the perspective, "I win; you lose." They don't care how much their anger and demands hurt the other person. They just want to win the argument. Others can become just as entrenched in their perspective and behavior: being passive and compliant to end the conflict as quickly as possible, or perhaps to fight just as hard to win the argument. Either way, the relationship is wounded in every encounter. Someone may win the argument, but trust is broken time after time.

- Every couple, every family, every friendship, and every relationship of any kind experiences *disagreements*. They're part of life. Knowing how and when to argue, and knowing when to step away from an argument that is too heated, can make the difference between progress and disaster.

- Couples need to learn the principles of good communication and conflict resolution to help them talk about their finances and restore trust to the relationship. However, many couples need to address the destructive *pattern of control and compliance* in their communication. When they see these patterns more clearly, they can make choices to *listen and compromise*.

ASSESSMENT INTERVIEW : 3

Explain the five Money Personalities. Help the client identify herself and her spouse and then ask:

1. What happens when the two of you talk about your finances (or anything else important to you and your relationship)? What are elements of your Money Personality profiles with which you complement each other? What are possible points of misunderstanding?

2. Describe the pattern of your communication. Is one of you dominating and the other compliant? When one gives in, how does the other feel? Or do both of you try to dominate? Or are both of you passive and compliant?

3. When did this pattern start? How did it become a permanent part of your communication?

4. What are your hopes and fears concerning talking to your spouse about your finances?

5. What are the most common triggers that propel you to try to dominate (or become passive)? Can you see them coming?

6. What are some choices you can make when you feel or see the triggers?

7. What can you do when you see your partner flare up or wilt?

8. What would you consider progress for you individually and for your relationship?

9. How can I help?

4 : WISE COUNSEL

Understanding how to fight fair—and making a commitment to fight this way—opens the door to rebuilding trust, lowering defenses, and sharing genuine love. Fighting fair requires skill and courage, but it is far less emotionally and relationally taxing than living through the pain of control and compliance. Fighting fair involves listening, sharing what's in your heart, and compromising so that both people win. In fact, the purpose is for each person to feel good about him- or herself, each other, and the decisions that are made.

The eight rules for a fair fight are:

1. *Commit to making it work*. This is a crucial beginning. Both people have to want to succeed in being better communicators and building the relationship. Make a strong commitment to respect each other, listen carefully, look for common ground, and forgive when the other person steps out of bounds.

2. *Start with new expectations*. Bad habits in communication and years of established perceptions don't change in an instant, but they can begin to change in significant ways. Assumptions may be based on a long history of past experience, but now it's time to carve out new hope for a better relationship. At the first sign of trouble (and bumps in the road are inevitable), each person can say, "This time, we're going to work through this," instead of "Here we go again!"

3. *Diffuse the situation*. One of the hardest things for people to learn and practice is to walk away, regroup emotionally, and come back for another try. Too often the dominating person presses even harder to win, and the passive person wants to run away and hide. Instead, either of you can say, "This is too tense for me right now. Let's take a break and come back later to try again." Making this choice isn't a loss. It shows self-control, perception, courage, and a commitment to the relationship.

4. *Stay focused on the problem at hand.* One of the techniques some people use to win an argument is to "cloud" the initial issue by bringing up different and irrelevant things or engaging in blaming instead of trying to solve the problem. When some couples experience tension in their conversations, one of them brings up a host of past offenses. These strategies are destructive. Instead, don't get distracted by other issues or finding fault. Focus only on the problem at hand and look for a solution together.

5. *Think about your Money Personalities.* Insight is golden. When you understand yourself and your partner, you will finally grasp why you've communicated so poorly for so long. It's not that your partner is a bad person; it's that he or she values different things than you do. But identifying your Money Personality isn't an excuse for irresponsible or controlling behavior. Your insights will help you understand, appreciate the differences, laugh a little more, and find a solution that works for both of you.

6. *Search for solutions.* Gaining the skills to fight fair lowers the level of animosity, establishes a platform for good communication, and fosters understanding, but you still have to find a workable solution for the financial problems in the relationship. The Money Personalities may have very different answers to each problem, so you shouldn't be surprised if you don't agree at first. But if you stay with it and listen a lot, you will be able to identify several plausible options from which you can choose the one that offers the best chance of success—regardless of whose idea it was.

7. *Expect to blow it.* The more wounded we are, the more we demand perfection from others—*our* definition of perfection, which means total respect, complete kindness, and absolute trust. But we're human. We make mistakes, we fail, we revert to old ways of thinking and acting, and we hide behind our previous forms of self-protection. As Peter wrote, "Love covers over a multitude of sins" (1 Peter 4:8). If you fail to show respect and reason, you must apologize, ask for forgiveness, and choose to build trust by acting with grace and integrity. If your partner is harsh or runs away instead of staying engaged, you should bring it up, express your hopes, and choose to forgive. When you choose to forgive and keep moving forward, even your sins and flaws become part of the new story of the relationship, making it stronger than ever.

8. *Extend grace.* Fighting fair involves a lot of love, forgiveness, and hope. Let go of the past, repent of your failures and flaws, and keep moving ahead to make the relationship stronger. When there's tension or disappointment, you may be tempted to go back to the old ways. But remember how gracious God is toward us. He forgives "seventy times seven" times—limitless—and keeps loving us. When you are certain of his grace for you, then you can extend grace to your partner. You can't expect perfection in your conversations about money or any other topic, but when you love each other enough to value the relationship above all else, you will stay engaged during good times and bad. You will love, laugh, listen, and keep searching for good solutions to money problems.

5 ACTION STEPS

1. Explain the five Money Personalities and help the individual or couple identify themselves. Discuss the way their Money Personalities complement each other and how they may conflict with each other.
2. Teach and model the principles of active listening and conflict resolution. You might want to ask the couple to have their first discussion with you as the facilitator or mediator.
3. Role play a conversation about a particular topic that has caused problems in the relationship.
4. Ask the couple to practice the rules for a fair fight in your presence. Coach them and give them feedback.
5. Support them as they use these rules to establish a new way of communicating with each other.

6 BIBLICAL INSIGHTS

Hatred stirs up conflict, but love covers over all wrongs.

Proverbs 10:12

The perspective "I win; you lose" makes losers of everybody, and running away from tension in a relationship doesn't resolve anything. When we truly love someone, we don't use bullying techniques to get our way and we don't hide from the other person to avoid conflict. We want the best for our partner and the relationship, so we stay engaged.

Above all, love each other deeply, because love covers over a multitude of sins.

1 Peter 4:8

We may tease and laugh at the other person's quirks, but when we sin against one another it hurts. Loving our partner means we choose to be honest about the pain we feel, but instead of lashing out or running away, we forgive and communicate to resolve the problem.

Bear with each other and forgive one another if any of you has a grievance against someone. Forgive as the Lord forgave you.

Colossians 3:13

Good communication skills can take us a long way in improving our relationships, but no matter how proficient we become, people will still get on our nerves. We "bear with" them by choosing to avoid negative reactions. We overlook as much as possible, address the things that are necessary, and graciously forgive because Jesus has forgiven us.

A bruised reed he will not break, and a smoldering wick he will not snuff out, till he has brought justice through to victory. In his name the nations will put their hope.

Matthew 12:20–21

When Jesus met people who were wounded and broken, he didn't use their weakness to crush them. Instead, he loved, supported, listened, and provided for their needs. In the same way, the strong person in any relationship can act like Jesus by showing humility and love to support the weaker person.

PRAYER STARTER 7

Jesus, this couple needs your help. They've been in a destructive pattern of communication for a long time, and it needs to change. Help both of them apply the eight rules of fighting fair so they can show genuine love to each other and move forward. May they trust you to change them and their relationship . . .

RECOMMENDED RESOURCES 8

Palmer, Bethany, and Scott Palmer. *First Comes Love, Then Comes Money: A Couple's Guide to Financial Communication*. HarperOne, 2009.

http://www.ronblue.com/

http://www.mvelopes.com/focusonthefamily/

http://www.daveramsey.com/home/

http://www.crown.org/

Credit

1 PORTRAITS

- Latoya was going off to college and she wanted to get a credit card. The bank in her neighborhood turned her down. When she talked to one of the officers, he said he'd be glad to issue her a card if her father's name was on the account as well. Her father agreed so she could begin to develop credit.
- Julie and Luke had been married for three years and they wanted to buy a house. When they applied for a loan, they were turned down because Luke's credit score before they were married was very low due to some late payments on a motorcycle he had bought several years earlier.
- Randy and Carol wanted to build up their credit so they could eventually buy a house. To make progress, they opened an account at a national chain and bought a big screen television, paying $50 a month for it. They made sure the company would report their payments to the major credit reporting companies.

2 DEFINITIONS AND KEY THOUGHTS

- *Credit* is a borrower's reputation and predicts the person's likelihood of repaying loans. *A person's credit is formulated from his borrowing history, especially credit reports.*
- A *credit report* contains massive amounts of information about a person's *borrowing history*. Lenders (retail stores, insurance companies, and others) provide information for credit reports, including how much the person borrowed, repayment of loans, and other details. Credit reporting agencies collect and distribute this information. If companies make faulty reports, a person's credit will suffer.
- *Numeric credit scores* are generated by a computer that examines and tabulates credit reports.
- Credit was originally used solely by lenders to evaluate borrowers. Today, however, credit reports are used in many other areas of life. They may be used to determine a person's suitability for employment and insurance.
- Ways to build credit:

  — *Obtain a secured credit card.* You make a deposit to a bank account and the bank issues a credit limit based on the amount of the deposit. The bank takes little or no risk, and you gradually build credit.

— *For large purchases, use store programs.* This works well for items like furniture, appliances, and electronics. It's easier to qualify for these programs, and they enable people to build credit. Be sure the retailer reports the loan and payments to the major credit reporting companies.

— *Obtain a credit card* from a reputable bank and pay at least the minimum amount on your charges before the due date. The danger, however, is in building a debt that one is not able to manage and to get stuck with exorbitant credit card interest and fees.

- People who have low credit scores can *rebuild their credit rating* by following the same path, but it may take longer to overcome poor choices from the past.
- Some people advocate building credit by asking someone (often a parent or friend) to *cosign a loan.* Then the lender considers the cosigner's credit when deciding on granting the loan. If the borrower pays the loan, he builds his credit. If he doesn't, the cosigner must pay, which often creates significant relational problems. For this reason, in most cases, we don't recommend this approach.

ASSESSMENT INTERVIEW : 3

Explain the Money Personalities and use these insights as the basis for a discussion about the couple's interaction regarding credit.

1. Are financial stresses causing problems for you? If so, tell me about them.
2. What is your Money Personality? What is your spouse's? As you think about these profiles, what are the areas in which you complement each other? What are some points of potential misunderstanding, differing perceptions, and tension?
3. Are you having trouble borrowing money? Tell me about that.
4. Has this problem affected your relationships? If so, how?
5. How have you tried to build (or rebuild) your credit? What has worked? What hasn't worked very well?
6. How would having a better credit score help you?
7. How can I help?

WISE COUNSEL : 4

The inability to borrow money can be a significant problem, either for young people who want to buy a first home or for those whose credit has been eroded by poor financial management. As you talk to people and this issue comes up, explore the implications. Quite often financial problems of all kinds create relational difficulties. Be sure to address these.

For individuals, families, and businesses, the modern financial system is based on credit. Building good credit, then, isn't just a good thing to do—it's a necessary part of living in today's world. However, a person's credit score is just one small piece of life. If the acquisition of things becomes too important, it's idolatry, and it poisons every part of the person's life.

Explain the different ways of building credit and explore which ones work best for the person you are counseling. One of the most important pieces of advice to give anyone building credit is this: Make payments on time. If you can't pay the debt in full, at least make the minimum payment due.

Show the person how to monitor his credit score by going online to one (or all) of the three main companies that record and report these scores.

Individuals and couples who come for counseling will benefit from the insights of the five Money Personalities. Review these and help clients identify themselves and others close to them. Explain the principles of active listening, good communication, and conflict resolution, and answer any questions.

5 : ACTION STEPS

1. Building credit is important, but very few (if any) people come to counseling for this issue. Instead, they come for emotional and relational difficulties. As you assess the problem, be aware that the inability to borrow money may contribute to a person's emotional distress and a family's sense of insecurity.
2. Giving advice on building credit may seem as though it's out of your range of expertise, but a little information and common sense will enable you to guide your client. Become familiar with the suggestions in the previous section, and offer the appropriate suggestions to your client.
3. Many people need help formulating a clear, workable plan, even if the steps are very simple. Take nothing for granted. Help the person come up with steps and a time line to contact stores, banks, or credit reporting companies for information.
4. Explain the five Money Personalities and help him identify himself and his spouse. Discuss the principles of good communication and help him learn how to apply these principles.
5. After a few weeks, ask the client what steps he has taken and encourage him to keep moving ahead. Talk about the impact this is having (or will have) on important relationships.

6 : BIBLICAL INSIGHTS

The plans of the diligent lead to profit as surely as haste leads to poverty.

Proverbs 21:5

The modern financial system doesn't just bestow good credit on people. We have to think and plan the best way to build credit so that we can borrow wisely.

By wisdom a house is built, and through understanding it is established; through knowledge its rooms are filled with rare and beautiful treasures.

Proverbs 24:3–4

A house—and a home—is established by wisdom and discipline in all areas of life, including finances. The treasures we enjoy include the things we buy, but far more are peace, love, hope, and joy with our family members. We are blessed when we learn to value these highly.

Be sure you know the condition of your flocks, give careful attention to your herds; for riches do not endure forever, and a crown is not secure for all generations.

Proverbs 27:23–24

From time to time, all of us need to know where we stand in the eyes of the world. Checking our credit score tells us how companies view us, as valued and respected partners or as risks. Our reputations as Christians are, to some degree, based on how we manage our money.

PRAYER STARTER 7

Lord, this man wants to use money wisely, including credit. He doesn't want to spend more than he earns, but sometimes he needs to borrow some money for big purchases. Give him wisdom, Lord, to limit his spending and to borrow only what's necessary. Help him use everything he has for you . . .

RECOMMENDED RESOURCES 8

Munchbach, Jim. *Make Your Money Count: Connecting Your Resources to What Matters Most*. Baxter Press, 2007.

Palmer, Bethany, and Scott Palmer. *First Comes Love, Then Comes Money: A Couple's Guide to Financial Communication*. HarperOne, 2009.

http://www.ronblue.com/

http://www.mvelopes.com/focusonthefamily/

http://www.daveramsey.com/home/

http://www.crown.org/

Credit Cards and Overspending

1 PORTRAITS

- When Carmen went to college, her father got her a credit card. He felt good about it because she was launching into her college career on her own and she had done a good job managing money in high school. Soon after she arrived on campus, however, she became friends with some girls who were from wealthy families. They spent money on anything without even thinking about it. To keep up, Carmen used her credit card. She knew she was over the limit her dad had given her but she didn't want to look foolish and cheap in front of her new friends. When the first bill came to her dad, he hit the roof. She had racked up more than $2,000 in the first month! When he called, she knew instantly she was in big trouble.

- Joel had been working at the same company for thirty years. When the company downsized, he was surprised that he was let go but he was even more surprised when he couldn't get a job for several months. Even though he and his family cut expenses to the bone, they burned through their savings pretty quickly. When that money was gone, Joel began putting groceries and other expenses on his credit card. Maxing out one card, he began using another card he had seldom used before. A few months later it was maxed out too. He didn't even have enough to pay the minimum on them. He owed $25,000, an amount that was increasing quickly due to the fees.

- Kathleen's husband, Lawrence, had no idea she drove fifty miles every Tuesday to gamble. She was at home when he left for work and she was there at the door when he came home. In between, she hurried to a casino and gambled as long as she could. Sometimes she won but most of the time she lost every penny she bet. She became a compulsive gambler who couldn't stop. To try to hide her losses, she opened a credit card account with a bank at the casino. When the bills came, she made sure she got to them before her husband could see them and she insisted on writing the checks each month. For more than a year she hid her secret life from Lawrence, but finally, he realized a lot of money was unaccounted for. When he looked at the checkbook and saw the payments to the bank, he confronted Kathleen. At first, she denied knowing what it was about. Finally, she came clean. It was a classic case of financial infidelity. Kathleen and Lawrence had a long road to travel to rebuild trust.

- When Linda's daughter Mary had her first baby, Linda was thrilled. Though Mary and her husband lived halfway across the country, Linda was determined to be there to help as much as possible. Linda's husband had died years before, and she lived on his pension and Social Security, which meant she didn't have much to spare. To pay for the plane tickets and gifts for the baby, Linda used her credit card. For the first time in her life, she couldn't make the full payment the next month. But she wanted to go back again to see Mary and the baby. After several trips over six months, Linda owed more money than she ever imagined possible. Each time, she had rationalized her expenses and told herself it was no big deal—but it became a very big deal. She experienced significant anxiety, headaches, and nausea. Her doctor said it was stress.

DEFINITIONS AND KEY THOUGHTS 2

- The *misuse of credit cards* is so common in our culture that it seems completely normal. People don't want to delay gratification, so they use these tools to get what they want immediately. For a while it seems like "free money," but when they can't make the payments, the mounting debt leads to anxiety and relational conflict.
- Some financial advisors (and spouses and parents) believe credit cards are almost demonic. Certainly the misuse of them causes big problems, but if they are used properly, they can be helpful tools. *Appropriate uses* include:

  — *Convenience.* Credit cards allow us to buy things over the phone or online.
  — *Record keeping.* Each statement provides a detailed accounting of the month's purchases. Many banks also provide data showing how much we spend in categories like food, clothing, and travel.
  — *Reservations.* Credit cards enable us to guarantee rental cars, hotel accommodations, and other things we want to reserve.
  — *Cash flow.* We may find an item that is offered at a steep discount for a short while when we don't have the cash to buy it. Using a credit card enables us to purchase it now and pay for it next month when we have the money.
  — *Emergencies.* Sometimes we have expenses for medical care, car repair, or some other emergency and we don't have enough cash or a checkbook with us.
  — *Services.* Many credit cards offer rewards, such as airline miles or cash back, as well as extended warranties, travel insurance, and discounts on selected items.

As many people know very well, there are *risks in using credit cards*, including:

  — *Increased spending.* People who use cash spend 30 percent less than those who use credit cards, so it's a good idea to use cash whenever possible to stay within the budget.
  — *Losing track of spending.* Whipping out a card is so easy that many people don't stay on top of the amount they're spending.

— *Additional fees and expenses.* Annual fees are charged for some cards, but the real culprit in this area is the interest rate banks charge on the unpaid balance. These rates may be from 8 to 35 percent, and the interest is paid on the accumulating balance each month. Some people think that paying the minimum is acceptable, but paying only the minimum means that it will take a long time to pay off the balance, and during that time, the total interest payment soars.

— *Obligations on future income.* When people sign the agreement to open a credit card account, they make a commitment to use future income to pay the balance. The more debt that is incurred, the more future income is obligated.

— *Worry and conflict.* Beyond the numbers on the statement each month, the emotional and relational costs of the misuse of credit cards is staggering.

3 | ASSESSMENT INTERVIEW

1. How is credit card debt causing problems for you? Are these difficulties only affecting you individually or are they creating problems in your relationships?
2. What is the current status of your credit card account? How did it get this way?
3. What attempts have you (or whoever incurred the debt) made to get out of this debt?
4. Have you been completely honest with others (like your spouse) who are affected?
5. Do you have a plan? If so, what is it?
6. Who else needs to get on board with this plan?
7. How can I help?

4 | WISE COUNSEL

People come to counseling regarding credit card debt if they are experiencing significant personal anxiety or relational conflict. In these cases, credit card debt is often just one piece of the puzzle. They may need help with this and several other areas of life, including depression, compulsive behavior, secrets and financial infidelity, and poor communication patterns with spouse or kids.

When people are deeply in debt due to the misuse of credit cards, they may need professional financial assistance, but warn them to beware of companies that advertise debt consolidation. These may be legitimate but they may also be scams.

Work with the individual or couple to deal with the presenting emotional and relational issues. In addition, suggest crafting a sound, workable budget. Help them understand the five Money Personalities and principles of good communication.

ACTION STEPS : 5

1. Explain the five Money Personalities. Help her identify her personality and that of her spouse to promote understanding.
2. Teach the client the principles of conflict resolution and help her apply these principles in her relationships.
3. Talk about the appropriate uses of a credit card. To relieve anxiety and promote trust, help her make commitments about how and when she will use her cards.
4. Address the issue of credit card misuse in the context of the larger issues in the individual or couple's life, such as trust, secrets, financial infidelity, and communication.
5. Monitor progress and provide additional insights and support.

BIBLICAL INSIGHTS : 6

It is better not to make a vow than to make one and not fulfill it.

Ecclesiastes 5:5

God takes commitments very seriously. When we sign up for any kind of credit, we make a solemn vow—to the bank or other lender, but also to God—to pay what we owe. Some of us may think that paying it eventually is good enough, but the proper use of credit cards means that we pay off the full amount each month.

Give to everyone what you owe them: If you owe taxes, pay taxes; if revenue, then revenue; if respect, then respect; if honor, then honor. Let no debt remain outstanding, except the continuing debt to love one another, for whoever loves others has fulfilled the law.

Romans 13:7–8

Credit cards give us the opportunity to put off the payment of debts, but we shouldn't take this opportunity. Instead, the pattern of our lives in every area should be to pay each person and institution what is rightfully due.

But the fruit of the Spirit is love, joy, peace, forbearance, kindness, goodness, faithfulness, gentleness and self-control. Against such things there is no law. Those who belong to Christ Jesus have crucified the flesh with its passions and desires. Since we live by the Spirit, let us keep in step with the Spirit. Let us not become conceited, provoking and envying each other.

Galatians 5:22–26

As we walk in the Spirit and experience his wisdom and strength, the fruit of God's life pours from us, including self-control, so we can say no to selfish desires.

For the Spirit God gave us does not make us timid, but gives us power, love and self-discipline.

2 Timothy 1:7

The spiritual life is filled with choices, often hard choices, but we are never alone. The Spirit lives in us to give us the power we need to honor Christ in everything we do.

7 : PRAYER STARTER

Father, everything we have is yours, and this woman wants to honor you with every dime you entrust to her. She's made some bad choices and she's let some things slip. She wants to correct this and establish a new, better pattern of taking care of money. Lord, thank you for your forgiveness, love, and strength. Help her trust you for her future . . .

8 : RECOMMENDED RESOURCES

Munchbach, Jim. *Make Your Money Count: Connecting Your Resources to What Matters Most.* Baxter Press, 2007.

Palmer, Bethany, and Scott Palmer. *First Comes Love, Then Comes Money: A Couple's Guide to Financial Communication.* HarperOne, 2009.

http://www.ronblue.com/

http://www.mvelopes.com/focusonthefamily/

http://www.daveramsey.com/home/

http://www.crown.org/

Debt

- Alex owns his own business, and Diana is an executive in a large local company. Together they make more than $300,000 a year. The problem is that they spend more than $320,000. "I don't know how this could happen," Alex lamented to a friend. "We're over $75,000 in debt." Diana was brutally honest, "It's because we can't say no to anything we want. Something has to change, but I'm not sure where to start."

- Scott and Tracy were in their late twenties when they got married. Friends and family gave them thousands of dollars as wedding presents, and they took this as a sign they could buy whatever they wanted. With the confidence of all that money in the bank, they rented a very nice apartment. They bought a new 3D television, two computers, smart phones, and a new car. Except for the apartment and the car, they put it all on credit cards. After about four months of a dwindling bank account, they realized what they'd done. They owed $4,000, their account was empty, and they had obligations for more each month than they were earning. "We're such fools," Tracy wept when they faced the facts. "It's all stuff you wanted," Scott whined. That conversation wasn't a good beginning in an attempt to resolve the problem.

- Darren worked as a regional manager for a national corporation for twenty years. During this time, he saw some of his friends start their own businesses and get rich. Finally, he mustered the courage to take a step. He researched a number of companies that were on the market and he borrowed more than a million dollars to buy a trucking company. He didn't know anything about shipping but he told his wife, "How hard can it be? I've run our region successfully for years. I can do this." In three years his company failed. After he sold the assets, he owed more than $500,000. The strain of those years, followed by the utter financial collapse of their world, caused a deep rift between Darren and his wife. She wanted a divorce, but he pleaded with her to stay. He said, "I'll get a good job. I can be a manager and make good money. It'll take time, but we'll dig out of this hole." She wasn't so sure.

- Tom and Terri both have good jobs. He's an insurance agent and she's a nurse. For many years, they lived comfortably with their three kids. They didn't save much but they enjoyed life. When the first son went to college, they scraped together enough savings to pay for his tuition and expenses. But by the time he was a senior, both of the other two kids were in college, and the costs skyrocketed.

They applied for grants and loans, but even with those, Tom and Terri had to come up with money for some expenses. By the time the last child graduated, the event was bittersweet. The parents were proud of their kids but they were more than $100,000 in debt.

2 DEFINITIONS AND KEY THOUGHTS

- There is a big difference between *good debt* and *bad debt*. Generally, good debt is at or below 10 percent interest and involves appreciating assets (like a home mortgage) or career opportunities (such as school loans). Bad debt is the result of foolish choices, bad breaks without a safety net, and the failure to plan effectively.
- People in debt may come to counseling with presenting problems of anxiety, depression, or relational conflict. The inability to effectively manage finances contributes to a feeling of shame, hopelessness, and anger.
- Quite often people slip into deep debt because of denial. They simply refuse to see the warning signs along the way that point to the growing problem. When they finally have to face the facts, they feel overwhelmed. At this point, they may look for someone to blame—sometimes themselves, but usually their spouse or someone else.
- The good news is that millions of people find the courage to face the reality of their crushing debts, make necessary adjustments, and climb back to solvency. This process is hard, but it builds character. Blame destroys trust, but working together to resolve debt problems builds relationships.

3 ASSESSMENT INTERVIEW

Explain the Money Personalities, and use them to stimulate discussion on the topic of debt.

1. How does debt contribute to how you're feeling today?
2. What is your Money Personality? What is your spouse's? What are points of agreement and tension between your two personalities, especially regarding debt?
3. Tell me about your financial condition. What is your current status?
4. What was the progression of choices that led to this trouble? Why do you think you didn't see the warning signals, or if you saw them, why didn't you do anything about them?
5. How is the debt affecting your mood, your outlook, and your relationships?
6. Do you have a plan to get out of debt? If so, what is it? If not, how will you construct one?
7. What are your biggest concerns as you take steps to get out of debt? What are your hopes?
8. How can I help?

WISE COUNSEL : 4

When debt is a contributing factor in a person's coming for counseling, he may not talk about his finances in the first session or two. It may take some digging to uncover debt as a significant cause of generalized anxiety, depression, despair, and relational turmoil. The counselor's role is to offer hope that change is possible—for the financial condition, the personal distress, and the strained relationships.

Counselors and pastors usually aren't equipped to help people with the details of financial matters, so it may be wise to refer clients to a competent professional financial counselor for help.

A few important principles can help a person take steps to get out of debt, including:

- *Spend less than your income.* This is a simple concept, but it's amazing how many people get into debt because they don't follow it. Individuals, couples, and families need to cut their expenses to have additional funds to pay down what they owe. They may also need to find a way to increase their income through additional work or the sale of assets.

- *Differentiate between good debt and bad debt.* Sometimes, even good debt can lead to trouble if the couple buys a house that's too expensive or if college loans are too extensive. Bad debt, however, is the prime target to help the couple or individual get out of debt.

- *Some people advise destroying all credit cards, but that's not necessary.* Determine which ones have the lowest rates, and use them for emergencies and reservations, but pay off the balance each month. Cut up all the others so there's no temptation to use them.

- *Be sure to pay at least the minimum payments on all cards each month.* Failure to make these payments creates significant headaches.

- *To pay down debts, put them all on the table and categorize them by the interest rate and the amount owed.* There are two different strategies debt counselors suggest. One is to begin with the smallest amount, pay it off, and then move to the next smallest. This "snowball effect" builds confidence. The other is to begin by focusing on the one with the highest interest rate and pay it off first, then work down toward the account with the lowest rate. Either way will work as long as people are tenacious in their commitment to lower expenses and use the money saved to pay down debt. No matter which strategy is employed, be sure to make at least the minimum payments on all the other cards and accounts.

- *Negotiate lower rates.* Many lenders will be willing to lower the interest rate if you ask them. They don't want anyone to default on their loans, so they may be willing to work with you to make it a bit easier to make the payments.

- *Celebrate each step forward.* Digging out of a big debt hole takes a lot of courage. It can be difficult to change living standards and financial goals, so be sure to have a party (an inexpensive one) each time an intermediate goal is reached.

Quite often debt grows because of secrets and other forms of financial infidelity. Feelings of resentment and betrayal are common, along with shame and the desire to blame others for the problem. For individuals and couples, understanding themselves and others involved can pave the way toward substantial progress. The five Money Personalities and principles of conflict resolution are valuable tools to help people move ahead.

5 ACTION STEPS

1. Review the five Money Personalities to help the client understand himself and his spouse.
2. Explain the principles of good communication and conflict resolution. Answer any questions about applying these principles.
3. Address the personal feelings of shame and hopelessness that often accompany significant debt and offer hope for resolution of the problem.
4. Refer to a financial counselor for additional assistance in helping the person or couple formulate a good plan to get out of debt.
5. Continue to monitor the level of tenacity to stick with the plan. It's common for people to start well, but the daily grind of cutting expenses can wear them down. They need assurance that their wise choices will make a difference.

6 BIBLICAL INSIGHTS

The rich rule over the poor, and the borrower is slave to the lender.

Proverbs 22:7

When people endure crushing debt, they become the slave of the lender—their lives revolve around the lender's demands to pay back the loan. We are called to put Christ first in our lives, but pressing debts have a way of dominating our thoughts. We need to get our debt problems resolved so Christ can be our first priority.

I am not saying this because I am in need, for I have learned to be content whatever the circumstances. I know what it is to be in need, and I know what it is to have plenty. I have learned the secret of being content in any and every situation, whether well fed or hungry, whether living in plenty or in want. I can do all this through him who gives me strength.

Philippians 4:11–13

Paul saw everything he enjoyed as a gift from God, not a right he could demand. When he had plenty, he didn't set his heart on living lavishly, and when he had little, he wasn't discouraged. He learned "the secret" of being content in every situation. We need to learn the same lesson.

So I say, walk by the Spirit, and you will not gratify the desires of the flesh. For the flesh desires what is contrary to the Spirit, and the Spirit what is contrary to the flesh. They are in conflict with each other, so that you are not to do whatever you want. But if you are led by the Spirit, you are not under the law.

Galatians 5:16–18

Often people get into debt because they didn't say no to their desires to have more stuff and better experiences. Self-control and wisdom are hallmarks of a person who walks in the Spirit.

Keep your lives free from the love of money and be content with what you have, because God has said, "Never will I leave you; never will I forsake you."

Hebrews 13:5

To the writer of Hebrews, contentment doesn't come out of thin air. It is a product of deep trust that God is with us, he loves us, and his purposes are best. With this assurance, we can make good choices and stick with them, trusting God to give us strength to carry them out each day.

PRAYER STARTER 7

Lord Jesus, this person has gotten into big financial trouble and he needs help to climb out of the hole. Give him wisdom, Lord, to face reality and craft a workable plan to get out of debt. He wants to be able to focus on you and his family and not on his creditors, but he realizes that, for a while, he must devote his energies to trusting you with this problem. Thank you that you will be with him each step of the way . . .

RECOMMENDED RESOURCES 8

Munchbach, Jim. *Make Your Money Count: Connecting Your Resources to What Matters Most.* Baxter Press, 2007.

Palmer, Bethany, and Scott Palmer. *First Comes Love, Then Comes Money: A Couple's Guide to Financial Communication.* HarperOne, 2009.

http://www.ronblue.com/

http://www.mvelopes.com/focusonthefamily/

http://www.daveramsey.com/home/

http://www.crown.org/

Estate and End-of-Life Planning

1 : PORTRAITS

- Doug's mother died a few years ago, and since then, his father's health has been steadily declining. Doug has tried to talk to him about taking good care of himself, but recently his heart and lungs have been the cause of medical concern. His dad has been in and out of the hospital several times. The last time, everyone, including his dad and the doctors, thought he was going to die. When Doug went to visit him after he regained consciousness, his dad told him bluntly, "Son, don't let them keep me alive like this. I want to go be with your mother. Isn't there some kind of paper I can sign to make sure they don't bring me back again?"

- Felicia's parents were in a horrible car wreck. Her father died instantly, and her mother died after a week in ICU. During that week, her brother Jack began making a list of the things he wanted out of their parents' home. Felicia was outraged by her brother's insensitivity. When she confronted him, he barked, "They didn't have a will, did they? It's all fair game. You make your list, and I'll make mine. There's some good stuff to divide between us." Felicia had talked to her mother several times about making a will, but she always put it off.

- Gretchen's mother's memory wasn't what it used to be. For many months, Gretchen thought it was no big deal, but when her mother got lost in the grocery store, she realized something was seriously wrong. The doctor diagnosed Alzheimer's. She told her mother, "Mom, before things get worse, we need to work some things out so I can take care of you. I've asked our lawyer to draw up a power of attorney."

- Randy and Juanita have three small children. One night as they talked about their future, Randy asked, "What would happen to the kids if we were both killed?" The thought horrified them, but they realized the "logical" solution wouldn't work. Randy is an only child, and Juanita's brother is an alcoholic who has been arrested four times for drunk driving. She thought about their best friends and asked Randy, "How about talking to the Phillips about being guardians? Can we put that in a will?" "Yeah," Randy replied, "but we need to talk to them first."

2 DEFINITIONS AND KEY THOUGHTS

- *Wills*, *living wills*, and *powers of attorney* aren't the most exciting topics for a family to discuss, but they can provide clarity and direction in the most difficult moments. Many of the conflicts families endure in the last stages of a parent's terminal illness or after a death can be avoided (or at least minimized) if these instruments have been drawn up.

- In counseling, these topics can arise as preparation or as regret. Families who adequately anticipate the need for these tools can lower levels of stress, but often those who have failed to create them endure additional heartache in the most painful times of their lives.

- A *will* directs the distribution of assets after a person's death. In many cases it is the most important written document that a person creates during her lifetime. Many people don't want to face their own mortality, so they avoid this topic, but they can do their families great harm by their passivity. Various forms of wills are available, and each one has different aspects for the testator and the executor of the will. The *testator* is the person who creates the will, and the *executor* is the person appointed by the testator to execute the will.

- A *living will* is a legal document used by those who want to make their wishes known regarding the use or avoidance of life-prolonging medical treatments. The instrument can also be referred to as an advance directive, health care directive, or a physician's directive. (A living will, however, should not be confused with a *living trust*, an instrument used to hold and distribute assets to avoid probate.) A living will directs health care providers and family members concerning a person's desires for medical treatment in the event she is incapacitated. Each state may have different requirements, so an attorney's assistance may be needed.

- A *power of attorney* is used when a person is no longer able to manage her own financial affairs. This document is notarized, tailored, and revocable. It can involve one or more people, but if more than one person is involved, gaining consensus for decisions is sometimes difficult.

  — A *durable power of attorney* remains in effect during incompetence or disability.

  — A *standby power of attorney* is implemented in the event a person is unable to manage her affairs.

  — A *temporary power of attorney* applies only if an emergency arises.

ASSESSMENT INTERVIEW : 3

The issues of anticipating the need for these instruments or the conflict that can arise from not having them, make the assessment interview complex. Some of the questions below apply to family members who anticipate loved ones being incapacitated, some apply to resolving problems after the death of someone who didn't have a will, and some apply to people who need their own will.

If a family member is incapacitated:

1. Are you or someone in your family in such poor physical or mental health that you are considering a living will or power of attorney?
2. What do others in the family think about this course of action?

3. Does the person want these instruments? If not, what are your options?
4. Have you consulted with an attorney? Do you have one you trust?

If a family experiences conflict because there was no will:

1. How has the lack of clear directions in a will affected your relationships with others in the family?
2. What were your expectations?
3. At this point, what needs to happen to find common ground?
4. If you and your family members can't find resolution, are you prepared to grieve the loss and forgive those who have wronged you?

For those who need to write a will:

1. Do you have a will? If not, what are some benefits you'd receive from having one?
2. What are some resources you can use to write a comprehensive will?
3. What are some important provisions, such as guardianship of your children, that you are considering?

4 : WISE COUNSEL

Severe illness and death are extraordinarily difficult events for a family to face, and quite often they are complicated by many other factors, including the pain of watching helplessly as a family member deteriorates physically and/or mentally, the anticipated loss at the person's death, conflict with family members about how to care for the loved one, and conflict over assets from the estate.

In counseling, look for the complicated and disturbing factors around a person's sense of loss due to a family member's sickness or death, as well as conflict with others in the family about how to care for the person or distribute assets after death. In many cases the pain from these issues is almost as great (and sometimes greater) than the initial loss. Individuals and couples who come for counseling will benefit from the insights of the five Money Personalities. In addition, discuss the principles of conflict resolution.

If a parent (or another relative) has died without a will, a power struggle may ensue. Usually the demands are framed as things "owed to me," "justice," and secret promises. Help the person sort out reality and respond with dignity, truth, and bold love. Help the person avoid being demanding, reacting out of hurt and anger, or caving in to demands out of fear.

Couples with children under eighteen years old may have concerns about guardianship of their children. Help them be honest with each other about the suitability of family members to care for their kids. In these discussions, a spouse may display naïveté or mixed loyalties that cause conflict, even when everyone is safe and healthy.

Your role isn't to draw up legal instruments, but to help people sort out personal fears and desires, as well as facilitating family dialogue to reach resolution. Many times, jealousy and greed cause great heartache and grief, necessitating forgiveness. You can help your client deal with these emotions.

Find an attorney or two in your community who can assist clients with their legal needs in this area.

ACTION STEPS : 5

1. In the assessment interview, uncover any legal issues revolving around sickness, incapacity, or death in the family. Explore emotional, relational, and financial complexities of these painful issues and offer understanding and empathy.
2. Explain the five Money Personalities and help the client identify herself and her spouse.
3. Help the person distinguish between actual issues and fears about the future. In some cases, these fears are realized but they can sometimes be minimized by careful planning and good communication. At the time of a parent or spouse's death or disability, people may find that they can't think clearly. Your assistance in asking questions and finding truth is valuable.
4. Explore the benefits of a will, living will, and power of attorney, but don't give legal advice.
5. Refer your clients to a competent attorney for legal advice and assistance in drawing up these instruments, or point them to online services.

BIBLICAL INSIGHTS : 6

Hope deferred makes the heart sick, but a longing fulfilled is a tree of life.

Proverbs 13:12

All of the legal instruments described in this chapter focus on circumstances when hopes are dashed. We can minimize the pain and relational conflict, however, if we use the tools available to us.

Whoever scorns instruction will pay for it, but whoever respects a command is rewarded.

Proverbs 13:13

It's sad that some family members value money and possessions more than the love of the dead and the living. This is the reason a will is important, so people will have to respect the wishes of the one who has died.

Good judgment wins favor, but the way of the unfaithful leads to their destruction.

Proverbs 13:15

We may not want to face the facts about the incapacity of a parent or our own mortality, but it's "good judgment" to be honest about the realities of life. If we fail to address these things with dignity and truth, we can enflame, instead of minimize, heartache and conflict.

All who are prudent act with knowledge, but fools expose their folly.

Proverbs 13:16

The time to think about wills, living wills, and powers of attorney is before we need them. Like the builder who needed to count the cost of the project before he began, we should count the cost of *not* taking action in providing for our family by having these vital legal documents.

7 : PRAYER STARTER

Father, this woman needs to face the hard facts (of a parent's incapacity, a loved one's death, or her own mortality) and make choices that honor you. Give her wisdom, Lord, to make good decisions that minimize conflict with those who remain. This time in her life may feel out of control, but you hold all things in your loving hands . . .

8 : RECOMMENDED RESOURCES

Munchbach, Jim. *Make Your Money Count: Connecting Your Resources to What Matters Most*. Baxter Press, 2007.

Palmer, Bethany, and Scott Palmer. *First Comes Love, Then Comes Money: A Couple's Guide to Financial Communication*. HarperOne, 2009.

http://www.ronblue.com/

http://www.mvelopes.com/focusonthefamily/

http://www.daveramsey.com/home/

http://www.crown.org/

Family Businesses

PORTRAITS 1

- Antonio and Melinda worked together at a nationally known company for several years before they started dating and eventually got married. After a few more years and many late-night conversations, they decided to leave the company and set up their own business. Since graduating from college many years before, Antonio had dreamed of owning his own company, but Melinda was more hesitant. He always painted a glowing picture of wealth, lavish vacations, and plenty of time to enjoy each other. She had heard horror stories of one-hundred-hour workweeks going on for years before a company began turning a profit. Soon after they opened the doors of their new business, Antonio and Melinda's relationship exploded. They just couldn't handle the tension running a business caused and the long hours of work.

- Paul had owned his own business for twenty years and he was looking forward to his sons joining him when they graduated from college. The older son, Albert, was a hard worker and grasped the business model very easily, but Robert, the younger son, never quite clicked with his father and brother. Albert and Paul carried Robert for a while, but one day, Albert's resentment boiled up and he yelled at his brother. Robert walked out and said, "I'm not working here another day!" Paul and Albert now have to figure out what went wrong and how they can handle this very difficult situation.

- Ray and Bethany had struck gold. Their plumbing supply business had been in operation for only five years, and they were making tons of money. As the business grew, however, Bethany's work as bookkeeper wasn't keeping pace with the needs of the company. Ray realized he needed to hire an accountant to handle all the work, but he didn't want Bethany to feel unneeded. Their business success had brought some unexpected complications to their marriage.

- William and his wife, Hanna, had operated a shoe store together for several years. Though they had very different roles, things seemed to be going along very well. After a while, William noticed that Hanna seemed resentful and withdrawn. When he asked what was wrong, she blurted out, "How long am I going to work like a dog for laborer's wages? I should be your partner in this business." William had no idea his wife felt this way, but he had no intention of making her a full partner in the business. He saw this as his business, one she benefited from as it provided for their family. William felt it would only drive them crazy if they made joint decisions.

2 DEFINITIONS AND KEY THOUGHTS

- It is estimated that 95 percent of businesses in this country are family owned and operated.
- For many couples and families, the idea of working together sounds heavenly. But we've seen many life partners try to be business partners and find that their finances—and their relationship—couldn't survive the shift.
- There are, however, couples who can make a business work. They work together and love it. So if couples or families are considering starting a business together, they need to know the following:

  — *The partners must be equals.* If one person reports to the other or is a subordinate, it will be a disaster. Equal means having equal responsibilities, equal benefits, equal decision-making power. That doesn't mean you have to have the same responsibilities. It means that you are true partners in making the business work.

  — *Know what's really involved.* Starting a business sounds like a great way to make a fresh start and spend time together. But being a business owner is anything but romantic. It's all about the details—salaries, hiring and firing, managing a building, budgets, insurance, marketing, and on and on. It's almost like building another family. And unless both partners are able to commit fully to making this work, it won't.

  — *Capitalize on each other's strengths.* Before jumping in, a couple should understand how their Money Personalities will help them work together. If they are going to build a business together, they need to spend at least a year figuring out who they are, what they are good at, and what they like to do. They have to know themselves and each other well before they go into business together. They should be able to answer these questions: What's going to make this venture fulfilling to each person? How will you solve the inevitable conflicts between you?

  — *This is a financial decision, not an emotional one.* Starting a business should be treated like any enormous investment. The couple must talk, talk, talk about what they're doing and why. They must take a long, hard look at their finances and use Money Huddles to continue talking about their plans and ideas. If it's not working, they must be willing to pull the plug. Their relationship is more important than a business.

  — *Conduct regular business meetings.* If a couple decides to move forward and start a business together, they should treat it like a business, not an extension of their relationship. In addition to their regular Money Huddles, they must hold monthly or quarterly meetings to stay on top of their business-related budget and other issues.

- In addition, a couple in business should stay connected to the numerous resources for family businesses, such as *Family Business* magazine and the Family Business Institute. It can be an incredible adventure for a couple to build a business together. It demands a lot of respect for each other, a clear sense of the risks involved, and strong financial communication skills. If they have all of that, then we wish them the best!

ASSESSMENT INTERVIEW : 3

Review the Money Personalities with the client and ask him to identify himself and other family members who will be involved in the business.

1. What is your Money Personality? What is the Money Personality of each member of your family?
2. Based on these personality profiles, what are some areas of commonality? What are some areas of potential conflict?
3. What are your hopes for a family business? Describe your goals. Are they realistic? Who, if anyone, thinks they're not?
4. Are you adequately capitalized? Do you have the resources you need for a good beginning?
5. What relationship struggles do you anticipate? How will you address them in a way that shows respect?
6. What are the traits you appreciate about your family members who will participate in the business? Do they know you feel this way about them?
7. What are your biggest fears? How will you deal with them?
8. How can I help?

WISE COUNSEL : 4

Encourage the client and his family to write a detailed business plan, whether they are starting a company or evaluating and making adjustments to an existing one. When money and power are involved, assumptions often prove to cause enormous strife. Ask them to balance blind enthusiasm about a hopeful future with hard-nosed discipline to ask the hard questions. The plan should include roles, capital, sales, distribution, costs, salaries, and so on, with realistic projections of income and expenses for a considerable period of time.

Ask your client to draft a partnership agreement for each person in the family who will be involved in the business. The agreement will spell out the specifications of the structure, responsibilities, capital contribution, ownership, and compensation. Failure to have clear expectations will lead to disappointment and conflict.

Even at the beginning of a company's existence, it's advisable to have a clear succession plan so that there are no destructive power struggles when an owner or partner leaves the company unexpectedly.

Of course, the person who came for counseling may have come primarily for help with existing or anticipated conflict in relationships. Address these by talking about good communication and conflict resolution skills.

5 ACTION STEPS

1. Review the Money Personalities and use these observations to facilitate good discussion about expectations in relationships.
2. In many new ventures, one person is brimming with excitement and may fail to see potential problems, while others are fearful about taking big risks. Help the client see that both traits are valuable and provide balance, but he and his partner must feel respected and both should be included in decision making.
3. Help the client set realistic expectations for the company and for each person's role and contribution.
4. Address any existing misunderstandings and points of conflict between the client and his partner or family members. Whether the company is brand new or has been around for decades, the quality of relationships is what makes life worthwhile.
5. Encourage him to craft a business plan, a partnership agreement, and a succession plan.
6. As the plan unfolds, stay in contact as needed to provide support and insight about the relationships.

6 BIBLICAL INSIGHTS

Do not forsake wisdom, and she will protect you; love her, and she will watch over you. The beginning of wisdom is this: Get wisdom. Though it cost all you have, get understanding.

Proverbs 4:6–7

Starting a family business is an adventure, and all real adventures involve a lot of risk. We need wisdom to anticipate opportunities and threats so we can respond appropriately. Those who rush in without thinking and praying are trusting in themselves, but people who want God's wisdom study his Word, pray, and listen to the whisper of his Spirit.

The simple believe anything, but the prudent give thought to their steps.

Proverbs 14:15

Assumptions kill, especially when we are trying something new. Careful analysis isn't a lack of faith—it's a sign that we're trusting God to give us direction.

My goal is that they may be encouraged in heart and united in love, so that they may have the full riches of complete understanding, in order that they may know the mystery of God, namely, Christ, in whom are hidden all the treasures of wisdom and knowledge.

Colossians 2:2–3

True riches aren't found in money or business success, but in knowing and loving Jesus Christ. When people dive into a new family business venture, they need to remember where their real treasure lies.

If any of you lacks wisdom, you should ask God, who gives generously to all without finding fault, and it will be given to you. But when you ask, you must believe and not doubt, because the one who doubts is like a wave of the sea, blown and tossed by the wind. That person should not expect to receive anything from the Lord. Such a person is double-minded and unstable in all they do.

James 1:5–8

God graciously leads his children who depend on him. When we ask him for direction, though, we need to pay attention to him. If we don't like God's direction and go off on our own, we won't enjoy his presence and blessings.

PRAYER STARTER : 7

Father, this couple is about to start something brand new and they need your help. They want their family business to honor you, not only with their success but also in their response to the inevitable setbacks and difficulties they'll face. Through it all, may they honor you and love each other. Help them, Lord . . .

RECOMMENDED RESOURCES : 8

Munchbach, Jim. *Make Your Money Count: Connecting Your Resources to What Matters Most.* Baxter Press, 2007.
Palmer, Bethany, and Scott Palmer. *First Comes Love, Then Comes Money: A Couple's Guide to Financial Communication.* HarperOne, 2009.
http://www.ronblue.com/
http://www.mvelopes.com/focusonthefamily/
http://www.daveramsey.com/home/
http://www.crown.org/

Financial Planning

1 : PORTRAITS

- Marge and Jack have been upwardly mobile since they graduated from college, got married, and found good jobs. They enjoyed a dual income and didn't worry much about all the money they were spending—and not saving. Now their two kids are teenagers and they have picked up on their parents' perspective about money: spend all you want. Marge and Jack bought their children nice cars when they turned sixteen and they've always invested in the finest clothes. The extravagant pattern of spending, though, has begun taking its toll. The couple is, for the first time in their lives, going deeply into debt. They argue about money all the time and they've begun fighting with their kids about all the spending.

- Michael and Letitia just had their first child and they're thrilled. They've barely made ends meet, but Letitia is determined to provide the very best of everything for her darling little girl. She has spent more than $10,000 on the baby's room in the little house they are renting. Michael has tried to get her to be reasonable, but she gets angry and complains that their daughter deserves the best.

- Martha told her counselor, "I have no idea where all the money goes. Both of us make a good income, but at the end of every month, I'm scrambling to pay the bills. It's driving me crazy." She wonders if her husband has a secret drug habit or is gambling away all the money. When she tries to talk with him about it, he becomes very defensive and storms out the door.

- Lloyd came to counseling for anxiety, but in the assessment, his therapist discovered that much of his stress is related to money. He is an impulse buyer and he can't stay out of electronics stores. His wife and children suffer from his compulsive behavior, and now the children, only seven and nine, are showing signs that they're catching their father's sickness. They demand more toys, a better television, and the latest gadgets and they whine when their mother tells them no.

- Rick's parents had to move out of their house and into an assisted-living facility. Their expenses every month are about $6,000, but Social Security doesn't cover all of that. Rick's dad worked as long as he could as a skilled machinist, but he wasn't in a union and didn't save any money. Now Rick and his wife have to figure out how to help his parents make it. He's reaching into his own pocket each month to provide for his parents. He's glad to do it, but his wife isn't as happy with the arrangement.

DEFINITIONS AND KEY THOUGHTS : 2

- Financial problems are often a contributing factor in family distress. In fact, it's probably the most common difficulty families face. It can surface at any time but tends to show up at transitional times, such as the first year of marriage, the birth of a child, when kids become teenagers, and when parents lose their independence.

- Resolving financial difficulties is a family affair, including parents and their children as needed (if the children are old enough), a team effort, not the responsibility of one person. Many times, taking steps to create and live by a budget increases stress and creates triangles of secret (or not so secret) alliances in which two people try to sabotage and control another.

- The benefits of good *family financial planning* include lower stress levels, better communication, good modeling for children, and the development of good habits that provide everyone with hope for the future.

- The elements of good *financial planning* for a family include:

  — an analysis of the *current status of finances*, *spending habits*, and *expectations*

  — a clear, workable *budget*

  — eliminating *wasteful spending*

  — reducing *debt*

  — putting money in a *strategic savings account*

  — creating a plan to *save and invest* for the future

- The transition from wanton spending and creating debt to *fiscal restraint and responsibility* isn't easy. Even if one or two people in the family are on board, others may be very resistant. Look for resistance, especially in either of the parents, and focus on the benefits of fiscal health, reduced stress, and richer relationships.

ASSESSMENT INTERVIEW : 3

Explain the Money Personalities and use these insights as a foundation for discussion about financial planning.

1. What is your Money Personality? What is your spouse's? What are points of agreement and potential misunderstanding in your two profiles—especially related to planning and budgeting?
2. How does financial stress affect your family?
3. What are some problems with spending that your family faces? Who is trying to curb bad habits? How is it going?

4. As you've tried to get a handle on your family finances, who has been supportive and cooperative? Who has been resistant? How is that resistance affecting you and others in the family?

5. What would be some of the benefits of getting out of debt, spending wisely, and saving money for the future?

6. What is the status of your family's budget?

7. How can I help?

4 : WISE COUNSEL

Though people may not initially present with financial distress, a few questions often bring out the fact that money troubles play a major role in conflict in the family. Spending habits may be one of the best and biggest windows on the family's dynamics, and a budget may provide an excellent proving ground for growth, courage, and communication for every member of the family.

When you ask about spending habits and resultant debt, you may get a flood of specific illustrations and explosive (or depressive) emotions. Money issues are quite emotional, and when family relationships are at the center of money troubles, they become significant issues.

You may or may not want to get into the specifics of analyzing their current spending patterns, motives, and expectations, but someone needs to help the family understand these important habits and feelings. If they don't know where the money is going, they won't be able to redirect it. They can examine current expenses, the major purchases of the past months or year, and the monthly costs for things they have considered necessary. In many cases these things are luxuries, not necessities.

Wasteful spending is a major problem for many families. Gradually they spend more and more, justifying every new level of debt. Some of the most common areas where costs can be cut include:

- *Food.* Many families eat out a lot and they shop at expensive grocery stores. Eating at home has many benefits, including saving money and teaching responsibility by involving family members in preparation, cooking, and cleanup. A $20 savings each week (which is minimal for most families) results in $1,000 savings over the year.

- *Car expenses.* Americans view cars as almost a sacred right, but many of us buy cars we can't afford and spend money we don't have to keep them going. Teenagers have come to expect a car, and usually a new one, when they are old enough to get a license. When insurance and gas haven't been figured into the anticipated cost, the expense soon goes out of control. Used cars aren't quite as flashy, but living within our means feels pretty good.

- *Insurance.* Raising the deductible may save hundreds of dollars in home and car insurance premiums.

- *Do it yourself.* Some of us are more skilled around the house than others, so we may need to hire a plumber or electrician for that work. But we can learn to paint and even lay tile instead of hiring a professional. Doing our own yard work can save thousands each year and it's good exercise too.

- *Eliminating or reducing luxuries*. If a family is in debt, extravagant travel needs to be curtailed, at least until they achieve financial stability and a measure of wealth. Expensive hobbies need to be replaced by ones that cost less.

Besides cutting costs, a family needs to cooperate in reducing existing debt and saving money for the future.

- *Debt reduction*. One of the most important elements of family financial planning is getting out from under the crushing load of debt. There are many different strategies, including first paying off the lowest amount that is owed to a creditor and working up the list. In many cases, people need to negotiate extra time and lower minimum payments for a time. Most lenders are eager to get their money, even if they have to wait a little while, as long as people are making significant progress in paying off the debt.
- *A strategic savings account*. When, or even as, debts are being paid, the family needs to put some money into a savings account as a cushion so that unexpected expenses don't wreck family finances.
- *Saving and investing for the future*. Impulse buying is about *now*, but a family needs to plan wisely for future expenses, including weddings, college costs, and retirement.

Individuals and couples who come for counseling will benefit from the insights of the five Money Personalities.

ACTION STEPS 5

1. In the assessment, determine the presence and severity of financial distress in the individual, couple, or family. Look for conflict over spending and high stress levels due to debt.
2. A couple or family may need to resolve many different issues, but financial issues often are the most immediate and concrete. Therefore, this topic can provide an opportunity for significant conversations about family dynamics and steps forward. Discuss issues of expectations, conflict, communication, and triangles (when two people oppose a third member of the family).
3. Offer some commonsense suggestions about the importance of having a workable budget to curb spending, reduce debt, and begin saving. Also talk about the importance of modeling responsible fiscal behavior to children. Address the conflict that may arise when parents rein in spending.
4. Explain the five Money Personalities and help the client identify herself and her spouse.
5. You may not have the skills and experience for detailed family financial planning beyond the basics of creating a budget, curbing spending, reducing debt, and

beginning to save. For further help, refer the person to a financial professional or online resources.

6. Continue to use the issue of financial distress as a window on family dynamics as you see the client. Monitor the progress that she and her family make and offer plenty of encouragement as they take courageous steps.

6 BIBLICAL INSIGHTS

Desire without knowledge is not good—how much more will hasty feet miss the way!

Proverbs 19:2

One of the biggest problems for families in our culture is comparison. When we look at what others have, naturally we make the assumption that we should have as much (or maybe more). We long to have lots of things to make us feel good about ourselves or to enjoy comfort and the thrill of having new stuff, but this desire often leads to heartache.

A sluggard's appetite is never filled, but the desires of the diligent are fully satisfied.

Proverbs 13:4

The benefit of wisdom and responsible behavior is that we don't have to look over our shoulders to see if anyone is chasing us and we aren't worried about the future. Good planning and following the plan lead to contentment.

But seek first his kingdom and his righteousness, and all these things will be given to you as well.

Matthew 6:33

Our first priority is to desire God—to experience his love, presence, and purpose. As we trust him and act wisely under his direction, he gives us many things to enjoy, including peace and love in our families.

Do nothing out of selfish ambition or vain conceit. Rather, in humility value others above yourselves, not looking to your own interests but each of you to the interests of the others.

Philippians 2:3–4

Misplaced desires and unrealistic expectations mean we will be focused on having what we want and having it now. Instead, God wants us to submit our hearts to him, trust him for leading, and be good examples to those around us, especially our children.

Children, obey your parents in everything, for this pleases the Lord. Fathers, do not embitter your children, or they will become discouraged.

Colossians 3:20–21

A home in which parents and children communicate well and make good choices produces peace and joy, and it prepares the children for a lifetime of responsible, godly living.

PRAYER STARTER : 7

Father, this family is full of hurt and anger over money. Help them climb out of the pit, learn to make good choices about money, and love each other instead of demanding their own way. They need your help, Lord, and they desire to do their part in making good choices to manage their money . . .

RECOMMENDED RESOURCES : 8

Munchbach, Jim. *Make Your Money Count: Connecting Your Resources to What Matters Most*. Baxter Press, 2007.

Palmer, Bethany, and Scott Palmer. *First Comes Love, Then Comes Money: A Couple's Guide to Financial Communication*. HarperOne, 2009.

http://www.ronblue.com/

http://www.mvelopes.com/focusonthefamily/

http://www.daveramsey.com/home/

http://www.crown.org/

Foreclosure

1 : PORTRAITS

- Randal and Lydia got swept up in the housing boom a few years ago when it seemed that all their friends were buying big houses in nicer neighborhoods. They didn't want to be left out, but the bar was set very high. To get a house that was as big as their friends' new homes, they had to get a 0 percent loan with payments of about half their monthly income. "We can make it," Lydia assured Randal. The economy looked good, and with assurances that the value of the house would only go up, they signed the papers. A couple of years later, the economy went into a recession and home values declined. Randal and Lydia realized they owed $50,000 more on their house than it was worth. "I don't know how long it will take before we get back to even," Randal lamented. "I think we should just walk away from the house and start over." He knew that nonpayment of the mortgage for several months would prompt the lender to initiate a foreclosure but he didn't care. He just wanted out. Lydia agreed with the decision but she began showing signs of depression.

- Lisa and Michael got a mortgage based on their dual incomes. When Michael lost his job due to a merger, he assumed he could get another one very quickly. For a year, he looked at job openings and went to dozens of interviews, but nothing seemed to fit. During all this time, Lisa watched their savings dwindle to nothing, and they began acquiring significant credit card debt to make it each month. "Just get a job!" she barked after he turned down a position that was "beneath" him. "I don't care what it is. You don't have to like it. We need the income." The rift between them had begun when the savings ran out. Now it was a canyon.

- Sarah had warned Pete not to buy an expensive house, but he assured her that they'd be fine. His company reassigned him two years later to a different division in another part of the country. They put their house on the market and rented an apartment in the new city. For months they hoped their realtor would call with good news, but there weren't even any bites. Pete asked his company to buy his house, but his boss said they couldn't. To make the house more attractive, they lowered the price several times. "I just want out," Pete said. After a while, however, the asking price was less than he and Sarah owed. "Maybe we should just let the bank have it," he announced to the realtor.

- In the good times, Dana and Cindy lived in style. He was only a midlevel manager, but his company gave him huge bonuses every year. He grew to expect them, but when the economy turned down, the company's revenues plummeted. The year without a bonus was tough, but the following year, the company let Dana go. He could find a job that paid his base salary, but the fat bonuses were a thing of the past. Dana and Cindy tried to cut back on expenses and for another year they scraped up enough money to pay the mortgage. Finally, they realized it wasn't working for them. They tried to sell the house but they owed more than it was worth. When the bank foreclosed, they blamed each other for the foolish decision to buy the house and spend every dime of the bonuses on luxuries.

DEFINITIONS AND KEY THOUGHTS : 2

- A *foreclosure* is a process in which a lender (or *lien holder*) obtains termination of a mortgage holder's equitable right of redemption, using the secured value of the item, usually a house, as specified in the mortgage documents. Through a court order or other statutory procedure, the lender, or secured creditor, takes possession of the house. When the house is then sold by the lender, the proceeds repay the debt. Other lien holders can foreclose to repay debts, including unpaid taxes, homeowners' association dues, or contractors' bills. Depending on the provisions of the mortgage agreement, if the sale doesn't completely pay the balance of the principal and fees, the lender can file a claim for a *deficiency judgment*.

- In most states, there are two primary types of foreclosures:

  — *Foreclosure by judicial sale*, commonly called *judicial foreclosure*, is available in every state. The lender initiates foreclosure by filing a lawsuit against the borrower. It involves the sale of the mortgaged property under the supervision of a court. In these sales, the proceeds first satisfy the mortgage, then other lien holders, and if any money is left, the remainder goes to the borrower.

  — *Foreclosure by power of sale*, also called *nonjudicial foreclosure*, is legal in many states if a power of sale clause is included in the mortgage or if a deed of trust with this clause (rather than a mortgage) was used. The sale of the property by the mortgage holder occurs without court supervision. It is usually faster and cheaper than foreclosure by judicial sale.

- The issues of a legal foreclosure are beyond the expertise of most counselors, but the emotional damage caused by the loss of a home and financial ruin may surface in the counseling room. To many people the home is an important source of their identity and stability. Losing a home is often emotionally devastating and considered a social stigma. During the long process of gradual financial collapse and the legal proceedings for the lender to acquire assets, people may experience significant anxiety, depression, and relational conflict. Problems that had been hidden or ignored during good times come to the surface during times of stress and loss.

3 ASSESSMENT INTERVIEW

1. How long have you been struggling to try to keep your home?
2. When did you realize you probably weren't going to be able to make the payments? How did the realization affect you at that time?
3. How did you communicate this truth to your family? How did they respond?
4. Do you have a good attorney and financial advisor to help you through this time?
5. What has your home meant to you? (*Consider the sense of failure, status in the community, stability, fear, anxiety that the client may feel.*) What are you losing through the foreclosure?
6. What are your hopes and fears at this point?
7. What are your immediate plans?
8. What are some lessons God can teach you and your family through this ordeal?
9. How can I help?

4 WISE COUNSEL

Foreclosure is a legal process, but it has profound emotional and relational impact. A client going through this ordeal may not talk openly about the failure, but a few questions about current stresses may open up this line of inquiry and insight.

It is imperative that the client find competent professional assistance from an attorney and/or a financial advisor. During times of stress, many people have clouded thinking, so they compound their problems by making poor decisions. Help them find sources of good advice and assistance.

Address issues of despair, hopelessness, failure, shame, resentment, blame, depression, and other emotional and relational difficulties that occur for many individuals and families when they face financial failure. The tension in marriage may have been simmering for years, but facing the foreclosure of a home may cause it to boil at a time when both spouses desperately need understanding, support, and encouragement. To facilitate understanding between them, use the five Money Personalities.

5 ACTION STEPS

1. Individuals and couples facing the prospect of foreclosure or the aftermath of the process come to counseling because they feel deeply discouraged and ashamed. For many couples the experience drives a wedge in their relationship. They need insight, emotional support, validation of their emotions, new ways of interpreting the difficulty, and help in communicating more effectively with each other. For significant emotional distress, consider a referral for appropriate medications and other therapeutic interventions.
2. If the person or couple doesn't have good legal and financial counsel, refer them to an attorney and financial professional they can trust.

3. To facilitate personal understanding and relational support, share the five Money Personalities and help the client identify himself and his spouse.

4. Discuss the principles of active listening, good communication, and conflict resolution, and answer any questions.

5. Continue to monitor progress and impart a sense of hope that God's ultimate purposes for the client haven't been derailed by the foreclosure.

BIBLICAL INSIGHTS 6

I waited patiently for the LORD; he turned to me and heard my cry. He lifted me out of the slimy pit, out of the mud and mire; he set my feet on a rock and gave me a firm place to stand. He put a new song in my mouth, a hymn of praise to our God. Many will see and fear the LORD and put their trust in him.

Psalm 40:1–3

Sometimes we find ourselves in "the mud and mire" of life because of our dumb choices, the failure of others, or circumstances beyond our control. Whatever the cause, God wants us to look to him, trust him with our past and our future, and sing songs of praise and hope because we're sure he's always in control.

For though the righteous fall seven times, they rise again, but the wicked stumble when calamity strikes.

Proverbs 24:16

Failure isn't the biggest problem we face. The most crushing problem is when we respond to failure with hopelessness instead of faith. No matter how many times we fall, God is there to help us get up again and start taking steps forward. His love never fails.

Because of the LORD's great love we are not consumed, for his compassions never fail. They are new every morning; great is your faithfulness. I say to myself, "The LORD is my portion; therefore I will wait for him."

Lamentations 3:22–24

When we experience financial failure, we may think our life is over. In this passage, Jeremiah assures us that God's tender love and strong hand are with us every day. In fact, they are as sure as the sunrise each day.

"For I know the plans I have for you," declares the LORD, "plans to prosper you and not to harm you, plans to give you hope and a future. Then you will call on me and come and pray to me, and I will listen to you. You will seek me and find me when you seek me with all your heart."

Jeremiah 29:11–13

Despair and depression rob us of perception and cloud our sense of hope. Even when the children of Israel experienced the tragedy of exile away from their homes, God assured them that his purposes for them were always good and right. They could trust in him because he had proven he was faithful, even in their darkest moments.

7 PRAYER STARTER

Father, this person would never have chosen the path he is on. He thought he was making good decisions about his house, but it didn't work out as he planned. But you aren't surprised. You know, you care, and you will help him take steps forward. Help him trust in you as he moves through this difficult time. May he and his wife learn to trust each other. Thank you for your grace, your love, your strength, and your good purposes for them . . .

8 RECOMMENDED RESOURCES

Munchbach, Jim. *Make Your Money Count: Connecting Your Resources to What Matters Most.* Baxter Press, 2007.

Palmer, Bethany, and Scott Palmer. *First Comes Love, Then Comes Money: A Couple's Guide to Financial Communication.* HarperOne, 2009.

http://www.ronblue.com/

http://www.mvelopes.com/focusonthefamily/

http://www.daveramsey.com/home/

http://www.crown.org/

Gift Giving

PORTRAITS 1

- Geraldo is a Spender. He loves to give gifts and he believes the amount he spends shows the extent of his love. Every Christmas and birthday he goes all out with lavish presents for his wife and kids. And each time his wife cringes. Greta's a Saver and she knows they can't afford all the things he buys. She loves his generous, giving heart but she takes back most of the things he buys for her and the kids. After a few years, their differences in gift giving and receiving have caused increased tension in their relationship.

- Marta spends hours creating beautiful or funny cards to give with her gifts. People love to get anything from her because they get such a kick out of her cards. Even if her gifts aren't expensive, she shows the depth of her love from the obvious devotion she has poured into the homemade cards. Her husband, Jimmy, however, is a bit dense. He feels as though he's done his duty if he runs to the store, buys something on sale, and wraps it with whatever paper he can find in the closet. When he gives Marta her gifts, he's perplexed when she isn't thrilled.

- Rhonda has wonderful memories of Christmases when she was a child and she wants to recreate those experiences for her children and her husband. She starts shopping in October for just the right gifts at just the right prices. When she sees the same item for less money at another store a week or a month later, she returns one and buys the other. She is a perfectionist about Christmas, but her behavior causes such stress—for her and the whole family—that Christmas has become a burden. Her husband has encouraged her to tone down her expectations and simplify her life during those months, but she still has dreams of the perfect Christmas.

- Sean and Jeri determined early in their marriage that they wanted to impart good values to their children. When Will and Sara were very young, Sean and Jeri began to teach and model the meaning of giving gifts. They talked about what would delight other people, how much they could afford, and how they could present these things in the most meaningful way. Sean and Jeri succeeded in helping their kids realize that the heart of giving is much more important than the cost of the gift. A hand-drawn picture was more treasured by their grandparents than anything they could ever buy at the store.

2 DEFINITIONS AND KEY THOUGHTS

- In his bestselling book, *The 5 Love Languages*, Gary Chapman identifies the *ways people give and receive love*, including *words of affirmation, quality time, receiving gifts, acts of service,* and *physical touch*. Actually, all of these are forms of "gifts" people give to one another, and they all involve some kind of expenditure—time, money, and/or effort. Most of the time, however, we think of tangible items when we talk about gifts.

- Birthdays, Christmas, anniversaries, graduations, and other special occasions are normal times for giving and receiving gifts, but *spontaneous presents* may say even more about a person's love.

- In our culture of comparison, many people have very high expectations about what they should give and receive. This pressure clouds motives and robs people of much of the joy that should surround expressions of love. Even when people get exactly what they want, a sense of demanding it takes the joy away.

- Each of the Money Personalities has different values and expressions in seeking, purchasing, giving, and receiving presents. When people understand their own Money Personality and their family members' personalities, they can make better choices *about how to communicate love through gifts*.

- In many cases, the issue of gift giving comes up in counseling only when a couple has experienced significant hurt and conflict in their relationship. In this case the perceptions and expectations about gifts become part of the therapeutic process of marriage counseling, not an isolated topic. Similarly, this subject can be an important subject for premarriage counseling.

3 ASSESSMENT INTERVIEW

Review the Money Personalities with your client before asking these questions.

1. What is your Money Personality? How does it affect your perceptions and behavior about giving and receiving gifts?
2. What is your spouse's (or fiancée's) Money Personality? How does this shape her behavior regarding gifts? How about your children (if you have any)?
3. What patterns in your spouse's (or fiancée's) giving habits do you appreciate? Give some examples.
4. What habits offend and hurt you? Give some examples.
5. What aspects of giving presents cause stress for you (such as shopping for just the right thing, the time it takes to shop, the expense, the pressure of expectations, and so on)?
6. What aspects bring you the most pleasure?
7. What are your hopes for mutually meaningful gift giving in your marriage and family?
8. How can I help?

WISE COUNSEL 4

Different Money Personalities view shopping and giving gifts from very different perspectives. If clients understand this fact, unrealistic expectations can gradually be reduced so that each person accepts the other.

Various aspects of giving presents offer a variety of challenges. For instance, some people are far more stressed out about finding the perfect gift, some about the cost, and others about the presentation. The issues that converge around this topic include personalities, timing, perfectionism, budgeting, creativity, and the willingness to do whatever is meaningful to the other person, even if it's uncomfortable.

To establish good and healthy communication and expectations, we recommend:

- *Setting expectations.* Before the holiday season shopping crunch, take time with your spouse to talk as a couple about what holiday shopping will be like. If funds are limited, talk about it. You should also explain to your kids that the coming holiday will be more modest in terms of gifts. If you normally exchange gifts with extended family and can't afford to do so this year, you should tell them early on. A simple phone call or email will let them know the change, and they may be happy to find other ways to celebrate that cost less.

- *Shopping smart.* The same rules that apply to sticking with a grocery budget can work for holiday shopping. Make a list and stick with it, avoid last-minute runs to the store when you'll be tempted to grab the first thing you see, and start shopping early to find discounts and be able to use coupons. And the internet can be a big help! Not only is it convenient, but shopping online can actually save money because it keeps us out of stores where we may be tempted to buy more than we need, and by helping us compare prices and find the best deal.

- *Knowing what causes stress.* While most of us get stressed out during the holidays, we tend to get stressed out for different reasons. Savers get stressed about spending money, while Spenders get stressed about getting all their shopping done. Before the holiday rush kicks in, make a plan for reducing the stress of the season by agreeing on a budget with your family, on a firm list of purchases, and on talking and working together no matter what.

- *Working as a team.* Even if one member of a couple loves to shop or entertain and the other hates it, it's essential that the couple tackle the holidays together. They need to agree on a budget, talk about spending, and plan events and activities together. Not only will this avoid financial frustrations, the couple will have a lot more fun too.

- *Plugging into the recipient's passions.* Whether a child is three or thirteen, she's got interests that can spark a desire to help others. If you think about what a child loves—stuffed animals, sports, trading cards, dance—and use it as a starting point, you can find an appropriate way to get the child involved in giving. For example, if the child loves football, consider involving him in donating to a Pop Warner program for underprivileged kids. If she's on a cheerleading squad, help her find ways the whole group can raise money for a cause. If he loves collecting trains, consider donating a train set to an Angel Tree project in town.

117

- *Turning hard times into helping hands.* If a family has suffered a loss, dealt with an illness, or struggled financially, the children of the family have an automatic connection with other kids in the same boat. And that connection can open up their hearts. When Bethany was diagnosed with breast cancer two years ago, our children learned that it takes money to support research and that the treatments discovered through that research saved her life. Donating to cancer research had an obvious appeal to our kids (such as Susan G. Komen for the Cure).

- *Keeping it up.* We know that the needs in our communities don't go away when the holidays are over, but donations often do. Encourage your children to stay involved for the long haul by checking in on the charity's website, reading about the organization and the people it helps, and attending related events. Then children realize that giving can happen anytime.

- *Matching the child's funds.* After your family decides on an organization to support, you can commit to matching your child's contribution dollar for dollar. If your child is doing a service project or donating toys, you can figure out how you can give an equivalent donation of time or effort. Your example will speak volumes to the child. By staying involved, being intentional, and encouraging the child's giving, parents can keep their child's generous heart beating strong.

One last note: *We need to give ourselves some grace.* We might not stick to our budget perfectly. We might not have the most gorgeous holiday decorations in the neighborhood. We might freak out over the little details of a family gathering. It's okay. We can regroup, keep talking to our partner, and enjoy the wonder of the season.

5 : ACTION STEPS

1. Review the Money Personalities with your client. Discuss the way her perceptions of money affect her behaviors in giving and receiving gifts.
2. Discuss the relevant issues that can cause misunderstanding and conflict in giving gifts, including time in shopping, perfectionism (the expectation of finding just the right gift), budgeting, creativity, and presentation.
3. Help the client understand her family, appreciate their strengths, and value their attempts to show love in their way of giving gifts. Quite often learning to appreciate the differences resolves a lot of the conflict for a couple and a family.
4. Take the focus off the gifts and put the focus on the client's and her spouse's hearts. Giving and receiving gifts isn't really about the things but about the love they share.
5. Change doesn't happen easily or quickly. Encourage the client to create a plan for how she'll handle the next birthday, holiday, or anniversary.
6. Offer insights and support to help parents impart to their kids good values about giving and receiving gifts.

BIBLICAL INSIGHTS : 6

What a person desires is unfailing love; better to be poor than a liar.

Proverbs 19:22

The guiding light in every aspect of our relationships is love. When we spend too much or become too absorbed with trying to find the perfect gift, our focus is more on us than the other person; and our gift is, in some respects, a lie.

Let us not become weary in doing good, for at the proper time we will reap a harvest if we do not give up. Therefore, as we have opportunity, let us do good to all people, especially to those who belong to the family of believers.

Galatians 6:9–10

When we are devoted to another person, we love without strings attached and we continue to show love even if we get little thanks in return. This is especially true in our relationships with teenagers, but it can also happen when we're trying to rebuild trust in a strained or broken relationship.

Not that I desire your gifts; what I desire is that more be credited to your account. I have received full payment and have more than enough. I am amply supplied, now that I have received from Epaphroditus the gifts you sent. They are a fragrant offering, an acceptable sacrifice, pleasing to God.

Philippians 4:17–18

When Paul received gifts from the church at Philippi, he realized that their expressions of love were far more valuable than the actual gifts themselves. He knew the people would experience great joy as a result of their giving.

For where you have envy and selfish ambition, there you find disorder and every evil practice. But the wisdom that comes from heaven is first of all pure; then peace-loving, considerate, submissive, full of mercy and good fruit, impartial and sincere. Peacemakers who sow in peace reap a harvest of righteousness.

James 3:16–18

Comparison is generated by envy and selfish ambition. When our shopping and buying are driven by these factors, nothing good comes from them, even if the person wanted the gift. We need to examine our hearts, trust God to purify our motives, and give out of sincere love.

7 | PRAYER STARTER

Father, we want our gifts to our spouse and kids to be a reflection of your kindness and love for us. Thank you for giving to us so lavishly in Jesus. Give this person wisdom, Lord, to understand her loved ones, to be wise about money, and to be creative in showing love . . .

8 | RECOMMENDED RESOURCES

Munchbach, Jim. *Make Your Money Count: Connecting Your Resources to What Matters Most*. Baxter Press, 2007.

Palmer, Bethany, and Scott Palmer. *First Comes Love, Then Comes Money: A Couple's Guide to Financial Communication*. HarperOne, 2009.

http://www.ronblue.com/

http://www.mvelopes.com/focusonthefamily/

http://www.daveramsey.com/home/

http://www.crown.org/

Giving and Contributions

PORTRAITS : 1

- Tim and Janice wanted help for their marriage. They've been fighting about a lot of things, particularly money. Tim has a friend from college who is a missionary, and Tim has made a commitment to support his friend financially. The amount is so large, however, that Tim and Janice have to do without some things to make the monthly contribution. Janice fumed, "Do you care more about your friend in Indonesia than you do about me?"

- Felicia grew up going to church. She has been religious in every sense of the word. She attends Sunday morning, Wednesday evening, and any other time the church meets for anything. Recently she has become depressed. She explained to her counselor, "God let me down. I read the promises about God blessing those who give generously. I gave. In fact, I gave the money I needed to pay the rent, but God didn't bless me. I was evicted. I'm disappointed that I lost a good place to live, but far more, I'm hurt that God didn't come through like he promised."

- Rob sat in the counseling office with his arms folded and a grimace on his face. His wife, Tina, explained to the counselor that she felt oppressed by Rob—sexually, emotionally, and financially. She related that Rob wanted her to account for every penny that went out of the checkbook. "I can't make any of my own decisions," she said, weeping. "I'd love to give some money to some kids who are going on a mission trip, but he won't let me." "Why should I?" Rob barked. "They're not doing anything to help *me*."

- Elizabeth came to counseling for help with anxiety attacks. The problem, though, is more pervasive than isolated instances of panic. In the assessment interview, Elizabeth explained that she lives under a cloud of guilt and shame. One of her comments was typical of others: "When it comes to my money, I give to our church, but not because I want to. Oh, I know I should want to, but I give because I feel so guilty when I don't put anything in the plate when it passes me."

DEFINITIONS AND KEY THOUGHTS : 2

- The concept of *generosity* isn't primarily about the amount of money a person gives. It's broader. Giving generously is the perspective that God is the creator and owner of all things, and we, his people, are his agents who use part of it for a while. Everything we have, including our ability to make money, is *a gift from God* to be used, invested, and enjoyed for his honor.

- As God's beloved children, we are *custodians* of everything he puts in our hands: *time, possessions, people, money, skills, and opportunities*. There isn't a sacred-secular dichotomy in which some things are God's and some we insist he keep his hands off. We belong to him all day, every day, in the boardroom and the bedroom, and our checkbooks and our scorecards are his.

- Being generous with money involves *wise saving, spending, investing, and giving*. Each component is as important as the others, and they influence each other.

- When we have this perspective about *God's ownership* and our privilege to use our resources to help others, we become wise in how we handle all the things he has put into our care. We don't cling tightly to our money and we aren't foolish and frivolous in our spending. When we give, we give *gladly, generously, and sacrificially*. We give gladly because we realize we're partners with God in the greatest enterprise the world has ever known—redeeming people and building God's kingdom. We give generously because we know that changing lives is far more important than anything else we can spend our money on. And we give sacrificially—willing to do without for the sake of God's cause—because we are convinced that God's purposes are more important than pleasure, comfort, and a few more possessions.

- Just as there are different Money Personalities, people give for different reasons. They give to God's causes to honor him because he loves them, to help people in need, or so their lives will count for eternity.

- Some church leaders have observed that 90 percent of the money donated to churches is given by people who are more than fifty years old. The older generation may have more resources than younger people, but not that much more.

3 ASSESSMENT INTERVIEW

In most cases, the topics of giving and generosity come up in counseling only if a couple's conflict touches on them or when individuals experience shame or discouragement because God didn't come through as they had hoped.

1. How do you feel about giving to God's work?
2. How do you see your possessions, time, relationships, and skills? Are they gifts from God for you to manage, or do you consider them your own to do with as you choose? Explain your answer.
3. Do you and your partner experience conflict over money? Do you argue about where and how much to give?
4. Are you satisfied with God's blessings? Is there any disappointment that God hasn't blessed as much as you had hoped? If so, how has that perspective affected your relationship with him?
5. When was the last time you were thrilled to give money, time, and energy to God's cause?
6. How can I help you?

WISE COUNSEL :4

Consider how the topic of generosity came up in the assessment interview or subsequent counseling sessions. In most cases, this issue arises only when there is conflict between partners or if an individual experiences shame, guilt, or deep discouragement related to God's promises.

The issue isn't about numbers in a checkbook. It's about the person's perspective about God's ownership and God's willingness to entrust some time, skills, and resources to us for a while. When people have this perspective, they are more willing to give generously and gladly instead of hoarding their possessions or giving foolishly with demands.

As we help people with issues related to money, we need to help them step back and understand God's perspective related to all their possessions, not just their money. Many people feel forced to give, and they either give out of guilt or defiantly refuse to give. A richer, deeper understanding of God's grace, his ownership, and our role as money managers helps us sort out the conflicting emotions.

People gravitate to one or more of the many different motivations to give to God's work. For instance, some want to give simply to show God how much they love him; others want to see people's lives changed. Some people grew up in churches that taught an oppressive message about giving, and these people feel oppressed or defiant or both. In many cases you'll have to address those ingrained but inaccurate views of giving as you impart truth about being partners with God.

Individuals and couples who come for counseling will benefit from the insights of the five Money Personalities. The principles of active listening and conflict resolution will help them communicate more clearly and positively as they discuss how, and how much, they want to give.

ACTION STEPS :5

1. In the assessment interview, determine the nature and severity of the person's issues related to possessions, expectations, demands, and giving.
2. If there is conflict in this area between partners, encourage them to talk openly, find common ground, and begin to take steps they can both support. Explain the five Money Personalities and help them identify themselves and each other. Discuss the principles of good communication.
3. If an individual feels oppressed and ashamed because she can't measure up to a church's standards of giving, talk about God's wonderful grace and the widow's mite.
4. If a person feels deeply disappointed that God didn't come through "as he promised," help the person understand that God's purposes are far bigger than our expectations, and he's not a machine that always acts in a predictable way.
5. In many cases, issues of generosity are woven into other complex problems of relationships, expectations and demands, shame, faulty teaching, poor models, and other money problems such as debt. Help clients sort out conflicting

emotions and thoughts, relate the truth of God's Word about these things, and provide hope for the future.

6 BIBLICAL INSIGHTS

David praised the LORD in the presence of the whole assembly, saying, ... "But who am I, and who are my people, that we should be able to give as generously as this? Everything comes from you, and we have given you only what comes from your hand."

1 Chronicles 29:10, 14

Everything we have comes from God's hand, even our talents and our ability to work hard and earn a living. When we grasp this truth, we'll hold possessions more loosely and give more generously.

Do not store up for yourselves treasures on earth, where moths and vermin destroy, and where thieves break in and steal. But store up for yourselves treasures in heaven, where moths and vermin do not destroy, and where thieves do not break in and steal. For where your treasure is, there your heart will be also.

Matthew 6:19–21

Ultimately things don't matter much. Our real treasure is making a difference in people's lives for God's sake. If we truly value that, we'll invest our money in his causes.

"Watch out! Be on your guard against all kinds of greed; life does not consist in an abundance of possessions."

And [Jesus] told them this parable: "The ground of a certain rich man yielded an abundant harvest. He thought to himself, 'What shall I do? I have no place to store my crops.'

"Then he said, 'This is what I'll do. I will tear down my barns and build bigger ones, and there I will store my surplus grain. And I'll say to myself, "You have plenty of grain laid up for many years. Take life easy; eat, drink and be merry."'

"But God said to him, 'You fool! This very night your life will be demanded from you. Then who will get what you have prepared for yourself?'

"This is how it will be with whoever stores up things for themselves but is not rich toward God."

Luke 12:15–21

Greed is part of our culture. All the ads we see and hear every day tell us we need more and more, but having more things can never really satisfy our soul.

Remember this: Whoever sows sparingly will also reap sparingly, and whoever sows generously will also reap generously. Each of you should give what you have decided in your heart to give, not reluctantly or under compulsion, for God loves a cheerful giver. And God is able to bless you abundantly, so that in all things at all times, having all that you need, you will abound in every good work.

2 Corinthians 9:6–8

If we understand that we are custodians, under God's leadership, of all he has given to us, we will want to honor him with everything we are and everything we have. We give generously and gladly to honor our Father who loves us and has given us so much, and we aren't devastated when he doesn't bless us immediately in the way we hoped.

PRAYER STARTER 7

Lord Jesus, you gave everything to connect with us and give us love, forgiveness, and eternal life. Thank you for your grace. And thank you for entrusting to us all the time, skills, relationships, and money you've given. Help this child of yours to be a wise, glad, and generous person . . .

RECOMMENDED RESOURCES 8

Munchbach, Jim. *Make Your Money Count: Connecting Your Resources to What Matters Most.* Baxter Press, 2007.

Palmer, Bethany, and Scott Palmer. *First Comes Love, Then Comes Money: A Couple's Guide to Financial Communication.* HarperOne, 2009.

http://www.ronblue.com/

http://www.mvelopes.com/focusonthefamily/

http://www.daveramsey.com/home/

http://www.crown.org/

Hoarding

1 PORTRAITS

- Gary has never thrown anything away. He's only thirty-four, but his home has been taken over by the stuff he wants to keep. His living room is filled with stacks of old magazines, his closets are jammed with old clothes, and his garage is full of everything and anything that won't fit in his house. He never has friends over. Still, Gary goes to garage sales and shops online to acquire more things, usually things he "might need someday."

- Alice and Joyce are sisters, but you'd think they were from different planets. Alice is one of those people you hate to get behind at the grocery store because she has to pull out a file folder of coupons and go through every one of them when the cashier rings up her purchases. This routine comes after long hours in the store carefully comparing the price of store brands to the national brands. Her pantry has enough food in it for a small army. When Joyce comes over, she pleads with Alice to throw away cans, jars, and bags of stuff that have been in the house for years, but Alice stands in front of her pantry doors to protect them. She shakes her head. "You never know when I might need some of these things. They'll come in handy." Joyce told a friend about Alice, adding sadly, "I don't know what's wrong with my sister!"

- Omar insisted that Marianne come with him to see a counselor. For years he has lived with closets stuffed with things they don't need. Every square inch of their home is piled with things he would like to throw away. After they got married, he was amused when Marianne kept things and insisted, "You never know when we might need this." After a while, however, he realized her strange habit was actually an obsession. Her life revolved around keeping things—often worthless things. He told the counselor, "My wife needs help, and now I need help too. I don't know where we can go from here, but this is my last shot at saving our marriage. I can't keep living like this."

- Stanley and Carla moved about five hundred miles away from their hometown after they were married. Now forty years later, they need to travel back home every month to try to care for his elderly parents. His father is suffering from dementia and is now in an assisted care facility, but his mother is going strong. She always saved things, but as she has gotten older, she has refused to throw anything away. In the last five years, her house has become unbelievably packed with stuff. Stanley told a friend, "It's amazing. It's hard even to walk from room to room. A couple of years ago, we had to walk around the piles of stuff but now we can't get in most of the rooms. I don't know how my mother has done it, but she's completely filled every room but the kitchen with junk."

- When Cheryl goes to the grocery store, she always picks up another package of toilet paper. Probably she has more than six hundred rolls, but she keeps buying more. Four closets at her house are dedicated to them. When a friend came over for coffee and tried to hang up her coat in one of these closets, she was stunned. She blurted out, "Cheryl, what in the world is all this? You're not hoarding, are you?" Cheryl laughed nervously. "Of course not. These were on sale, and I thought it would be good to stock up." She quickly closed the closet door and steered her friend into the kitchen, away from the rest of the house and the other closets.

DEFINITIONS AND KEY THOUGHTS 2

- *Compulsive hoarding* (also known as *disposophobia*) is the excessive acquisition of possessions and the failure to discard or use them, even if the items are worthless. It is generally considered to be a subtype of *obsessive compulsive disorder* (OCD). Like other compulsive behaviors, hoarding is an attempt to manage the anxiety caused by obsessive doubts. Varying levels of hoarding behavior may be observed. A diagnosis of OCD of the hoarding type is made when there is significant distress or disruption to feelings of self-worth, interpersonal relationships, education, occupation, housing, finances, legal issues, or health as a result of hoarding behavior.

- As things accumulate, the person experiences *impaired mobility* and *interference with basic functions*, such as sleeping, cleaning, and cooking. The person may borrow things from family, friends, and neighbors but refuse to return them. Sometimes this obsession leads to shoplifting and other types of theft.

- Even thinking about discarding items creates *anxiety* and *intense distress*, and causes *conflict* with the person who is suggesting or demanding that things be thrown out.

- Often obsessive thoughts arise as *self-directed questions*, such as:

  — "What if I run out?"
  — "What if I need to know something and don't have the papers easily available?"
  — "What if I put it away and can't find it?"
  — "What if the way I organize it isn't the right way?"
  — "What if I throw it away but the day comes when I really need it?"

ASSESSMENT INTERVIEW 3

1. How do you feel when you think about running out of something or throwing things away?
2. Describe your criteria for acquiring things and keeping them.

3. What is your sorting method? How do you keep things in order?
4. How is this behavior affecting your most important relationships, your career, your health, your finances?
5. Can you connect this behavior with the modeling of your parents?
6. How secure did you feel as a child? Tell me about your relationships with your parents and siblings.
7. What do you really want in life? How can you get there?
8. How can I help?

4 WISE COUNSEL

Therapy, medication, and the imparting of new life skills can be effective in helping people with OCD. Therapeutic interventions such as cognitive-behavioral therapy help the client explore entrenched patterns of thought, triggering situations, and intense emotions. Medications used to treat anxiety and OCD can be considered. Depression and other comorbid conditions may also be present and require attention.

OCD isn't based on logic, so "why" questions—asked by the counselor or the client—may not be profitable. Instead, address the underlying cognitive distortions that are powered by intense and anxious feelings.

People who hoard can learn to practice some practical skills to help them make better choices about their things, including:

- put items into a limited number of piles, such as recycle, sell, give away, throw away, or keep
- handling things only once (instead of evaluating and sorting multiple times)
- accepting imperfection, such as not alphabetizing sheets or refolding towels that aren't folded perfectly the first time
- determining to have clear paths through the house and usable rooms
- organizing systematically rather than randomly collecting everything
- valuing friendships and creativity instead of a false sense of security based on things acquired and isolation
- asking for assistance to deal with feeling stuck or emotionally out of control

Many people who come for counseling for OCD related to hoarding experience significant financial and relational disruptions. The five Money Personalities can provide insights for the client and family members.

5 ACTION STEPS

1. Determine through consultation with a psychiatrist or related expert the severity of the OCD problem with hoarding and begin to use therapeutic interventions to help stabilize the person and begin to impart skills and hope.

2. Address the underlying cognitive distortions (such as excessive reassurance, overestimation of danger and consequences, and the need for certainty) and powerful, intense emotions.

3. When it is appropriate for the individual or couple, describe the five Money Personalities and help them identify themselves and each other.

4. Explain the principles of good communication and conflict resolution and answer any questions about applying these concepts.

5. Continue to monitor the individual's progress and the couple's communication.

6. If the person or couple is experiencing significant financial problems, refer them to a professional financial advisor.

BIBLICAL INSIGHTS 6

*Trust in the L*ORD *with all your heart and lean not on your own understanding; in all your ways submit to him, and he will make your paths straight.*
*Do not be wise in your own eyes; fear the L*ORD *and shun evil. This will bring health to your body and nourishment to your bones.*

Proverbs 3:5–8

To a person with OCD, all the thoughts and fears seem perfectly logical. To change, he has to realize that he needs God's perspective, wisdom, love, and strength. At first, the change of direction will seem odd, even wrong, but if the person stays with it, he will develop new, healthy neural pathways that become good habits of thinking and acting.

Do not be anxious about anything, but in every situation, by prayer and petition, with thanksgiving, present your requests to God. And the peace of God, which transcends all understanding, will guard your hearts and your minds in Christ Jesus. Finally, brothers and sisters, whatever is true, whatever is noble, whatever is right, whatever is pure, whatever is lovely, whatever is admirable—if anything is excellent or praiseworthy—think about such things. Whatever you have learned or received or heard from me, or seen in me—put it into practice. And the God of peace will be with you.

Philippians 4:6–9

As they learn to perceive and think differently, hoarders need to pray diligently, asking God for help but also thanking him for his kindness and the hope of change. Such prayers lead to right thinking, which eventually produces genuine peace.

That, however, is not the way of life you learned when you heard about Christ and were taught in him in accordance with the truth that is in Jesus. You were taught, with regard to your former way of life, to put off your old self, which is being corrupted by its deceitful desires; to be made new in the attitude of your minds; and to put on the new self, created to be like God in true righteousness and holiness.

Ephesians 4:20–24

As we read and study God's Word, our minds are gradually renewed, we "put on" new and healthy habits, and our lives reflect more of God's power, love, and kindness.

In the same way, the Spirit helps us in our weakness. We do not know what we ought to pray for, but the Spirit himself intercedes for us through wordless groans. And he who searches our hearts knows the mind of the Spirit, because the Spirit intercedes for God's people in accordance with the will of God.

Romans 8:26–27

Reorienting our minds, hearts, and actions is some of the hardest work we'll ever do. At times, we want to give up because we don't see as much progress as we'd like. In these pivotal moments, Paul assures us that the Holy Spirit is praying for us according to the Father's will, that we'll stay strong, learn important lessons, and keep taking one step forward at a time.

7 PRAYER STARTER

Father, this person's life has been out of control. His attempts to take control of things to make him feel more secure have only made him feel more anxious and isolated. He needs your help. Thank you for your love, forgiveness, and strength. Keep him from fear and help him to start taking steps out of this hole he's in. Give him grace for the next step . . .

8 RECOMMENDED RESOURCES

Munchbach, Jim. *Make Your Money Count: Connecting Your Resources to What Matters Most.* Baxter Press, 2007.

Palmer, Bethany, and Scott Palmer. *First Comes Love, Then Comes Money: A Couple's Guide to Financial Communication.* HarperOne, 2009.

http://www.ronblue.com/

http://www.mvelopes.com/focusonthefamily/

http://www.daveramsey.com/home/

http://www.crown.org/

Home Real Estate Purchases

- Tom and Brittany have been married for two years. They both have good jobs and enjoy the neighborhood where they rent an apartment. In the past few months, however, they have begun to look at their rent check as a waste of money. "This could be going toward our own home," Brittany observed. They had long talks with each other and friends about the advantages of owning a home and they've started looking at neighborhoods they like. "The prices aren't quite what they used to be," Tom said, "but they're still way out of our price range."

- Tammy and Phil bought a small house soon after they moved to a new city where Tammy got a new job. Now, after having three children, the house seems to have shrunk. "We've either got to build on or get a bigger house," Phil observed.

- Gwen's husband walked out on her a year ago, leaving her with the dog and the house—and the mortgage. She found a job soon after they split up, but she doesn't make enough money to make ends meet. She sighed, "I'm going to have to sell the house but I don't know where to begin."

- Randy and Kathy have done well financially. Randy's career in banking has given them a bulging income, and with last year's bonus, they want to buy a vacation home. Kathy smiled. "We can't decide if it's going to be in the mountains or at the beach. I'm so excited." "Yeah," Randy agreed, "but we don't want to throw our money away. We still need to make a good investment decision."

DEFINITIONS AND KEY THOUGHTS 2

- *Home ownership* is an important part of the American dream, but it's a frightening proposition for those who are buying their first home. For the vast majority of people, buying a home is the largest investment they'll make in their lives.

- Those who consider purchasing their first home, and those who are buying for the second or third time, need to weigh carefully the advantages and disadvantages of home ownership. *Renting* may seem like throwing money away each month, but renters don't have the headaches owners face with repairs and upkeep. And those who are transient should realize that selling too quickly can seriously erode their return on investment. Other reasons it's not a good idea to buy include a bad credit report, high existing debt, a tenuous job situation, and a dislike of maintenance.

131

- In any real estate market, local knowledge is vitally important. *Home values* can change across a street or down the block. The prospective buyer should find a knowledgeable person, probably an agent, to assist in the search.
- Before getting too far down the road, it's a good idea to find a reputable lender and become *prequalified* for a loan. This provides a good idea of the price range of houses that can be purchased.
- Whether it's buying or selling, real estate is usually negotiated, so it's important to sharpen (or learn for the first time) some skills in *negotiating the best deal*.

3 ASSESSMENT INTERVIEW

1. Tell me your thoughts about buying or selling a home.
2. What are your fears and hopes regarding your home?
3. How are you gathering information about your credit score and existing debt load? What have you found out?
4. Do you have an agent you can trust? How is it going so far in relating to this person?
5. Do you have any particular fears or concerns you want to share with me?
6. How can I help?

4 WISE COUNSEL

A house is much more than boards, paint, and the land it sits on. Quite often a person's sense of identity is tied up in the place of residence. For this reason, issues surrounding buying or selling a home can come up in counseling, especially when such a transaction comes with a job change, a divorce, or some other difficult life change.

As you ask the assessment questions, determine the nature and level of stress the person is experiencing, and pursue those topics so she feels understood and supported.

Individuals and couples who come for counseling will benefit from the insights of the five Money Personalities. Use these perceptions to stimulate discussion and understanding. If you feel comfortable, offer some commonsense input about the benefits and liabilities of home ownership and sales negotiations, but it's not appropriate to give real estate advice.

For the particular issues regarding the market, loans, and other topics, refer the person to a trustworthy real estate agent, but continue to talk about the person's hopes and fears.

5 ACTION STEPS

1. When people come for counseling, they may bring up the topic of home ownership if it is causing undue concerns. This is an important issue when people move from one city to another, when they divorce, or when a couple disagrees

about how to manage their money. Explore the emotional and relational issues surrounding their concerns about buying or selling a home.

2. Explain the five Money Personalities and help the client identify herself and her spouse. Discuss the principles of good communication and conflict resolution, and help her apply these principles.

3. If possible, refer the client to a reputable real estate agent who can answer questions and provide a full range of services.

4. As counseling progresses, continue to address the person's fears and hopes related to buying or selling a home, but don't give specific advice about real estate.

BIBLICAL INSIGHTS : 6

Do not be one who shakes hands in pledge or puts up security for debts; if you lack the means to pay, your very bed will be snatched from under you.

Proverbs 22:26–27

Often home ownership looks more attractive before the purchase than after it. Most people should not consider buying if the total payment each month is more than 30 percent of their monthly income.

Suppose one of you wants to build a tower. Won't you first sit down and estimate the cost to see if you have enough money to complete it? For if you lay the foundation and are not able to finish it, everyone who sees it will ridicule you, saying, "This person began to build and wasn't able to finish."

Luke 14:28–30

Avoid impulse buying. Carefully consider every aspect of the purchase, including price, payments, upkeep, travel expenses to and from work, and potential resale value.

See, I have given you this land. Go in and take possession of the land the LORD swore he would give to your fathers—to Abraham, Isaac and Jacob—and to their descendants after them.

Deuteronomy 1:8

Throughout the history of Israel, the land has been a vital part of their identity. In our lives, too, the place we call home is very important. We need to trust God for wisdom to know when he gives us the land. We do not want to pursue a purchase apart from his leading and his wisdom.

7 PRAYER STARTER

Father, you are our heart's true home, but we also need a place to live. Lead this person clearly. Give her wisdom about every aspect of buying (or selling) so that she honors you in every aspect of it. Thank you for your grace . . .

8 RECOMMENDED RESOURCES

Munchbach, Jim. *Make Your Money Count: Connecting Your Resources to What Matters Most*. Baxter Press, 2007.

Palmer, Bethany, and Scott Palmer. *First Comes Love, Then Comes Money: A Couple's Guide to Financial Communication*. HarperOne, 2009.

http://www.ronblue.com/

http://www.mvelopes.com/focusonthefamily/

http://www.daveramsey.com/home/

http://www.crown.org/

Inheritance

PORTRAITS 1

- "You're going to ruin him!" Betty almost shouted at Henry. "You've given him everything he's ever wanted, and if you leave him millions after we're gone, he'll just throw it all away." "What else do you suggest we do with everything we've earned and bought?" Henry asked icily. Betty didn't miss a beat. "We can give most of it to charity and leave him only enough to force him to finally get a job."

- Samuel and Kim got married in their fifties. It was the third time for him and second for her, with children from each of these marriages. Both of them had started successful companies, but as they sat down to update their wills, they realized the barely concealed jealousies of their large blended family would probably boil over when the assets were divided. "We need help," Samuel said. Kim added, "Not just with the will. We need help with all the demands and hurts in our complicated family. It's an explosion waiting to happen."

- Kay and Robby are retired and are updating their will. They have two children. Katherine has always been a model daughter, responsible and attentive. But their son, Rob, has been the black sheep of the family since he was a kid. As Kay and Robby talk about assigning their assets, Kay wants to give almost everything to Katherine. "She's been there when we've needed her," she explains, "but Rob, he's an addict who has thrown away or poisoned everything he's ever touched." Robby disagreed. "That's not fair. Both of them are our children, and we should split the assets equally." Their net worth is about 3 million dollars.

- Jason's wife died years ago, and his three children have never gotten along. For years his eldest daughter was named executor of his estate, but recently, she's been in bitter arguments with her two siblings. "I don't know what to do," Jason lamented. "I need to decide who is going to be the executor of my estate. Right now, I'd just as soon give it all away. Then they'd all be angry with me instead of each other."

DEFINITIONS AND KEY THOUGHTS 2

- An *inheritance* is the *real property* bequeathed to survivors after a person's death.
- In counseling, people may come for wisdom and direction in determining how to distribute their assets to their heirs, or people may come after the will is

probated and they don't feel they were treated fairly. Many of the most bitter family disputes are enflamed by unfulfilled expectations about an inheritance.

- The *distribution of assets* brings out the best and worst in heirs—either generosity and humility or greed and arrogance. Too often people are disappointed, resulting in hurt, bitterness, and estrangement from family members. Perceptions of inequality and injustice in the distribution of an inheritance can cloud family relationships for years.

- On the other hand, good communication and wise distribution can extend a legacy of love, trust, respect, and success to the next generation.

- The distribution of assets can include everything that has value, and even some things that seem to have only sentimental value, including real estate, cash, investment funds, business interests, jewelry, and so on, but also diaries, scrapbooks, photographs, and other items that keep the legacy of family affection alive. Many people make a detailed list of particular items they want to leave to specific family members, but others give instructions for the heirs to make a list and then take turns picking what they want, and some use a combination of these approaches.

- One of the most common desires is to reward the good behavior in some family members by giving them a disproportionate share of the assets. Usually other family members feel betrayed, creating deep resentment.

- Some assets require the *transfer of title* to the new owner.

- The selection of an *executor* is a crucial task of those who are writing wills. This person carries out the prescribed intent of the deceased.

3 : ASSESSMENT INTERVIEW

For those who are deciding how to divide their assets:

1. What are your goals for distributing your assets in your will?
2. Have you made a list of specific items you want to give to particular people?
3. Do you plan to give more to one person than another? If so, have you communicated your intentions to the one who might feel overlooked?
4. How can you leave a legacy of love and success to your heirs?
5. How can I help?

For those who are disappointed by the distribution of assets:

1. Tell me about the distribution. How do you feel about it?
2. What were your expectations? What would have been fair to you?
3. How has this affected your relationships with other heirs?
4. Do you plan legal recourse? Why or why not?
5. What will it take for you to be grateful for what you have, grieve your losses, and move on with your life?
6. How can I help?

WISE COUNSEL : 4

The distribution of an inheritance can be the source of a wide range of responses, from elation to heartbreak. In the assessment interview, determine if the person needs help in dividing assets among heirs. If the person is an heir, uncover perceptions of fairness or injustice.

Comparison means everything in an inheritance. Children may receive a million dollars, but if their brother or sister received two million, they feel angry and resentful—at the sibling and at the parents. Look for perceptions and feelings under the numbers and possessions.

If the person has come for wisdom about distributing assets, talk about the importance of communicating love to each person, not just making a list of things to leave behind. A letter of affection and pride in each person may mean more than a vase, a set of dishes, or a painting on the wall. Help the person leave a legacy of love.

Individuals and couples who come for counseling will benefit from the insights of the five Money Personalities. In addition, principles of active listening, communication, and conflict resolution will help them communicate more clearly and positively.

If the person feels resentment because someone else got more, help him process the feelings and find resolution—spiritually, emotionally, and relationally.

If you or your client suspect that genuine wrong has been committed in the distribution of assets, suggest that he see a competent attorney for assistance.

ACTION STEPS : 5

1. In the assessment interview, discuss the client's goals of distributing assets, perceptions about family members, and feelings of hope, love, anger, and resentment. All of these could be present, depending on which family member the client is thinking about. Fairness is in the eye of the giver.
2. If the person feels slighted by the deceased and heirs who received more than the client thinks they should have received, provide a safe place to talk about emotions and perceptions. Quite often the hurt experienced when assets were distributed is only the tip of the iceberg, and a lifetime of hurt and anger lurks under the surface.
3. Help the person sort out facts and feelings. If there has been a violation of the will, he may choose to pursue legal action. If, however, the violation is of dignity, the person may pursue honest conversations with a goal of reconciliation. In many cases, however, hurt feelings and distrust remain. Help the person learn to trust in the sovereignty and goodness of God, as well as his provision.
4. Explain the five Money Personalities and help him identify himself.
5. Discuss the principles of good communication.
6. If appropriate, refer the person to an attorney who can provide legal assistance.

6 : BIBLICAL INSIGHTS

And he gave their land as an inheritance, an inheritance to his people Israel.

Psalm 135:12

The concept of an inheritance is woven throughout the Scriptures. The land of Israel, the promises of God, and in fact, the presence of God were the legacy of God's people from the time of Abraham until today. Though an inheritance sometimes causes heartache in our families, it is meant to be a source of blessing, joy, and strength.

Ill-gotten treasures have no lasting value, but righteousness delivers from death.

Proverbs 10:2

Family members who connive to get more from an inheritance hurt themselves and everyone else, but those who trust God and walk with him, especially when they feel betrayed, experience God's grace and strength.

A good person leaves an inheritance for their children's children, but a sinner's wealth is stored up for the righteous.

Proverbs 13:22

Possessions, wisely handled, can be tools in the hands of a good parent or grandparent to leave a legacy of wisdom for years to come.

For this reason, since the day we heard about you, we have not stopped praying for you. We continually ask God to fill you with the knowledge of his will through all the wisdom and understanding that the Spirit gives, so that you may live a life worthy of the Lord and please him in every way: bearing fruit in every good work, growing in the knowledge of God, being strengthened with all power according to his glorious might so that you may have great endurance and patience, and giving joyful thanks to the Father, who has qualified you to share in the inheritance of his holy people in the kingdom of light. For he has rescued us from the dominion of darkness and brought us into the kingdom of the Son he loves, in whom we have redemption, the forgiveness of sins.

Colossians 1:9–14

In his prayer, Paul explains that our greatest inheritance is the grace of God and our position as his dearly beloved children. This inheritance is more valuable than anything here on earth and it can never be taken away.

PRAYER STARTER : 7

Lord Jesus, thank you for all you've given us, especially your grace to rescue us from sin and hell. This person wants to be a good manager of the possessions in his life. Give him wisdom to give (or receive) so that he can reflect your love . . .

RECOMMENDED RESOURCES : 8

Munchbach, Jim. *Make Your Money Count: Connecting Your Resources to What Matters Most.* Baxter Press, 2007.

Palmer, Bethany, and Scott Palmer. *First Comes Love, Then Comes Money: A Couple's Guide to Financial Communication.* HarperOne, 2009.

http://www.ronblue.com/

http://www.mvelopes.com/focusonthefamily/

http://www.daveramsey.com/home/

http://www.crown.org/

Insurance

1 PORTRAITS

- Bev and Anthony are in their early thirties and have two children. Anthony has a good job but he's concerned about what would happen to his family if he should die. For several years he's thought about getting life insurance but he gets conflicting messages about the benefits of whole life and term.
- Rhonda is a single mom trying to make ends meet. She's held a job since the divorce but she hasn't had the energy or time to look after a lot of details. A month ago her home burned to the ground. When the adjuster came, he told her that her policy was out-of-date and would cover only a fraction of her loss. She feels doubly devastated.
- Charles and Sherry celebrated their sixtieth wedding anniversary at an assisted living facility. More than twenty years ago, he had the foresight to take out a long-term care policy for both of them, and now it's saving them—and their kids—an enormous amount of money.
- Nathan is self-employed, and his business has struggled to gain traction. When he opened his doors, he bought disability insurance. In the last few years, however, he cut costs every possible way, and the disability policy lapsed. He is in reasonably good shape but he worries that, if he got sick—really sick—and the business collapsed, it would leave his wife and kids without any income at all.

2 DEFINITIONS AND KEY THOUGHTS

- Most people have insurance on their homes and cars, but they may need to consider policies for other purposes, including *property in a rented apartment, disability,* and *long-term care.*
- When considering ways to manage risk, examine the stability and reputation of the insurance company. Information can be found online. Always work with highly rated companies. Some companies offer low rates, but they may not provide adequate service when customers really need them.
- Many people are *underinsured*. It's wise to carve out thirty minutes each year to review and update policies. If the agent doesn't have time for a review and adjustment, the insured should find a new provider. One of the most painful things about major loss is when someone discovers that the insurance doesn't fulfill expectations.

- Today most people prefer *term* instead of *whole life* (or cash value) policies, but there are pros and cons on each side. Do your homework, talk to an informed and neutral person, and make the best choice for you and your family.
- Healthy people may think they won't ever need *disability insurance*, but accidents and major illness can wreck family finances. This kind of risk management doesn't cost much and it provides peace of mind.
- *Long-term care* policies have become increasingly popular as the Baby Boomer generation enters retirement. Living longer has its benefits, but longevity in poor health or mental instability can quickly sap a family's resources.

ASSESSMENT INTERVIEW 3

1. What are your concerns about managing risk at this point in your life?
2. What options are you considering?
3. Do you have people you trust to advise you?
4. What are your next steps in determining the type of insurance you need?
5. How can I help?

WISE COUNSEL 4

Typically, people don't come to a therapist, pastor, or lay counselor because they have questions about insurance. However, if they come because they've experienced the trauma of a fire, accident, or disability, they may need some help with the emotional pain and some advice about insurance.

Another reason people may bring up the topic of insurance is that they are obsessing about their risks. They may be depressed about traumas in the past or paranoid about potential risks in the future. Their worries about insurance are only the surface issue. Don't get sidetracked there. Go deeper into their obsessive doubts and worries.

If people bring up the issue of insurance, ask the diagnostic questions and determine the nature of any complicating emotional or relational problems. If there are, indeed, significant issues related to insurance, refer the person to a competent professional.

Individuals and couples who come for counseling will benefit from the insights of the five Money Personalities. In addition, principles of active listening and conflict resolution will help them communicate more clearly and positively.

ACTION STEPS 5

1. If the topic of insurance surfaces in the assessment interview, determine the nature of the problem and the current level of difficulty or need.
2. Quite often worries about the present are rooted in painful past wounds. Take time to uncover those pains, if they exist, and address the hurt, fear, doubt, and uncertainty caused by unresolved events.

3. Explain the five Money Personalities and help the client identify herself and her spouse. Discuss the principles of good communication, which will be needed when discussing insurance with a spouse.
4. If there are genuine concerns about the type and sufficiency of insurance coverage, refer the person to a trusted agent.
5. If you continue to meet with this person, monitor the level of worries and the steps taken to resolve present problems.

6 BIBLICAL INSIGHTS

I am sending you out like sheep among wolves. Therefore be as shrewd as snakes and as innocent as doves.

Matthew 10:16

Life is unpredictable. Evil, accidents, sickness, and natural disasters can disrupt or destroy our lives. As stewards of our lives, our families, and the resources God has entrusted to us, we need to be shrewd in taking care of them. Learning to trust God and seeking his guidance in such decisions is a daily task.

Plans fail for lack of counsel, but with many advisers they succeed.

Proverbs 15:22

We need to do our homework to find insurance companies with sterling reputations and agents who can advise us with skill and care.

Speak up for those who cannot speak for themselves, for the rights of all who are destitute. Speak up and judge fairly; defend the rights of the poor and needy.

Proverbs 31:8–9

God has called us to care for those who can't take care of themselves, and this begins with providing an umbrella of protection for our families.

Husbands, love your wives, just as Christ loved the church and gave himself up for her. . . . In this same way, husbands ought to love their wives as their own bodies.

Ephesians 5:25, 28

We provide insurance protection for our spouse because we are dedicated to her in the same way Jesus is dedicated to us. We may need to sacrifice some conveniences to provide this protection, but that's what love does.

PRAYER STARTER : 7

Father, we treasure the people you treasure. Give this person the ability to make wise decisions about protecting her family from financial ruin. Guide her to the right people to help her, and give her direction about the kind of coverage she needs. Thank you . . .

RECOMMENDED RESOURCES : 8

Munchbach, Jim. *Make Your Money Count: Connecting Your Resources to What Matters Most*. Baxter Press, 2007.

Palmer, Bethany, and Scott Palmer. *First Comes Love, Then Comes Money: A Couple's Guide to Financial Communication*. HarperOne, 2009.

http://www.ronblue.com/

http://www.mvelopes.com/focusonthefamily/

http://www.daveramsey.com/home/

http://www.crown.org/

Investing

1 PORTRAITS

- Frank has always admired his brother Jim and been amazed by Jim's optimism about investment opportunities. A year ago Jim proposed a business deal. "It can't miss," he assured Frank. But it missed in a big way, and Frank lost every penny of the $100,000 he put into the deal. He didn't tell his wife about it, and when she found out, she hit the roof. She went for counseling because she's not sure she can ever trust Frank again.

- Ed and Nadine are polar opposites. When they were dating, they were enamored with their different ways of looking at life, but after fifteen years of marriage and three kids, these differences grate on their relationship. It shows up in many ways, including their view of investing their 401(k) funds. Ed's Money Personality is Risk Taker. He is always looking for the next big upward swing in the market, so he wants to put both their investments in aggressive growth funds. Nadine is risk averse. She feels much more comfortable with bond funds. They are seeking counseling to help them find common ground on a wide array of conflicting areas, including how to raise their kids, sex, budgeting, and how they invest for retirement.

- Samuel grew up in a poor part of a major city. He got the opportunity to go to college and did very well. Now he's a regional manager for an engineering firm, which pays him a very good salary and benefits. He has some money in individual stocks and worries about their performance. A dozen times each day he checks the Dow Jones average and his stock on his smart phone. His obsessive nature is considered a strength in the highly detailed world of engineering, but his worry about his investments is driving him up a wall.

- Michael has been a real estate developer through many cycles of boom and bust. Over the last twenty years, he's made and lost millions of dollars. He's gotten used to the roller-coaster ride, but his wife, Bonnie, can't stand it any longer. She felt uncomfortable when he bought her luxury cars, furs, and diamonds during the boom times and she felt ashamed when they had to move out of their house because his company was bankrupt. When she tried to talk to him about all the strain she felt, he just shrugged and said, "The ups and downs go with the territory. I'm a developer. I make and lose money all the time." But recently she filed for a divorce.

DEFINITIONS AND KEY THOUGHTS 2

- Today, for people of almost any income level, a vast and varied array of *investment opportunities* are available, including *stocks, bonds, mutual funds, tax-free funds, savings accounts, real estate, start-up businesses, venture capital investments*, and many variations of each of these.

- In relationships, opposites attract, and this can be true of investments too. Conflict can arise when one partner is *risk tolerant* and one is *risk averse*. Their perception about risk isn't just about the numbers on a page—the type of investment they prefer is shaped by their sense of identity and safety. And usually they can't understand how their spouse can be so irresponsible with money or anal about holding on to it.

- The topic of investments isn't the presenting reason most people come to counseling but it can play an important part in common presenting problems, including marital conflict over all areas of managing money, disappointment and blame over past investment failures, and the splitting of assets in a divorce.

- For particular investment questions, refer the clients to a qualified financial professional.

ASSESSMENT INTERVIEW 3

Explain the Money Personalities and use the insights gained to stimulate discussion.

1. What is your Money Personality? What is your spouse's? What are some areas where your profiles complement each other? Where do you sometimes find misunderstanding and tension?
2. In what way is financial management, and particularly investments, contributing to your difficulty today?
3. What is your track record with investments? Are you satisfied with your decisions? Why or why not?
4. If married: Do you and your spouse usually agree about investment decisions or do you experience a significant level of disagreement? Who usually wins?
5. Have disagreements affected the level of trust between you?
6. How has this conflict affected other areas of your relationship and your family?
7. How would finding common ground build trust and lower the level of tension?
8. How can I help?

WISE COUNSEL 4

Many people who have experienced past financial failures, including failed investments, carry a load of blame and shame. Even though the client does not currently have distress over investments, he may have unresolved anger, hurt, and mistrust as a result of things that happened years before. Explore this possibility with the client.

People can be obsessive about almost anything, but especially about sex, power, and money. Look for any signs that the person is overly worried about the performance of an investment. This may simply show that he has chosen an investment instrument that is over his level of risk tolerance, or it could reveal a deeper psychological issue of obsessive-compulsive disorder.

Many couples experience conflict over money, including investments. If money is a problem for a couple, explore the issue of investments to see if disagreement about this issue is a significant factor.

Help the couple see that the differences that were so attractive and beguiling when they were first together have become a wedge dividing them. Now they may be personalizing these differences ("I'm right and you're wrong") and making them seem more catastrophic than they really are ("If we do what you want, it's the end of the world!"). Help them see that differences aren't bad or wrong, but despising differences will lead inevitably to conflict and distance.

Individuals and couples who come for counseling will benefit from the insights of the five Money Personalities. The principles of active listening and conflict resolution will help them communicate more clearly and positively.

It's not unusual for the issue of investments to come up in counseling people who are going through a divorce. Some split their assets amicably, but others fight tooth and nail and use investments as a tool to hurt the other person. Address topics of forgiveness, grace, honesty, and boundaries in these cases.

Find financial professionals in your area to help your clients with specific direction for their investments. If you aren't trained in this area, avoid giving this advice.

5 ACTION STEPS

1. In your assessment interview, determine if the presenting problem of discouragement, conflict, or any other issue is related to disagreements with a spouse about investments or anger due to past failures in investing.

2. Address the underlying assumptions of the individual or couple. Discuss the meaning of money, the different perceptions and comfort with risk, and how the client is communicating with his spouse about this issue. Look for signs of discouragement, shame over past failures, and obsessive thoughts about current investments.

3. Explain the five Money Personalities and help the client identify himself and his spouse. Discuss the principles of good communication and answer any questions.

4. As counseling a couple continues, strive to help them understand one another, find common ground, and offer support to each other instead of despising their differences.

5. For couples and individuals, address issues of responsibility, wisdom in decision making, financial goals, experiencing and expressing forgiveness, and trusting God's sovereignty to use even failures to teach valuable lessons.

6. When it's appropriate, refer the couple or person to a qualified financial professional for investment counseling.

BIBLICAL INSIGHTS 6

You may say to yourself, "My power and the strength of my hands have produced this wealth for me." But remember the LORD your God, for it is he who gives you the ability to produce wealth, and so confirms his covenant, which he swore to your ancestors, as it is today.

Deuteronomy 8:17–18

The ability to make money, through hard work or investments, comes from the Lord. We need to see every good gift as coming from his hand, including the growth of our investments.

Plans fail for lack of counsel, but with many advisers they succeed.

Proverbs 15:22

Some people have a God-given knack for investing, but most of us need some help from qualified professionals who can give us sound advice.

A faithful person will be richly blessed, but one eager to get rich will not go unpunished.

Proverbs 28:20

Poor investment choices come at either extreme—too cautious or too risky. Usually those who look for slow, steady growth reach their goals, but often those who try to get rich quickly make foolish investment choices and harm their most valued relationships.

Ship your grain across the sea; after many days you may receive a return. Invest in seven ventures, yes, in eight; you do not know what disaster may come upon the land.

Ecclesiastes 11:1–2

There are few guarantees in investing. Apart from government-backed savings accounts, investors have to weigh the potential gain against the real risks. Most investment counselors recommend diversification to minimize risk.

PRAYER STARTER 7

Father, everything we have is yours, including our ability to make money and the gain we get on our investments. This person wants to be a good steward of what you've given him. Shape his heart to use money for good purposes instead of selfish ends and give him direction to invest wisely. And, Lord, help him find common ground with his spouse so that their relationship is strengthened instead of harmed by their investment choices . . .

8 RECOMMENDED RESOURCES

Munchbach, Jim. *Make Your Money Count: Connecting Your Resources to What Matters Most.* Baxter Press, 2007.

Palmer, Bethany, and Scott Palmer. *First Comes Love, Then Comes Money: A Couple's Guide to Financial Communication.* HarperOne, 2009.

http://www.ronblue.com/

http://www.mvelopes.com/focusonthefamily/

http://www.daveramsey.com/home/

http://www.crown.org/

Major Purposes

- Candy was tired of driving her old car, but it was only two years old. "I can't stand that old thing," she told a friend. "I need a new car—one that's really fun to drive." She had been looking at ads in magazines, and when she saw a beautiful model from an ad in living color, she had to have one like it. She drove to the nearest dealer, picked out the color she liked, signed the papers, and drove away. The salesman was surprised when she agreed to full price and all the maintenance agreements.

- Joseph and Maria were attracted to each other because they are polar opposites in many ways. Recently, however, these differences have begun to wear on their relationship. Maria is a Saver and Security Seeker, but Joseph is a Flyer, seldom giving a thought to the money he spends. When they looked for their first house, they almost came to blows several times. "I don't know what gets into her," Joseph told the counselor. "She analyzes everything. It takes all the fun out of shopping, and to be honest, out of our relationship."

- Tammy and Manuel wanted to buy new outdoor furniture and a nice grill—with a total cost of more than $4,000. Manuel wanted to get it all at once and put it on their credit card, but Tammy planned to put money away each month until they had enough to buy it without going into debt. "We're having people over next week," Manuel pleaded. "We've got to have something for people to sit on." Tammy reacted angrily. "We just got through paying off your golf clubs. We're not going into debt for a grill and some chairs to sit outside once in a while." It wasn't long before a simple disagreement escalated to the point where it threatened to destroy their marriage.

- "That big screen looks good," Justin told Sheila. "Let's get it." Sheila looked astounded. "It's the first one we've looked at." Justin shrugged. "So. It's just what I was looking for. Why do we need to waste time looking all over town for a better price. We'll probably end up here buying this one. We can get it now and save all that time and trouble." Sheila walked out and sat in the car. She refused to shop anymore with Justin.

2 : DEFINITIONS AND KEY THOUGHTS

- The different Money Personalities have widely varied ways of making major purchases. Savers and Security Seekers are cautious and want to save money; Spenders, Risk Takers, and Flyers are much more free spending.
- Often each partner in a marriage comes from the opposite side of the equation, so misunderstanding and conflict occur quite frequently. One is cautious and analytical; the other is impulsive.
- In families, the kids, grandparents, aunts, uncles, and everyone else has a Money Personality that can add to the conflict. The closer the family, the more opportunity for these personalities to collide, especially when there are significant financial decisions, such as major purchases.
- A few guidelines about major purchases can help clarify the direction of conversations and the expectations of each personality. These guidelines include:

  — *Establish a range of prices for the item.* Internet searches can take only seconds but they provide a good baseline for expectations.
  — *Compare prices and look for bargains.* Without leaving home, people can look online, make calls to local stores, and use apps on their smart phones to locate the best deals. Depending on the item, stores may offer deep discounts on particular days or in certain seasons.
  — *For large ticket price items, it's not out of place to negotiate the price.* Some people try to bargain for a lower price on groceries, but that seldom works. For cars, it's expected. People can also ask for the best price for appliances, furniture, computers, and other major purchases.

- The principles of active listening, communication, and conflict resolution will help clients understand one another and find common ground.

3 : ASSESSMENT INTERVIEW

Individuals may experience insecurity and anxiety over major purchases. Couples and families may endure significant conflict. And of course many people experience individual anxiety and mutual conflict at the same time. Begin by explaining the Money Personalities.

1. What is the cause of your anxiety or conflict?
2. When you look back at the history of your relationship with your spouse and/or family, is this event unusual or do you see a pattern? If it's a pattern, describe other times you've experienced this.
3. What is your Money Personality? What is your spouse's (or that of other members of your family)? How might the differences between you contribute to the tension you've experienced?
4. How would good communication and understanding change the way you interact with family members?

5. If you learn to understand and value each other, how might shopping for major purchases actually draw you closer?
6. How can I help?

WISE COUNSEL : 4

The anxiety and conflict many people experience when shopping together for major purchases are probably symptomatic of a more pervasive pattern in the relationship. It just surfaces in this way at this time. The item to be purchased isn't the real issue but it may represent something very important to each person, such as status, control, authority, or freedom. When these are the underlying values, identity is tied up in the thing to be bought, and people become demanding and defensive in their pursuit of these values.

One of the biggest issues in many families is the comfort level with debt. Some family members don't mind debt at all and they resent having to pay it off. But others, especially Security Seekers and Savers, don't feel comfortable with owing anything to anybody (except, perhaps, having a mortgage on their home). To resolve the tension, family members need to understand each other better and find common ground, valuing each other more than the things to be purchased and even more than the hidden values of status, security, control, and freedom.

The Money Personalities and the principles of good communication apply to this aspect of the relationship.

ACTION STEPS : 5

1. After listening to the nature of the presenting problem, explain the Money Personalities and ask the client to identify herself and other family members.
2. Review the principles of active listening and conflict resolution and answer any questions.
3. Help the client examine her relationship with the person she's having problems with to look for any pattern of miscommunication and misunderstanding. This can be a subject for further discussion in counseling and as homework for a Money Huddle.
4. Monitor the family's progress in communicating what's in their hearts, finding common ground, and building trust.

BIBLICAL INSIGHTS : 6

Be devoted to one another in love. Honor one another above yourselves.

Romans 12:10

Power struggles don't turn out well. One person may "win" and get her way but she does so at the expense of the relationship. When we are devoted to one another, we look out for the other person's interests, seek to understand, and graciously forgive wrongs.

Therefore let us stop passing judgment on one another. Instead, make up your mind not to put any stumbling block or obstacle in the way of a brother or sister.

Romans 14:13

Criticism and demands are big stumbling blocks in many relationships. When we insist on finding fault instead of finding common ground, we alienate the one God has given us to love and support.

Accept one another, then, just as Christ accepted you, in order to bring praise to God.

Romans 15:7

We aren't commanded to agree with others all the time, or to remain quiet when we have a different opinion, but we are to love and accept the person, seeking to understand so we can appreciate instead of criticize.

May the God of hope fill you with all joy and peace as you trust in him, so that you may overflow with hope by the power of the Holy Spirit. I myself am convinced, my brothers and sisters, that you yourselves are full of goodness, filled with knowledge and competent to instruct one another.

Romans 15:13–14

In our most important relationship, the person sleeping next to us (or our kids down the hall) is far more important than status, security, or freedom. As we understand, we are more able to be patient, to love, and to look for ways to support each other.

7 PRAYER STARTER

Father, the thing this person wants to buy is meaningless, but her relationship with her family means everything. Thank you for forgiving her for being judgmental and competitive. May she seek to love her spouse, understand her family, and build trust as they live together. Thank you for your wisdom and grace . . .

8 RECOMMENDED RESOURCES

Munchbach, Jim. *Make Your Money Count: Connecting Your Resources to What Matters Most.* Baxter Press, 2007.

Palmer, Bethany, and Scott Palmer. *First Comes Love, Then Comes Money: A Couple's Guide to Financial Communication.* HarperOne, 2009.

Money Huddles

- Joyce and Ken had been struggling in their relationship for years. Secrets, resentment, and a cloud of suspicion had almost caused them to give up hope. In the counseling session, as the secrets were exposed, they nearly came to blows but gradually they gained hope that the marriage could be saved. The counselor told them how to conduct a Money Huddle to help them communicate more effectively about their finances. They were very reluctant and put it off for several weeks because they were afraid they'd blow up at each other again. Finally, the counselor helped them have limited goals for their first meeting, and it proved to be a good start.

- David and Marie had been living separate lives under the same roof for years. When their secrets and resentments finally surfaced in counseling, they forgave each other and made a new commitment to their relationship. "It's like we're dating again," David told a friend. "I think we can talk about anything!" Their counselor trained them in how to conduct a Money Huddle, and they loved every minute of it. "The first one was a blast," Marie told her counselor. "So many of the old hurts are gone, and we have hope for our future together."

- When Danielle found out that Gary had blown his entire 401(k) gambling, she was furious. For months, she fussed and fumed. He quit gambling, joined a 12-step group, and showed her every penny he spent each week, but it wasn't enough. Their counselor told them how to have a Money Huddle, but Danielle didn't want anything to do with it. "How can I trust him to tell me the truth?" she growled. The counselor asked if she'd give it a try and see if they could make some progress—even a single step of talking for a few minutes without blaming and defending. Very reluctantly Danielle agreed. "I'll give him five minutes. After that, we'll see where we go with it." To his credit, Gary was willing to go as slowly as Danielle needed him to go. The first meeting lasted, in fact, only five minutes. She kept looking at her watch to keep track of time. But she agreed to have another meeting the next week, and then the next. Gradually the distrust, rage, and suspicion began to melt as Gary proved his love and integrity.

- Christy and Les got off to a good start in the first month of having their Money Huddles, but when school started for their kids and their lives got hectic, they postponed their next meeting, and then forgot to schedule another one. After three or four months, they forgot about them completely. Very quickly they reverted to the same behaviors that had driven them apart. Les became more demanding, and Christy withdrew into passivity. They poured their lives into their kids and avoided each other.

2 DEFINITIONS AND KEY THOUGHTS

- We call regular times for couples to talk about their finances *Money Huddles*. The key to a good money relationship is being intentional in *communicating about finances*. We suggest a regular time set aside to talk about current money (inflow and outgo) and dreams for the future—at least once every month.

- A Money Huddle is a great time to TALK:

  — T = *Time together*. Set a positive tone and get away from distractions.
  — A = *Assign duties*. Each member of the couple needs to have specific things he or she does for their financial household.
  — L = *List of goals*. The couple should review their goals and remind themselves what they are working for.
  — K = *Keep it consistent*. They must meet regularly.

- If a couple is in the process of resolving *financial infidelity*, the prospect of looking at each other and talking about the things they've avoided for years can be overwhelming. They need to have *realistic expectations, a clear process, limited goals*, and lots of *encouragement*.

- To get a good start, couples should meet weekly for the first month, then every two weeks for the next three months, and then monthly for the rest of their lives.

- Money Huddles are a combination of a *date, a business meeting*, and *a brainstorming session*. The components include:

  — *Setting a date* to talk about values, personalities, and finding common ground in finances.
  — *Getting rid of distractions*, like the kids, work, and the phone.
  — *Getting comfortable* so it's a pleasant experience. This isn't a confrontation; it's a conversation between friends and lovers.
  — *Setting the tone* by speaking words of affirmation, love, and hope, really making it like a date.
  — *Focusing on successes*, not failures and problems. There should be an atmosphere of gratitude and hope.
  — *Talking about priorities*. Every problem can't be solved immediately, so the most important things need to be the focus of the conversation. In many cases this is where the different personalities and values surface, and each person may have a different set of priorities. The couple should not blame each other or insist on their own way. Instead, they must listen, ask questions, and look for common ground.
  — *Setting goals* that are clear, mutually agreeable, and achievable. Once goals are determined, they should be written down. The couple assigns

responsibilities and sets target dates to accomplish them. It is best to start with "easy wins" to build confidence and encourage both partners to stay engaged in the process.

— *Scheduling the next Money Huddle.* Persistence is important, not only in managing money but in creating a healthy pattern of communication, so a time and place should be set for the next huddle. For the first month, the couple has a meeting once a week, then every two weeks for the next three months, and then once a month for the rest of their lives.

— *Celebrating.* When the huddle is over, the couple can take a deep breath, give each other a big kiss, and thank God they're changing the atmosphere of their relationship.

ASSESSMENT INTERVIEW : 3

Explain the five Money Personalities. Help the couple identify themselves and each other. Explain the nature of a Money Huddle and then ask:

1. What have you learned about yourself and each other from the Money Personalities?
2. How does your Money Personality complement your partner's? How do they conflict?
3. What do you hope to accomplish by having a regular Money Huddle?
4. What will be the long-term benefits in your relationship? What obstacles do you anticipate, such as communication, lack of trust, scheduling, differing expectations?
5. What are some realistic goals for the first huddle?
6. When and where will you have it?
7. How can I help?

WISE COUNSEL : 4

Some couples are eager to talk openly about money, but if the wound of financial infidelity is deep, one or both members of the couple may encounter significant resistance. After all, they're considering talking about something that has caused great pain. They need hope for the future of the relationship, assurance that their conversations will be worth the effort, and a clear understanding of the process.

Typically, one partner is more willing to participate in the Money Huddle than the other. This may be the result of past experiences, personality differences, or greater hope that it will work.

The five Money Personalities approach the huddles in very different ways. Flyers would rather have a root canal than talk about details of finances, but Security Seekers want to have two huddles a day to be sure they stay on track with every penny. Savers want to be sure they keep enough money in reserve, but Spenders are ready to end the meeting as soon as they have a dollar figure they can spend.

Advise the couple that if the discussion in the huddle becomes too hot or too cold, they should step away for a while, get a snack, watch TV, or do something else to take their minds off the discussion. Before they disengage, however, they need to agree on when to resume. The goal isn't to be right or to demand their way. The purpose of these conversations is to work out financial problems, which will build the relationship as the couple works together.

Quite often in huddles, past patterns of attack and withdrawal surface, especially in the first few huddles. The couple should do whatever it takes to keep moving forward by focusing on the positives, affirming truth and integrity, and celebrating each step forward.

5 ACTION STEPS

1. Explain the five Money Personalities and help the couple identify themselves. Discuss the way their Money Personalities complement each other and how they may conflict with each other.
2. Explain the goals and procedure of a Money Huddle. Answer their questions. You might want to ask them to have their first one with you as the facilitator or mediator.
3. Teach the principles of active listening, good communication, and conflict resolution, and answer any questions.
4. Encourage them to schedule regular Money Huddles to continue to build the relationship and communicate about their finances.
5. Monitor their progress as they continue to come for counseling. The huddles provide a strong foundation for communication about every area of their lives and their relationship.

6 BIBLICAL INSIGHTS

But now you must also rid yourselves of all such things as these: anger, rage, malice, slander, and filthy language from your lips. Do not lie to each other, since you have taken off your old self with its practices and have put on the new self, which is being renewed in knowledge in the image of its Creator. . . . Therefore, as God's chosen people, holy and dearly loved, clothe yourselves with compassion, kindness, humility, gentleness and patience.

Colossians 3:8–10, 12

We have the power to choose what we say and how we say it. In conversations we can inflict wounds or heal old ones, shatter trust or rebuild it. As we walk with God, we can trust him to renew us, give us wisdom, and fill our hearts with love for our partner so that our words heal and build.

My dear brothers and sisters, take note of this: Everyone should be quick to listen, slow to speak and slow to become angry, because human anger does not produce the righteousness that God desires.

James 1:19–20

The goal in a Money Huddle isn't to win an argument, but to understand each other and find a mutually beneficial way forward. The more we listen, the more we understand. Participants should stop talking, stop thinking about what they're going to say next, and stop angling to win the point. Instead, they must listen carefully, ask questions, and affirm the other person's feelings—even if they disagree with the point.

Remind the people to be subject to rulers and authorities, to be obedient, to be ready to do whatever is good, to slander no one, to be peaceable and considerate, and always to be gentle toward everyone.

Titus 3:1–2

Gentleness is a mark of true humility. In these huddle conversations, we must be aware of our tone of voice, facial expressions, and body language. We need to practice sitting back, smiling, and asking questions until we're sure we understand our partner's point.

When we put bits into the mouths of horses to make them obey us, we can turn the whole animal. Or take ships as an example. Although they are so large and are driven by strong winds, they are steered by a very small rudder wherever the pilot wants to go. Likewise, the tongue is a small part of the body, but it makes great boasts. Consider what a great forest is set on fire by a small spark. The tongue also is a fire, a world of evil among the parts of the body. It corrupts the whole body, sets the whole course of one's life on fire, and is itself set on fire by hell.

James 3:3–6

Words matter. They aren't magical but they're powerful. An unkind remark can inflict a deep wound, but a sentence or two of genuine affirmation can bring healing. Before a couple has a Money Huddle, they should ask God to help them see each other the way he sees them and help them speak to each other the way he would.

PRAYER STARTER 7

Father, this couple wants to talk openly, honestly, and positively about money, but they have some hurdles to overcome. Thank you for your grace and kindness. You have a wonderful plan for their relationship, and we trust you to guide them as they talk about money. They are committed to talking regularly because their marriage is worth the investment of time and energy . . .

RECOMMENDED RESOURCES 8

Palmer, Bethany, and Scott Palmer. *First Comes Love, Then Comes Money: A Couple's Guide to Financial Communication*. HarperOne, 2009.

Nagging

1 PORTRAITS

- Shannon is a Security Seeker; her husband, Dwayne, is a Flyer. Initially opposites attract, but eventually they can fiercely oppose one another. That's what happened to this couple. Dwayne seldom thinks twice about buying something he wants. He spends money on golf, his workouts at the gym, lunches with friends, and gifts for the family. Since they got married, Shannon has taken responsibility for their finances—because Dwayne seemed so oblivious. To try to keep him in line, Shannon points out every time he goes over the budget she set for him. She doesn't seem to realize that Dwayne has no intention of living by it. For the first few months, they laughed about their differences. They're not laughing anymore.
- Kathleen feels emotionally abused. Russell is a tightwad and he demands to know where every dime is spent. Each day when he gets home from work, he asks her for an accounting of everything she spent that day. If there is any hint of discretionary spending or any suggestion she didn't get the very best deals, Russell treats her like a disobedient dog. Actually he treats their dog better than he treats her.
- In his first year of marriage, Gary made some dumb decisions about spending money. It's been five years, but Monique still reminds him that he "isn't smart with money." Gary has long since mended his ways, but Monique won't (or can't) trust him.
- Javier put Debra in charge of the checkbook and paying bills online, but several times a month he checks each account to be sure she's done her job. Several times, she's asked, "Don't you trust me?" He replies, "Well, we can't be too careful. People make mistakes." She has tried to turn the responsibility back to him, but he refuses. Debra told a friend, "I can't stand it. He doesn't say much but he doesn't have to. I know he doesn't trust me with our money. I feel like he's standing over me all day scowling at me. That's no way to have a relationship!"

2 DEFINITIONS AND KEY THOUGHTS

- Nagging. We all do it, whether it's a little reminder about picking up his laundry, a subtle mention that she still hasn't paid that bill, a nightly hint about washing the dishes. Being on the receiving end of another person's persistent faultfinding always feels lousy. That's especially true when it comes to nagging about finances.

- *Nagging* is essentially a control mechanism. It is designed to encourage or shame the person into compliance. Even if it seems to work, it fails in the long run because it eventually poisons the relationship.

- Because money impacts every part of our lives, being reminded of our money failures—the big ones and the little ones—feels personal. To really deal with financial conflict, couples need to stop nagging each other and figure out what's really behind their discontent. The problem might have one of these three causes:

  1. *One partner doesn't feel heard.* If a person is constantly needling his spouse about money, he should step back and ask himself what he really wants to say. Chances are, he feels as if his partner doesn't listen to his fears or concerns about finances and nagging seems like the only way to get his feelings heard. Understanding our Money Personality helps us see how people can have such different ideas about money. Once we see that these differences don't have to get in the way, we can try starting fresh by saying something like, "I feel like I nag you about our money all the time, and you probably don't like that. I'm sorry. I have some concerns about our money and I'd like to talk with you about them this week."

  2. *There's a lack of trust.* We tend to nag when we worry that the other person isn't going to take care of an issue on his own. And that suggests a lack of trust. If a person has actual reasons to distrust his partner when it comes to money, it's time to get to the root of this problem and talk about what happened and how the couple can work together to get back on track. But just because one of them likes to spend money (the Spender) and one likes to save it (the Saver), that doesn't mean they can't trust each other. It means they need to practice strong financial communication, set realistic expectations for their finances, and stay committed to their Money Huddle.

  3. *The person has a bad track record.* Sometimes one partner's financial fears are based on the other person's mistakes. But if they want to move forward, one partner has to muster up the grace to forgive the other's mistakes and start over. Reminding one's partner about that bad real estate deal ten years ago doesn't help anyone. We have to let it go.

ASSESSMENT INTERVIEW 3

Explain the Money Personalities, and then ask these questions:

1. What is your Money Personality? What is your spouse's?
2. What are areas where the two of you complement each other? In what areas do you experience misunderstanding and conflict about money?
3. Describe the problem in your relationship. How does this communication affect you and your closeness with each other?
4. How have you used nagging to try to resolve the problem? What happened?
5. What were things like before the onset of this problem? How did you resolve differences then? What changed?
6. What would you like to see happen in your pattern of communication?

7. What is your responsibility? What is your spouse's?
8. How can I help?

4 WISE COUNSEL

A person who nags may be responding inappropriately to another person's pattern of irresponsible behavior, but some people use nagging to try to control people who have consistently proven to be responsible. So the issue may lie with both people or with only one.

The Money Personalities can help people understand their differences. Often the insight gained goes a long way in dissolving resentment and beginning to build unity.

Even when another person is irresponsible, we can use clarity and respect when communicating with him. Progress is made when a path for resolution of the irresponsibility is mutually agreed upon, including consequences for failure.

5 ACTION STEPS

1. Explain the Money Personalities and ask the client to identify himself and his spouse. Then discuss points of commonality and differences of perception. Use this conversation as a platform to build understanding.
2. Teach the principles of active listening, good communication, and conflict resolution, and answer any questions.
3. Clarify responsibilities and boundaries in the relationship regarding money. Usually nagging happens because one person feels the need to control another who seems out of control. Help the client set clear consequences for their own irresponsible behavior.
4. Negotiate a good plan for the next hour, the next day, and the next week to help the couple deal with the flashpoints that have produced nagging behaviors. Develop scripts to help them respond more appropriately to each other in those moments.
5. Discuss the importance of Money Huddles and offer the following advice: "In your next Money Huddle, make a commitment to put an end to nagging each other about money. Instead of nagging, write out your financial concerns and agree to focus on two of those concerns for the next few months. Once those fears are out in the open and you have a plan for addressing them, you'll find there's no more need to nag."

6 BIBLICAL INSIGHTS

Better to live in a desert than with a quarrelsome and nagging wife.

Proverbs 21:19

This observation is just as true about husbands. Nagging makes life miserable. But that's the point. People who nag are trying to use shame and degradation to force compliance with their wishes. The natural consequence, however, is a ruined relationship.

No good tree bears bad fruit, nor does a bad tree bear good fruit. Each tree is recognized by its own fruit. People do not pick figs from thornbushes, or grapes from briers. A good man brings good things out of the good stored up in his heart, and an evil man brings evil things out of the evil stored up in his heart. For the mouth speaks what the heart is full of.

Luke 6:43–45

If we want a snapshot of the condition of our heart, we need look no further than the words that come out of our mouth each day. When our heart is full of gratitude, we speak words of affirmation and love, but if it's full of resentment, we will try to control others by condemning what they do.

Do not let any unwholesome talk come out of your mouths, but only what is helpful for building others up according to their needs, that it may benefit those who listen. And do not grieve the Holy Spirit of God, with whom you were sealed for the day of redemption. Get rid of all bitterness, rage and anger, brawling and slander, along with every form of malice. Be kind and compassionate to one another, forgiving each other, just as in Christ God forgave you.

Ephesians 4:29–32

In this passage Paul connects our verbal messages with our heart attitude toward God and other people. He gives clear directives to stop speaking harmful words, deal with the bitterness in our hearts, and allow the love of Christ to expel resentment from us so that we love and forgive those around us—especially those who would normally annoy us.

Finally, brothers and sisters, whatever is true, whatever is noble, whatever is right, whatever is pure, whatever is lovely, whatever is admirable—if anything is excellent or praiseworthy—think about such things. Whatever you have learned or received or heard from me, or seen in me—put it into practice. And the God of peace will be with you.

Philippians 4:8–9

We have the responsibility to control what goes on in our mind. We can choose to dwell on past hurts and dashed hopes, or we can focus our attention on the love, forgiveness, and majesty of God. When our heart is right, our words are sweet and powerful.

7 PRAYER STARTER

Lord Jesus, you spoke truth to everyone around you, but you never nagged. You gave people options and you described consequences but you never nagged. Help us be like you. Fill our hearts with your grace . . .

8 RECOMMENDED RESOURCES

Munchbach, Jim. *Make Your Money Count: Connecting Your Resources to What Matters Most*. Baxter Press, 2007.

Palmer, Bethany, and Scott Palmer. *First Comes Love, Then Comes Money: A Couple's Guide to Financial Communication*. HarperOne, 2009.

http://www.ronblue.com/

http://www.mvelopes.com/focusonthefamily/

http://www.daveramsey.com/home/

http://www.crown.org/

Prenuptial Agreements

PORTRAITS 1

- Nick and Alyssa have been married before—this will be his fourth time and her third. Their lives are complicated, and they want to be sure they enter this marriage with their eyes wide open. They both have grown children, and some of them are against their parents getting married. Nick owns his own business and he wants to be sure his son takes over after he's gone. Nick has talked to Alyssa about his desire for a prenuptial agreement. "I don't want to leave it in the hands of attorneys," he explains. "I've seen that movie before, and it's not pretty."

- Krystal and Travis are planning to get married, but he's concerned about all the debt she'll bring into the relationship. After talking to a CPA, he explains to Krystal, "I don't like the idea of a prenuptial agreement, but my financial planner tells me that if we get married and you default on your loans, they can come after me. I can't let that happen."

- Gerald and Diana have wanted to get married for a while, but they've waited because Gerald's daughter despises Diana. She doesn't even attempt to conceal her hatred. "She's nothing but a gold digger," the daughter fumes. "She's just after my dad's money." To try to soothe his daughter's wrath and clarify everyone's expectations, Gerald says he wants a prenuptial agreement to spell out the financial arrangement in case he and Diana get divorced. Now he's got another angry woman on his hands.

- Jay and Stacy have planned a wonderful wedding and honeymoon. Both of them own their own businesses and are very successful. To make sure his children are protected in case of a divorce, Jay announces that he wants them to have a prenuptial agreement. He's shocked when Stacy is upset. "Is that all this is to you, a business relationship?" she cries. "If that's what you want, buy a wife! The Bible says a marriage is forever, but you want a parachute so you can bail out if there's any trouble. That's not the kind of marriage I want." They're getting counseling to try to resolve the hurt and anger. Their future together is hanging in the balance.

DEFINITIONS AND KEY THOUGHTS 2

- A *prenuptial agreement* is a binding, legal agreement between two people to outline the financial arrangement when and if the marriage ends. Sometimes such an agreement is made when two older people marry to be sure that their money is kept separate for their adult children when they die.

- To many Christians, the idea of a prenuptial agreement is antithetical to the teaching of Scripture. To them, marriage is sacred and inviolable—"until death do us part." Divorce isn't an option, or at least, it's a tragedy that should not be part of the planning before the wedding day.

- People who have been previously married and experienced bitter divorce proceedings may be much more cautious the next time they want to marry. To provide a sense of peace and trust, they want an agreement up front about the financial consequences if things don't work out. To them, a prenuptial agreement seems just and right.

- Several factors may cause one or both parties to consider the value of a prenuptial agreement. Any of the following circumstances may warrant such an agreement: when the upcoming wedding is a remarriage with complications in finances and relationships, when one or both partners have excessive debt and there is the threat of bankruptcy, when one of the partners owns a business, or when there is conflict with children over the marriage.

- In the Christian community, prenuptial agreements are controversial. Counselors and pastors need to think carefully about the nature of marriage, the clients' desire for this arrangement, what the agreement says to both parties, and the impact on the extended family.

- As couples consider the need for a prenuptial agreement, it is important that they understand the principles and processes of good communication about money, including the five Money Personalities and the Money Huddle.

3 ASSESSMENT INTERVIEW

In most cases, people bring up the topic of prenuptial agreements in counseling only if there is a significant disagreement about this issue. When this happens, be sure the couple (or individual) understands the Money Personalities, the principles of conflict resolution, and the process of communication using the Money Huddle. In this process, you can ask:

1. What is the nature of your disagreement? How has it affected your relationship?
2. Why is a prenuptial agreement attractive (or unattractive) to you? What does it imply about your relationship?
3. How would this kind of agreement affect your trust in each other?
4. How might it be valuable?
5. What might be some other ways to accomplish the goals the agreement is designed to accomplish?
6. After you found your Money Personalities on the Money Personality Profile (free on www.themoneycouple.com), what did you learn about yourself and each other?
7. How might regular Money Huddles help relieve financial fears in your relationship?
8. How can I help?

WISE COUNSEL : 4

Prenuptial agreements are essentially legal agreements to clarify financial consequences in case the marriage ends. Counselors need to examine the motives, fears, and hopes of both people entering the marriage and address them. If one or both see this agreement as "an out," the counselor may want to talk more about the meaning of marriage and the commitment it takes to make a marriage work.

In some cases, only one person wants the prenuptial agreement and the other is deeply offended by the request. If this hurt isn't resolved, it can become a serious impediment to trust in the relationship and derail the marriage. In this instance, a prenuptial agreement becomes a self-fulfilling prophecy.

Still, the couple may need to address real financial and relational issues before they get married. These may include conflict with the children of one of the partners, excessive debt brought by one or both of them into the marriage, business ownership, disparity of income, and other factors. Tools and processes outlined in other places in this guide can help the couple clarify their expectations, resolve hurt, and build trust. Take the time to work with the couple (or individual) using the five Money Personalities, principles of conflict resolution, and the Money Huddle.

The counselor's responsibility is to focus on the relationship to facilitate understanding and build trust. For legal and financial advice, refer the couple to a trusted attorney and/or financial advisor.

ACTION STEPS : 5

1. Discuss the five Money Personalities and help the couple identify themselves and each other.
2. Explain the principles of active listening and good communication and answer any questions.
3. Explain the significance of the Money Huddle. Help them use this process of communication to discuss the pressing financial issues that will have an impact on the marriage.
4. Address the pressing relational issues that have surfaced as they've talked about the need for a prenuptial agreement. Discuss the benefits and liabilities of having such an agreement.
5. If necessary, refer the couple to an attorney or financial advisor for professional advice.
6. Continue to help the couple create a healthy pattern of communication—about money and other issues in their relationship. Monitor and celebrate their progress.

6 BIBLICAL INSIGHTS

Trust in the Lord with all your heart and lean not on your own understanding;
in all your ways submit to him, and he will make your paths straight.

Proverbs 3:5–6

God wants us to plan well and trust him completely. The two aren't mutually exclusive. As people consider marriage, there are many unknowns. Sometimes it's prudent to anticipate them, but for others, we can't predict the outcome. People who are considering a prenuptial agreement need help in sorting out their hopes and fears for the new relationship.

Therefore, I urge you, brothers and sisters, in view of God's mercy, to offer your
bodies as a living sacrifice, holy and pleasing to God—this is your true and
proper worship. Do not conform to the pattern of this world, but be transformed
by the renewing of your mind. Then you will be able to test and approve what
God's will is—his good, pleasing and perfect will.

Romans 12:1–2

We are all affected by our culture and the world's values. To know God's will and follow it with all our heart, we need the Word of God, the Spirit of God, and wise fellow Christians to give us input and guidance.

Do not be anxious about anything, but in every situation, by prayer and
petition, with thanksgiving, present your requests to God. And the peace of
God, which transcends all understanding, will guard your hearts and your
minds in Christ Jesus.

Philippians 4:6–7

When the purpose of prenuptial agreements is to deal with very real and anticipated problems, they may be appropriate, but in many cases, they are a proclamation of a person's fears. God wants us to trust him and bring our requests to him with a heart of gratitude. When we do, his Spirit works deep in us to produce a sense of his presence and peace.

If any of you lacks wisdom, you should ask God, who gives generously to all
without finding fault, and it will be given to you. But when you ask, you must
believe and not doubt, because the one who doubts is like a wave of the sea,
blown and tossed by the wind.

James 1:5–6

When we don't know what to do, we can ask God for his wisdom. But when we ask, we need to be willing to take action in the way he directs us.

PRAYER STARTER : 7

Father, as this couple enters marriage, they are filled with hopes and fears. They need your help in anticipating problems but they want to trust you no matter what. Give them direction, Lord, so their relationship is based on the solid rock of your truth, grace, and love . . .

RECOMMENDED RESOURCES : 8

Palmer, Bethany, and Scott Palmer. *First Comes Love, Then Comes Money: A Couple's Guide to Financial Communication*. HarperOne, 2009.

http://www.ronblue.com/

http://www.mvelopes.com/focusonthefamily/

http://www.daveramsey.com/home/

http://www.crown.org/

Retirement

1 PORTRAITS

- "We thought this would be the happiest time of our lives," Sarah said sadly, "but it's been so hard." She and Marvin saved and planned for years to live on Social Security and their retirement funds. They dreamed of traveling abroad, visiting their children and grandchildren more often, and enjoying each other in their "golden years." Marvin's heart attack and subsequent ill health put a big dent in their plans, and the added medical expenses have seriously depleted their nest egg. They're worried that they may have to ask their kids for help and they don't want to be dependent on them.

- Randall worked for the same company for thirty years. He began when he was in college and rose to be a regional vice president. His pension was substantial and he wasn't thinking much about retirement because he enjoyed work so much. To his surprise his company was bought out, and he was offered early retirement. He had a lot to think about, including the sense that his work world would never be the same.

- Kristin had always assumed that she and Steven would live happily ever after. They didn't need much. Their house was paid for and they owned their old car. When Steven died and her son helped her look at her finances, she realized the Social Security benefits would barely enable her to make ends meet each month. Suddenly, as she tried to absorb the loss of her lifelong partner, she had to face the reality that any unexpected expense could prove disastrous. Grief was now mixed with worry and dread.

- Janet had always been a person who got things done. She was a manager at her company and she earned the respect of everyone there. When the financial downturn occurred, she experienced something she never imagined could happen to her—unemployment. In her late fifties, she wasn't on the top of any employer's applicants list. As the months went by, she burned through virtually all of her savings. Finally, she took a job at half her previous salary but she realized she'd have to work until the day she died. The emotional toll of the past months had taken a lot out of her. She was angry, resentful, and depressed.

DEFINITIONS AND KEY THOUGHTS 2

- A person is considered to be *retired* when she is no longer employed or seeking employment. Some people *semiretire* by reducing their work hours. And some people choose to change jobs instead of retiring, pursuing something they've wanted to do for a long time but lacked the financial resources and time to do it.
- In the United States, *early retirement* is at age sixty-two and normal retirement with full Social Security benefits has been age sixty-five but is rising to sixty-seven.
- The three primary sources of funding for retirement are *pensions*, *investments and savings*, and *Social Security benefits*. The total amount needed in these funds depends on anticipated expenses over time. Many investment companies offer online retirement calculators for investors to determine their goals.
- Studies show that *wealth* plays a major role in retirement choices. The more wealth a person or couple has, the more options they can consider, including retiring early.
- Those who are retired may come for counseling for any number of reasons, including the death of a spouse, stress from a lack of funds, boredom, sickness, dementia, loss of friends, the effects of moving out of a home, the need to find a job to make ends meet, and relational tension with a spouse or grown children over any of these issues.
- Middle-aged people may come to counseling for help in dealing with retired or retiring parents who are sick, financially strapped, or becoming mentally impaired.

ASSESSMENT INTERVIEW 3

For those who are considering retirement:

1. What are your hopes and fears about retiring?
2. Are you concerned about your finances, your health, your relationships with family members or close friends?
3. What are your goals and purposes for these years?
4. How can I help?

For those who are retired:

1. What are your concerns today about your life, your finances, and your relationships?
2. Aging almost certainly brings multiple losses—including health, friends, memory, expectations. What are the losses you've experienced? How are you handling them?
3. What kind of support are you receiving?
4. How can I help?

For those whose parents (or other loved ones) are struggling with retirement:

1. What stresses are you experiencing because of your parents' retirement? What additional needs or expectations are now on your shoulders?
2. How have you tried to help? How has your help been received?
3. Are any other family members involved in trying to help? What impact are they having?
4. What are your most pressing questions about helping your parents?
5. How can I help?

4 : WISE COUNSEL

The financial issues regarding retirement may be the most significant stressors in the life of the person who comes for counseling, but look beneath the numbers at the hurt, confusion, resentment, or relational tension in the person's life. These are the topics you'll address in counseling, and if the person needs financial advice, you can refer her to a professional financial counselor.

As people age, losses multiply quickly. It's not uncommon for retired people to attend many funerals of friends and family members, for health to decline, and for memory to deteriorate. If the person or couple has had to move (or has chosen to move), a full array of challenges and adjustments comes with the decision. One of the most difficult problems of aging is the loss of independence. Many people anticipate retirement as a glorious, happy, carefree time they've dreamed about, and it may be deeply discouraging when these happy times don't last very long.

Managing money in retirement is just as important as it was during the person's career. In fact, more available time may cause the person to be more attentive than ever, but also she may be even more worried about money than ever in her life. Anxiety over money can be especially pronounced if a spouse has died and the remaining person feels lonely and isolated. Suddenly everything looks dark and hopeless.

Usually, health and financial problems for the elderly bring other family members into the circle. Some offer quick fixes, some want to dominate, and some want to avoid the problem (and the people) entirely. The family dynamics in the lives of the retired and elderly can be quite complicated. In many cases, confusion, miscommunication, and distrust cloud the conversation and poison relationships, so it can be useful to get all the people involved in a room and help them communicate clearly, find resolution, and take steps forward.

Individuals and couples who come for counseling will benefit from the insights of the Money Personalities. In addition, the principles of good communication and the Money Huddle will help them share their thoughts and concerns more clearly and positively.

ACTION STEPS : 5

1. In the assessment interview, determine the nature of the underlying problem. Financial trouble may be the presenting problem, but almost always emotional and relational distress are present as well. Also explore the dynamics of the extended family to uncover demands, isolation, and miscommunication.
2. Help the person process feelings and thoughts. Challenge faulty thinking and false perceptions, and point her to truth and hope. Sometimes people just need a listening ear and then they find a new sense of hope.
3. Because losses are so numerous and painful in the lives of retired people, offer support and help her find other sources of love and encouragement.
4. Explain the Money Personalities and help her identify herself and her spouse. Discuss the principles of communication and how to have Money Huddles. Give her the assignment of having a Money Huddle with her husband before the next counseling session, or ask her to bring her spouse to the office to have one so you can facilitate the conversation.
5. For financial questions that are beyond general knowledge, refer her to a qualified financial planner.

BIBLICAL INSIGHTS : 6

Is not wisdom found among the aged? Does not long life bring understanding?

Job 12:12

Retirement isn't a time to do nothing. Instead, we can use all the wisdom and experience acquired over a lifetime to mentor younger people and share the experiences we've had.

Plans fail for lack of counsel, but with many advisers they succeed.

Proverbs 15:22

Especially in retirement, we need to keep a close eye on our finances, budget well, and spend wisely.

By wisdom a house is built, and through understanding it is established; through knowledge its rooms are filled with rare and beautiful treasures.

Proverbs 24:3–4

Some of the treasures we enjoy in retirement are tangible, but even more valuable is the time we have to spend with those we love and those in whose lives we want to invest.

And whatever you do, whether in word or deed, do it all in the name of the Lord Jesus, giving thanks to God the Father through him.

Colossians 3:17

We are not our own; we've been bought with a price. Our desire at every time of our lives is to honor God and have an impact for him. As his children, that's what gives us the most pleasure and fulfillment.

7 PRAYER STARTER

Father, our times of life are in your hands. This person wants to use her retirement resources—time, money, wisdom, and relationships—in ways that honor you. She realizes that she owes all she has to you. Thank you for what you've given her . . .

8 RECOMMENDED RESOURCES

Munchbach, Jim. *Make Your Money Count: Connecting Your Resources to What Matters Most.* Baxter Press, 2007.

Palmer, Bethany, and Scott Palmer. *First Comes Love, Then Comes Money: A Couple's Guide to Financial Communication.* HarperOne, 2009.

http://www.ronblue.com/

http://www.mvelopes.com/focusonthefamily/

http://www.daveramsey.com/home/

http://www.crown.org/

Savings

- Two years ago Patti lost her job, and it took six months for her to find a new one. Unemployment checks helped, but in the last two months before she started working again, she missed payments on her mortgage and credit cards. Her credit score took a hit, but her emotional stability was shaken even more. Since then, she's lived in fear that she won't have enough every month to pay her bills. She has gotten used to living on the edge, and it hasn't even crossed her mind that saving some money over the period of a few months would do wonders to lower her levels of fear and stress.

- Joel had enjoyed a good income and had a significant savings account for many years. Three years ago he started a new business and he put everything he had into it. He got a second mortgage on his home and used every penny of his savings. Now that the business is doing well, he has put four months of expenses in a savings account where he banks. "It gives me a wonderful feeling to know it's there," he says.

- Laura and Will had been fairly diligent at managing their money. Even with two little kids, they had a significant savings account. Then their third baby was born. "I don't know what happened," Laura remembers. "I thought we had enough money put aside, but somehow the expenses grew more than we expected." After a year, however, they began putting some money away again and built up their savings to cover three months of expenses. "It's made a huge difference in our sense of security," Will reports.

- Mark's parents enjoyed good health into their seventies, but then a series of medical problems seriously eroded their financial status. Mark realized his father was unusually worried and, when he asked him about it, his dad explained that he didn't have the money to pay the out-of-pocket for a recent surgery. For years Mark had kept money for about six months of expenses in a savings account. He didn't know when or if he'd ever need it. This was the day. That afternoon Mark went to the bank and withdrew $10,000 for his father. "You have no idea how much this means to your mom and me," his father told him. Mark said, "It means as much to me to be able to help you."

2 DEFINITIONS AND KEY THOUGHTS

- Most financial planners recommend putting *three-to-six-months' worth of expenses* in a *savings account*. The account needs to be *liquid* and *readily accessible* so it can be used when unanticipated expenses hit. Savings accounts don't earn much interest but they are easy to access.
- *Unexpected expenses* can take many different forms, such as major car repairs, health problems, or home repair from fire or flood.
- Savings can also be used judiciously for unique investment opportunities, but these should be considered very carefully, and the savings should be replaced as soon as possible.
- *Strategic savings* can also be used for expected expenses, such as weddings, family vacations, education, graduations, and upgrades for the home.
- Having a readily available *financial cushion* gives people more peace of mind, relieves stress, and reduces worry. Instead of dwelling on the risk of financial ruin or embarrassment, they can enjoy their families, focus on God's calling, and relax.

3 ASSESSMENT INTERVIEW

1. How do your finances contribute to your daily worries and concerns?
2. Have you missed any payments lately?
3. Have you experienced any recent unforeseen expenses or loss of income? If so, what happened?
4. Do you anticipate any upcoming expenses, such as a wedding, graduation, vacation, home repairs?
5. What are your average monthly expenses? How would it help you to have three to six months of expenses in a savings account?
6. Do you want to figure out how to build a significant savings account so you'll have several months' worth of expenses?
7. Are you willing to cut your current expenses to build your strategic savings? Why or why not?
8. How can I help?

4 WISE COUNSEL

Having a significant cushion of savings gives a wonderful sense of security and peace of mind. It's sad that our insatiable consumer age causes many people to buy more things instead of enjoying the security and peace of having savings.

We never know what can happen to cause unanticipated expenses. People experience all kinds of financial bumps in the road, including major car repairs (or the insurance deductible), medical procedures, fires, floods, hurricanes, and other sudden calamities. People also incur expenses they can anticipate for months or even years in advance, such as major home remodeling, elective surgery, a wedding (or two), graduations, and family vacations.

As people live longer, many elderly parents require the financial help of their grown children. This expense is seldom anticipated when the parents are in good health. And today many college graduates are moving back home while they look for a job, and some are staying at home even after they get good jobs so they can save money (and enjoy good cooking). This puts some adults in the sandwich generation—they provide care for elderly parents and for their kids at the same time—suffering the financial strain of caring for three generations.

Some people have seen their parents make wise financial decisions, such as having a strategic savings account, and they eagerly follow their example when they become adults. Many others, however, had poor parental models of money management. To them, saving is a foreign concept.

In some homes, the pressure to have more and do more stretches the monthly budget to the breaking point. To build a significant savings, these people have to make some changes, first in their values and then in their spending habits. Building a family's savings account requires good communication, sacrifice, and discipline.

Individuals and couples who come for counseling will benefit from the insights of the Money Personalities. In addition, the principles of active listening, good communication, conflict resolution, and the Money Huddle will help them share their thoughts and concerns more clearly and positively.

ACTION STEPS 5

1. When people come for counseling, they often talk about their worries, sleeplessness, shame, and relational conflict. In your assessment interview, determine if financial problems are contributing to the client's struggles.
2. Facilitate understanding and communication. Explain the five Money Personalities and help him identify himself and his spouse. Discuss the principles of good communication and how to have Money Huddles. Give him the assignment of having a Money Huddle with his wife before the next session, or ask him and his spouse to have one in your office so you can facilitate the conversation.
3. If debt or living on the edge is a problem, determine the cause. It could be some recent and significant unexpected expenses, loss of income, or out-of-control spending habits.
4. Look at the person's current financial condition, including debt, spending, income, and savings.
5. Help him come up with a workable and effective budget to get a grip on income and expenses. Explain the necessity of honesty and sacrifice, and encourage him to "pay" himself and his wife first by saving. If saving is the last item on the budget list, it will probably be overlooked.
6. Examine signs of resistance. Building a strategic savings account may make perfect sense to you, but the person may come up with any number of excuses to avoid trying it, including denial, shame, self-pity, and blaming others for

the problem. Each of these may feel right and provide a convenient excuse for staying stuck in poor habits.

7. Offer a strong sense of hope. The benefits of having several months of expenses in savings are lower stress levels, better communication with people we love, and peace of mind. No matter where people are starting, they can, with wisdom and determination, get to a point of financial security.

8. As the weeks go by, monitor the person's progress in making changes in spending and saving. Notice any forms of resistance, address them, and celebrate every step forward.

6 BIBLICAL INSIGHTS

Dishonest money dwindles away, but whoever gathers money little by little makes it grow.

Proverbs 13:11

We may love to hear stories about people who get rich quickly, but God's purpose for us isn't just about money and wealth—he wants us to grow in wisdom. Learning patience in every area of life, including building our savings, is God's plan.

The wise store up choice food and olive oil, but fools gulp theirs down.

Proverbs 21:20

Solomon has a lot to say about the benefits of wisdom. In this passage he says that wise people store up their resources, but foolish people waste them. When we store up our resources—not hoarding them, but wisely building up our supplies—we can help others, give to God's causes, and enjoy financial peace.

By wisdom a house is built, and through understanding it is established; through knowledge its rooms are filled with rare and beautiful treasures.

Proverbs 24:3–4

Good money management isn't just about numbers on a page. It's about knowing and following God's plan for our lives. As we walk with him, we learn more of what he values, we love people instead of using them, and we see our possessions and money as God's good gifts to enjoy.

7 PRAYER STARTER

Father, this person wants to be wise with the money you've entrusted to him. He's made some poor choices (or he's experienced some unexpected difficulties). Give him the wisdom and courage he needs to manage money in a way that honors you. Help him build up a significant savings account so he doesn't worry about money all the time. Thank you . . .

RECOMMENDED RESOURCES : 8

Munchbach, Jim. *Make Your Money Count: Connecting Your Resources to What Matters Most.* Baxter Press, 2007.

Palmer, Bethany, and Scott Palmer. *First Comes Love, Then Comes Money: A Couple's Guide to Financial Communication.* HarperOne, 2009.

http://www.ronblue.com/

http://www.mvelopes.com/focusonthefamily/

http://www.daveramsey.com/home/

http://www.crown.org/

Second Marriages and Money

1 PORTRAITS

- After her divorce Danielle went to a support group at her church. There she met Charles, who was also recovering from a painful divorce. As months went by, they began spending time together and they fell in love. Both of them, though, were still hurting. When they talked about the future, Danielle soon brought up the subject of her past. She was bitter toward her ex and she complained that he had taken advantage of her vulnerability in the settlement. Charles wanted to marry Danielle but he was afraid that her anger about money would somehow bite him.

- Cliff and Beth were single for several years after their divorces, but when they got married, they were sure things would be different this time. They weren't. Both of them had endured years of secrets and distrust in their previous marriages. They had lied and been lied to about sexual relationships and money. Soon after they were married, they both slipped back into old habits. When Cliff found out Beth had lied to him about money she'd been spending, he left her. He wasn't sure he could go through all that again.

- Alicia loved Mark and planned to marry him, but she didn't want to tell him about all the debts she incurred before her first marriage. When her first husband found out she owed $150,000 in school loans and credit card debt, he left her. Now she was afraid Mark would leave too if he found out. She talked to her counselor to get her advice about how to keep it a secret—without feeling guilty.

- Lindsey and Hank were having enough problems adjusting to each other, but to make matters worse, their grown children by their first and second marriages were hounding them about their relationship, their money, and how they felt neglected. Hank's son wanted to go to graduate school. When he asked his father for help, Hank told him he couldn't afford it because they were already supporting two of Beth's kids in college. Before long, everybody was angry with everyone else, and the new marriage was in deep trouble.

2 DEFINITIONS AND KEY THOUGHTS

- Remarriages are often quite complicated. Each spouse brings shattered dreams and new hopes, past hurts and new plans for the future, old habits and a commitment to new behaviors, children's expectations and the prospect of a new beginning. And of course some people have gone through these cycles several times by this point.

- When a couple plans to remarry (or if the remarriage has already happened), honesty is essential. The secrets of the past may have wrecked previous relationships, and old habits are hard to break, but both spouses need to be deeply committed to frank and open conversations about the realities of their lives, including their money.

- In these relationships, significant misunderstandings and disagreements are inevitable, especially because they involve multiple generations and multiple sets of children. The principles of good communication and conflict resolution will help create an environment of honesty, understanding, and healthy compromise.

- The five Money Personalities will help the couple understand each other and make progress in their communication.

- The couple can learn to talk openly and productively by following the process of the Money Huddle. Topics to discuss thoroughly (before and after the remarriage) include income, debt, estate planning, child support, and everything else of financial interest to either person.

- In some cases a prenuptial agreement may help the couple clarify their financial condition and expectations. If either or both of the spouses have been married multiple times, it's even more important to be clear about the past and the future. A prenuptial agreement can include all types of property, income, debts, savings, retirement accounts, and insurance policies. Some may say that this kind of agreement anticipates and invites failure, but instead, it may provide needed clarity and stability so the relationship can thrive.

ASSESSMENT INTERVIEW 3

For the individual planning to remarry, explain the five Money Personalities. Help her identify herself and her fiancé. Explain the nature of a Money Huddle. Then ask:

1. How does your Money Personality complement your fiancé's? How do they conflict?
2. If you and your partner have a regular Money Huddle, what do you think you can accomplish? What will be the benefits long term in your relationship?
3. What obstacles do you anticipate in your relationship, such as communication, trust, scheduling, expectations?
4. What are your hopes for your new relationship? How will it be different from the previous one(s)?
5. Did you and your ex have difficulty communicating about money? Were there any secrets that caused problems? Explain your answer.
6. Have you talked to your prospective spouse about your financial status and expectations? How did the conversation go?
7. What issues did you avoid or hesitate to talk about? Why did you avoid them?
8. How would it help your new marriage if you and your new spouse talked openly and freely about your finances?
9. How can I help?

For a remarried individual, explain the Money Personalities. Help her identify herself and her spouse. Explain the nature of a Money Huddle. Then ask:

1. How does your Money Personality complement your partner's? How do they conflict?
2. If you and your spouse have a regular Money Huddle, what do you think you can accomplish? What will be the benefits long term in your relationship?
3. What obstacles do you anticipate in your relationship, such as communication, trust, scheduling, expectations?
4. In your previous marriage(s), how did you and your spouse communicate about money? Were there any secrets? If so, how did they affect your relationship?
5. What are your hopes for this relationship regarding honesty about money?
6. Have you talked to your spouse about your income, debt, expenses, spending habits, and expectations? If so, how did it go? If you have not talked about these things, why haven't you?
7. What issues regarding money do you avoid or hesitate to talk about? Why do you avoid them?
8. How would openness and honesty about finances help your marriage grow stronger? What are the risks?
9. How can I help?

4 : WISE COUNSEL

Some remarried couples want to distance themselves from past problems in relationships. If the wound of financial infidelity from the previous relationship is deep, they may resist talking about money at all. Some people think that keeping secrets will prevent the pain, and it will, but only in the short term. In the long run, secrets will cause more financial infidelity, hurt, and broken trust. Couples need hope for the future of their relationship, assurance that their conversations will be worth the effort, and a clear understanding of the process.

Usually one partner is more willing to participate in the Money Huddle than the other. This may be the result of past experiences, personality differences, or greater hope that it will work. The different Money Personalities approach the huddles in very different ways. Flyers would rather have a root canal than talk about the details of finances, but Security Seekers would do two huddles a day just to be sure they stay on track with every penny. Savers want to be sure they keep enough money in reserve, but Spenders are ready to end the meeting as soon as they have a dollar figure they can spend.

Advise the client that if the discussion in the huddle becomes too hot or too cold, the couple should step away for a while, get a snack, watch TV, or do something else to take their minds off the discussion. Before they disengage, however, they need to agree on when to resume. The goal isn't to be right or to demand their way. The purpose of these conversations is to work out financial problems, which will build the relationship as the couple works together.

Quite often in these huddles, past patterns of attack and withdrawal surface, especially in the first few huddles. The couple should do whatever it takes to keep moving forward by focusing on the positives, affirming truth and integrity, and celebrating each step forward.

ACTION STEPS : 5

1. Explain the five Money Personalities and help the client identify herself and her spouse. Discuss the way their Money Personalities complement each other and how they may conflict with each other.
2. Teach the principles of active listening, good communication, and conflict resolution, and answer any questions.
3. Explain the goals and procedure of a Money Huddle. Answer her questions. You might want to ask her to invite her spouse to have their first Money Huddle with you as the facilitator or mediator.
4. Encourage her to schedule regular Money Huddles to continue to build the relationship and communicate about their finances.
5. Continue to monitor the couple's progress and offer support and assistance as needed.

BIBLICAL INSIGHTS : 6

My dear brothers and sisters, take note of this: Everyone should be quick to listen, slow to speak and slow to become angry, because human anger does not produce the righteousness that God desires.

James 1:19–20

As a couple discusses money, the goal isn't to win an argument but to understand each other and find a mutually beneficial way forward in handling their finances. The more we listen, the more we'll understand. When we stop talking, stop thinking about what we're going to say next, and stop angling to win the point, we will develop understanding. The goal is to listen carefully, ask questions, and affirm the other person's feelings—even if we disagree with her point.

But now you must also rid yourselves of all such things as these: anger, rage, malice, slander, and filthy language from your lips. Do not lie to each other, since you have taken off your old self with its practices and have put on the new self, which is being renewed in knowledge in the image of its Creator. . . . Therefore, as God's chosen people, holy and dearly loved, clothe yourselves with compassion, kindness, humility, gentleness and patience.

Colossians 3:8–10, 12

We have the power to choose what we say and how we say it. We want to understand, not control; to love, not win arguments. When we talk about our finances, we can inflict wounds or heal old ones; shatter trust or build it. As we walk with God, we can trust him to renew us, give us wisdom, and fill our hearts with love for our partner so that our words heal and build.

Remind the people to be subject to rulers and authorities, to be obedient, to be ready to do whatever is good, to slander no one, to be peaceable and considerate, and always to be gentle toward everyone.

Titus 3:1–2

Gentleness is a mark of true humility. When remarried couples have these conversations, they must be aware of their tone of voice, facial expressions, and body language. When they have Money Huddles, they should sit back, smile, and ask questions until they understand what their partner is saying.

When we put bits into the mouths of horses to make them obey us, we can turn the whole animal. Or take ships as an example. Although they are so large and are driven by strong winds, they are steered by a very small rudder wherever the pilot wants to go. Likewise, the tongue is a small part of the body, but it makes great boasts. Consider what a great forest is set on fire by a small spark. The tongue also is a fire, a world of evil among the parts of the body. It corrupts the whole body, sets the whole course of one's life on fire, and is itself set on fire by hell.

James 3:3–6

Words matter. In remarriages people are often wounded and vulnerable—though probably they don't want others to know it. An unkind remark can inflict a deep wound, but a sentence or two of genuine affirmation can bring healing. Before we have conversations about difficult issues, we should ask God to help us see our partner the way God sees us, and then speak accordingly.

7 PRAYER STARTER

Father, this person wants to have a successful marriage. She is committed to honesty and love, and she wants to deal with problems sooner rather than later—even to anticipate them before they surface. Help her, Lord. Give her and her husband wisdom and strength to keep moving forward toward you and each other instead of trying to run away. Help them trust you to guide them . . .

8 RECOMMENDED RESOURCES

Palmer, Bethany, and Scott Palmer. *First Comes Love, Then Comes Money: A Couple's Guide to Financial Communication.* HarperOne, 2009.

Parrott, Les and Leslie. *Saving Your Second Marriage before It Starts.* Zondervan, 2001.

Smalley, Gary and Greg. *The Heart of Remarriage.* Regal, 2010.

Secrets

- Diane and Gary came for counseling as a last resort. After their children graduated from high school and left for college, the house seemed very empty. All they had was each other, and long-buried resentments began to surface again. The tension was so intense that they planned to get a divorce but they wanted to give it one more try. The counselor asked them to talk about the good times in their relationship as well as the tough times. Diane remembered, "When we first got married, we talked about everything—and I mean everything. But one day when the children were little, I found out that Gary had been spending money we needed for other expenses. I thought it was just a misunderstanding, but when I asked him about it, he hit the roof. From that day to this, we haven't been able to talk about money, or for that matter, anything important at all. We've been emotionally distant for the past fifteen years."

- Jennifer told her counselor that she was afraid of her husband, Jack. When the counselor asked more questions, she resisted, but she finally explained, "He micromanages everything around our home—the kids, our money, how we spend Saturdays, what's on television—everything. If I even ask a question about money, like a request to buy some new clothes, he explodes. I don't know if I can take it anymore."

- James and Ruth argued about money for a long time and then they came up with a solution. James would keep the money he earned in one account, and Ruth would keep her salary in a separate account. They decided from the beginning to assign the responsibility to pay bills equally, with James paying the mortgage and Ruth paying for almost everything else. They never asked how the other spent money. At first, this seemed like a perfect answer to their bickering, but it led them to lead separate lives. They were roommates instead of lovers.

- Ted asked the bank to send the credit card statement to his office because he didn't want his wife to know how much he was spending, and he certainly didn't want her to find out that he was racking up hundreds of dollars in bills every month on online porn sites. When she asked if she could see the bill because she wanted to see if a dress she returned was credited on the account, he mumbled excuses and promised he'd check on it. She wondered out loud, "I don't know why you're having the bill go to your office. All the rest of our bills come here. You aren't hiding anything, are you?" A few months later, she called the bank and asked for a copy of the most recent statement. When she looked at it, she was stunned. She had wondered why she felt some distance in their relationship in the past couple of years. Ted had insisted he was just working too hard and wasn't himself. The problem between them wasn't his work schedule; it was his pattern of secrets and betrayal.

2 DEFINITIONS AND KEY THOUGHTS

- The famous line in the movie *Cool Hand Luke* is applicable here: "What we have here is a failure to communicate." And the failure is intentional. Secrets poison relationships, but they often begin with small acts of self-protection in response to hurt. The hurt can be caused by a simple misunderstanding, an overblown reaction to a minor issue, or a genuine offense. If it isn't resolved, mistrust drives a wedge between people, and self-protection becomes the primary goal. Great relationships aren't based on self-protection. They're the result of courageous honesty and genuine love.

- When misunderstandings aren't corrected and hurts aren't resolved, people may respond in several ways. Some couples avoid the topic like the plague (whether it's sex, money, children, relating to in-laws, or any other important subject), but in some relationships, one person becomes controlling and domineering as the other takes a passive role. Both may experience a complex jumble of emotions, but the ones that appear on the surface are anger (in the dominant one) and fear (in the one who is passive).

- Each of the Money Personalities has strengths and weaknesses. In open, healthy relationships, each person appreciates the strengths of the other and helps to minimize any shortcomings. But when conflict and disagreement become the norm, each one is tempted to keep secrets. Spenders and Risk Takers are most prone to lie to protect themselves from the wrath of Savers and Security Seekers who want to account for every penny. Usually Flyers don't care what people know about their habits with money, but if others chew on them enough, they withdraw and refuse to engage about money or anything else meaningful.

- Secrets promise freedom, relief, and the thrill of not being found out, but eventually, everything comes into the light. When the secrets are exposed, those who trusted feel deeply betrayed, even if the secret concerned a small amount of money. Truth, honor, and integrity form the foundation of any good relationship. When these are shattered, deep wounds result.

3 ASSESSMENT INTERVIEW

Encourage the client to discuss the Money Personalities with his spouse to identify differences and misunderstanding, and especially areas in which they feel one of them hasn't been honest. The one who is withdrawn out of fear, however, may have a very good reason to protect himself if the other is demanding, harsh, and controlling. Ask these questions:

1. What did you learn about your relationship from the Money Personalities?
2. Have you or your spouse been withholding information from the other out of fear? If you are fearful, how would you describe your fear? What exactly are you afraid will happen if you speak honestly about money (or anything else)?
3. Can you remember a time when you felt free to have honest dialogue with your spouse about money? When was that? Describe your relationship during that time.
4. What happened that caused distrust? Was there an incident or a series of events that caused you or your spouse to begin withholding information?
5. What would it mean to you and your relationship to trust each other enough to have open, honest conversations about money?
6. Where do you want to go from here?
7. How can I help?

WISE COUNSEL 4

Couples who have experienced the ravages of exposed secrets have three options:

1. They can commit to a long process of forgiving each other and gradually restoring trust by exhibiting integrity and communicating fully.
2. They can focus on the pain of the past and the long, hard road to rebuild the relationship and conclude that it's too much work. Then they can call an attorney and end the marriage.
3. They can say they want to change but refuse to do the hard work of repentance and restoration. They talk the talk but they keep walking in deception, half-truths, and outright lies. They may remain married, but their relationship is distant and cool.

To live without the damage of secrets in a relationship, couples need to do three important things:

1. *Commit to transparency.* It's one thing for couples to have separate accounts—his and hers checking or separate cash reserves. But *secret* accounts are something altogether different. They mean that someone in the relationship doesn't trust the other person with financial decisions. And since money touches every part of our lives, that financial mistrust usually points to a deeper level of mistrust that will infect the whole relationship. This is the reason hiding has to stop if the relationship is going to survive.
2. *Talk through the fears behind the secrets.* Hiding finances from your spouse is usually a response to fear, fear that he will spend you into debt, fear that she will control your spending, fear that you won't have a financial leg to stand on if the relationship ends. So the only way to get out from under the crushing weight of these secrets is to bring them into the light.
3. *Try to stay calm and be honest.* You might find that your spouse has fears of his own. Consider how your Money Personalities play into these secrets. Then commit to honest financial communication from now on.

185

Some well-intentioned couples rush to get the past behind them. They uncover some of the pain and quickly forgive, leaving most of the iceberg of resentment and distrust hidden. It takes time and effort for a counselor and a couple to excavate past wounds, uncovering events and emotions that need to be resolved. Often people make one of two mistakes in forgiveness: they forgive too quickly or too late. If they try to get beyond the pain too quickly, the hidden hurts will continue to poison the relationship, but if they refuse to forgive at all, the continued resentment will drive them apart.

Betrayal of any kind is a serious matter. The perpetrator needs to come clean, repent, and demonstrate a new commitment to truth and integrity. The victim needs to forgive, grieve, and begin to take steps forward to rebuild trust, but only as much and as quickly as the other person proves to be trustworthy.

When secrets and financial infidelity are exposed, things may get a lot worse before they get better. There may be violent outbursts of emotions, expressions of rage and hopelessness, and quick decisions to end the relationship. Be calm and patient with the client. Stay with the issue and offer hope to the client that the relationship can be mended and even flourish over time. It can, but it may be the hardest thing the two people have ever done in their lives.

5 ACTION STEPS

1. Use the Money Personalities to help the individual or couple become objective about communication, truth, and integrity in the relationship.
2. Take time to bring specific secrets and patterns of deception to the surface. Expect resistance because they have a history of hiding these things from each other.
3. Explain the meaning and process of repentance, forgiveness, and rebuilding trust in a broken or strained relationship. Encourage the betrayer to ask for forgiveness and the victim to grant it, but of course, in many relationships, both have committed wrongs, especially in harboring resentment instead of pursuing love, forgiveness, and restoration.
4. Discuss the ways different Money Personalities perceive the meaning of money and how the client and his spouse can support each other instead of misunderstanding each other.
5. Teach the individual or couple the principles of active listening and conflict resolution. Teach them how to have a Money Huddle. This process will help the couple learn to communicate and make genuine progress in their relationship.
6. Monitor progress, especially over the course of the first few weeks, and then for a few months as the couple faces opportunities and obstacles in their communication.

6 BIBLICAL INSIGHTS

I said, "I will watch my ways and keep my tongue from sin; I will put a muzzle on my mouth while in the presence of the wicked." So I remained utterly silent, not even saying anything good. But my anguish increased; my heart grew hot within me. While I meditated, the fire burned; then I spoke with my tongue.

Psalm 39:1–3

Silence isn't always golden. Sometimes it's best to be quiet, but when misunderstanding or genuine offenses occur in relationships, we need to go to the person and make every effort to resolve the problem—the sooner the better.

Do not let any unwholesome talk come out of your mouths, but only what is helpful for building others up according to their needs, that it may benefit those who listen. And do not grieve the Holy Spirit of God, with whom you were sealed for the day of redemption.

Ephesians 4:29–30

Secrets are like a pressure cooker. When the lid finally comes off, there's often an explosion of long-held anger and hurt. As we prepare to speak to one another to resolve past wounds and feelings of betrayal, we need to carefully consider our words. The Spirit of God will guide us as we prepare, and he'll lead us as we speak.

Get rid of all bitterness, rage and anger, brawling and slander, along with every form of malice. Be kind and compassionate to one another, forgiving each other, just as in Christ God forgave you.

Ephesians 4:31–32

We choose to forgive those who hurt us whether they repent or not, whether they are sorry or not, and whether they ever change or not. Our ability and motivation to forgive come from the deep well of our own experience of being forgiven by Christ for all our sins. Forgiveness isn't the same thing as reconciliation. We forgive unilaterally to free ourselves from resentment, but trust must be earned and built on proven integrity demonstrated by both sides.

Therefore confess your sins to each other and pray for each other so that you may be healed.

James 5:16

Confession is the gateway to spiritual, emotional, and relational healing. Without heartfelt apologies and asking for forgiveness, resentments can continue to fester, but amazing things can happen when people are willing to say, "I'm so sorry. Will you forgive me?"

PRAYER STARTER : 7

Lord Jesus, you are the source of truth and you want us to live with others in openness and honesty. This couple needs your help. Thank you for loving them and forgiving them. They want to make a commitment to you and each other to leave their secrets behind, live in truth, and honor each other in everything they say and do . . .

8 RECOMMENDED RESOURCES

Palmer, Bethany, and Scott Palmer. *First Comes Love, Then Comes Money: A Couple's Guide to Financial Communication*. HarperOne, 2009.

http://www.ronblue.com/

http://www.mvelopes.com/focusonthefamily/

http://www.daveramsey.com/home/

http://www.crown.org/

Separate Accounts

PORTRAITS 1

- Zoltanne and Mia argued about money before they married and they argued after their wedding day. After a couple of years, he'd had enough. He announced that he couldn't stand it anymore. "I'm opening my own checking account and getting my own credit card." Mia was surprised but she thought it might be a good solution. A few months later, they didn't argue as much about money, but their relationship had become colder and more distant.

- Matt and Jessica talked regularly about their financial condition. They planned well, saved regularly, and tried to get good deals on everything they bought. They decided to set up separate accounts so Jessica could keep track of her responsibilities for groceries, the phone bills, and a few other expenses she took care of each month. For this couple, separate accounts proved to be a very good idea because it helped them accomplish their mutual goals more effectively.

- Oliver came in one day after work and told Dana that he wanted to have his own credit card. She asked why, but he only said, "I've been thinking about it for a while and I think it would be a good idea." Dana shrugged and agreed but she was a bit perplexed. A year later, she happened to see his credit card statement that had fallen out of his coat. It contained a long listing of charges from porn sites. She was livid!

- Anne and Charles were both busy in their respective careers. He worked for an oil company, and she ran an interior design business out of their home. For about three years, she deposited her income in their joint checking account and kept records to identify the income stream. Finally, this proved to be too time-consuming, and she worried that an IRS audit might cause her trouble. She decided to set up a separate account for her business.

DEFINITIONS AND KEY THOUGHTS 2

- Individuals may have many different reasons to set up separate checking accounts and credit cards. Some of these reasons make good sense and build the relationship, but others are based on secret behaviors that threaten to destroy it.

- When couples get married, their finances may be complicated by several factors, including student loans, existing credit card debt, mortgages or other debts, child support, alimony, or distrust related to past hurtful experiences.

189

- Are separate accounts a good idea? If there's any financial question that can make a couple's heads spin, it's the question of separate accounts. Some financial planners say it's a necessity; others say it's asking for trouble. Parents and friends will give conflicting advice, leaving couples wondering how they will ever get it right. To make a wise choice, couples should consider these factors:

  — *Remember your partnership.* Separate accounts can be very helpful. They make it easy to see who's spending what. But they can also open the door to hidden spending and other secrets that are the core of financial infidelity. Remember, strong financial communication is based in partnership.

  — *Know yourselves.* Make your decision based on the strength of your financial communication. If you find it easy to keep each other up to speed on your individual accounts, then separate accounts can work just fine for you.

  — *Commit to regular Money Huddles.* We tell couples to think of themselves as a partnership, a kind of "life business" where financial decisions are made together in the "boardroom"—the kitchen table or the couch or wherever you want to meet—during routine Money Huddles. Just as business partners need to talk through financial decisions, even when they work for different departments, life partners need to talk about money no matter who writes the checks.

3 ASSESSMENT INTERVIEW

Explain the Money Personalities and use these insights as a foundation for discussion about the relationship. The reason people come for counseling isn't primarily about the dollars but about the relationship.

1. Can you identify your Money Personality? Can you identify your spouse's?
2. What are the ways your two Money Personalities complement each other? What are some possible (or real) sources of controversy and misunderstanding related to money?
3. Were there complicating factors, such as alimony or debt, that either of you brought into the marriage? How are these being resolved?
4. Why are you considering separate accounts? Is it to avoid the pain of arguments, or is it to manage money more effectively? Or perhaps some other reason?
5. How will separate accounts build trust?
6. How will they help you manage money?
7. How can I help?

WISE COUNSEL : 4

Look for patterns of communication, warmth, and conflict in the relationship. If a person brings up money in counseling, and particularly the possibility or reality of having her own separate account, it may be because she's experiencing significant stresses in the relationship.

If you determine that the couple is considering separate accounts to avoid dealing with conflict, shift the focus of conversation to uncover the source of the tension. Focus on that issue. Quite often money is only one source of tension for couples. The four major causes of stress in marriage are money, sex, children, and in-laws.

Use the Money Personalities, principles of communication and conflict resolution, and Money Huddles to facilitate open and honest dialogue for the couple.

Probably the underlying tensions won't be resolved quickly, so help the couple have realistic expectations of themselves, each other, and the marriage.

ACTION STEPS : 5

1. Discuss the Money Personalities. Identify each person's personality and the potential points of agreement and disagreement about money matters.
2. Explain that the issue of separate accounts isn't right or wrong. More important, they need to discuss their reasons. If they want to avoid facing conflict by setting up separate accounts, they will only create more distance in the relationship. If, however, they want to use these accounts as a money management tool, separate accounts can be effective and helpful.
3. Teach the principles of active listening, good communication, and Money Huddles. In a counseling session with the couple, role play a conversation about money and provide feedback.
4. Encourage the couple to have regular Money Huddles to stay on top of their finances and build their relationship.
5. If necessary, stay in touch with the couple to provide support.

BIBLICAL INSIGHTS : 6

When pride comes, then comes disgrace, but with humility comes wisdom.

Proverbs 11:2

When people demand their own way, especially to have power over others or to hide secret behavior, they lack God's wisdom and cause plenty of trouble for themselves and others around them.

Love must be sincere. Hate what is evil; cling to what is good. Be devoted to one another in love. Honor one another above yourselves. Never be lacking in zeal, but keep your spiritual fervor, serving the Lord. Be joyful in hope, patient

in affliction, faithful in prayer. Share with the Lord's people who are in need.
Practice hospitality.

Romans 12:9–13

The goal in any relationship is to give and receive authentic love with no strings attached. That's what it means for love to be "sincere." In considering the value of setting up separate accounts, each person should honor the other and practice joy, patience, and faithfulness in the relationship. When these traits are present, the couple will find a way to make one account or separate accounts work.

Therefore if you have any encouragement from being united with Christ,
if any comfort from his love, if any common sharing in the Spirit, if any
tenderness and compassion, then make my joy complete by being like-minded,
having the same love, being one in spirit and of one mind. Do nothing out
of selfish ambition or vain conceit. Rather, in humility value others above
yourselves, not looking to your own interests but each of you to the interests of
the others.

Philippians 2:1–4

In the conversation about the wisdom of setting up separate accounts, the attitude of each person is of primary importance. Power struggles lead only to distance and pain, but a humble heart opens doors for understanding and the ability to find a solution that works for both people.

Love is patient, love is kind. It does not envy, it does not boast, it is not proud.
It does not dishonor others, it is not self-seeking, it is not easily angered, it keeps
no record of wrongs. Love does not delight in evil but rejoices with the truth. It
always protects, always trusts, always hopes, always perseveres.

1 Corinthians 13:4–7

The way a couple handles money is a reflection of their love—or lack of love—for each other. Usually conflicts about money, sex, children, or in-laws aren't the real issue at all. They're just flash points of demands and resistance. Love covers a multitude of sins and it paves the way for a wide range of solutions to any problem.

7 PRAYER STARTER

Father, this couple wants to give and receive love in every part of their relationship. Give them the ability to really listen to each other, to value each other, and to discover your wisdom about setting up separate accounts. Thank you for your leading . . .

RECOMMENDED RESOURCES : 8

Munchbach, Jim. *Make Your Money Count: Connecting Your Resources to What Matters Most*. Baxter Press, 2007.

Palmer, Bethany, and Scott Palmer. *First Comes Love, Then Comes Money: A Couple's Guide to Financial Communication*. HarperOne, 2009.

http://www.ronblue.com/

http://www.mvelopes.com/focusonthefamily/

http://www.daveramsey.com/home/

http://www.crown.org/

Tracking One's Current Financial Position

1 PORTRAITS

- Deborah came to counseling because she doesn't know what to do with her daughter. Anne has been in and out of three drug abuse treatment programs, and she's currently in jail, originally for possession and then for contempt when a drug test showed she was still using. A few minutes into the conversation, the counselor learned Deborah is in debt for $50,000 for her daughter's treatment. Her pain about her daughter's wayward life and her inability to help her change is compounded by her financial distress. "I don't know how I'm going to make it," she lamented.

- Joan's husband, Paul, walked out on her and their three children. Before he left, she learned he had gambled away all the money he had said was put into savings and investments. Paul left Joan for a younger woman, leaving her with no money, no income, a mortgage, and three kids to raise. She hoped the divorce settlement would provide enough for her to live on, but it was far below her expectations.

- Joel was completely entranced by his friend's business opportunity and he gladly wrote a big check to get in on the deal. His wife, Mary, didn't trust the friend, but Joel assured her that it would make them rich. A few months later Joel found out that the deal bombed and he lost all he had invested. Mary came to counseling because she was so mad at her husband. "That was our future he threw away!" she almost yelled.

- Steve couldn't tell which came first, the depression or unemployment. Both had dogged him for many years. He had a few jobs here and there, but nothing seemed to last. To keep his apartment and buy some food, he borrowed money from his brother and his parents, but they finally said they couldn't keep sending him money. "They cut me off," he complained, "and I don't know where I'm going to get enough money to pay the bills."

2 DEFINITIONS AND KEY THOUGHTS

- Some people go to a financial planner seeking personal counseling, while others go to a professional for psychotherapy or marital counseling not realizing that money is causing the problems in the relationship. Money troubles are a major part of their stress, and these difficulties cloud every goal and relationship.

- Some of the people who are in financial trouble have very poor habits and little discipline in handling money. They are chronically poor money managers. Others, however, are victims of others' poor choices, theft, or natural disasters. And in many cases the client's financial problems occurred because they've trusted an irresponsible person, such as an addict.

- People may need help in figuring out where they can find sources of income, how to negotiate with debt collection agencies, and how to lower their expenses. If there are immediate needs, they need help assessing their current financial position.

- It's important to help clients figure out how to pay this month's bills, but beyond the immediate need, help them develop a sound short-term (3–6 month) goal based on the realities of their situation.

- In determining the current status, look carefully at every expense and every possible source of income. Be aware that many people don't want to list some of their expenses because they're ashamed to be spending money on foolish and unnecessary things.

ASSESSMENT INTERVIEW : 3

1. Are financial problems part of why you're seeing me today? If so, how are they affecting your mood and your relationships?
2. What are your chief worries about money?
3. Do you have enough to pay the bills this month?
4. Look at your checkbook or credit card statement. Let's list your expenses from last month, including housing, food, transportation, entertainment, insurance, and everything else.
5. Is there anything you didn't want to put on the list that you need to?
6. Now let's list your sources of income.
7. Are there any other potential sources of income?
8. Look at these total expenses and income. Where do they put you?
9. How can I help?

WISE COUNSEL : 4

Double-check the client's list of expenses by looking at the total for the past month and adding up the individual items. It may be that he hasn't included things like trips to a casino, magazine subscriptions, alcohol, expensive dinners, health club dues, or other expenses that seemed reasonable at the time but now are luxuries.

Often when people who come for counseling take stock of their current financial position, they feel overwhelmed by the problem. They may withdraw into self-pity and hopelessness and they may deeply resent the people who let them down. These perceptions and responses are normal but they need to be addressed as part of the problem.

Courage is essential in taking the first steps out of the quagmire of debt. Blaming others and self-pity feel right, but they are poisonous. Individuals and couples who come for counseling will benefit from the insights of the five Money Personalities. In addition, the principles of conflict resolution and the Money Huddle will help them communicate more clearly and positively.

Help to craft small steps that can pay big dividends, such as cutting expenses by canceling magazine subscriptions and cable, cutting up credit cards and paying with cash, and not going out to eat. The person can raise some money by selling some things that have been in the closet for years and perhaps downsizing the apartment, selling a house, selling an expensive car with a big monthly payment, and paying cash for a much cheaper car.

Determine where the hottest fires are burning. If creditors are calling, teach the client to negotiate with them to work out a payment schedule.

If the person needs more help than you can give, refer him to a professional financial planner or to a church benevolence program.

5 ACTION STEPS

1. Offer empathy and support. Most people have avoided taking stock of their financial position because it makes them feel so ashamed or resentful or both. When you ask the assessment questions, look for these forms of resistance and encourage the person to be completely honest with you.

2. Facilitate understanding and communication. Explain the Money Personalities and help him identify himself and his spouse, if married. Discuss the principles of good communication and how to have Money Huddles. Give him an assignment of having a Money Huddle with his wife before the next session, or ask them to come to your office so you can facilitate the conversation.

3. Dig into the numbers. A person's resistance may cause him to "forget" some important expenses and debts. Gently ask for full disclosure. Address the fear of feeling exposed by saying, "I know this is hard but I can't help you unless we look at things objectively. We've all made bad choices with our money. Let's take a good look so you can take steps forward."

4. Determine a clear, workable plan to cut expenses and raise some money. Many people are so far in debt that they can't imagine a way out. Become a partner in finding expenses to cut and celebrate every decision to trim the fat. Some of the larger expenses, such as the mortgage and car note, may require action soon because they drain so much money every month. And look at ways to bring in some extra income. Be creative and encourage the person with each new idea.

5. Prioritize. People get into financial quicksand over years of poor decisions, and it will take some time to get out. If they think they have to do it all today, they'll feel overwhelmed. Develop a plan with several stages. Start with clear, small steps so the person can feel like a success. Monitor steps forward and move to the next phase as each one is completed.

6. If necessary, refer the person to a professional financial planner. Anyone with common sense and some experience managing his own money can help someone who is struggling with an out-of-control budget, but sometimes a client's financial struggles are too much for us. Find a competent professional in your area, perhaps one who will help people pro bono.

BIBLICAL INSIGHTS 6

Be sure you know the condition of your flocks, give careful attention to your herds; for riches do not endure forever, and a crown is not secure for all generations.

Proverbs 27:23–24

Most of the time, financial problems aren't the result of a single poor choice. They are usually the product of countless thoughtless decisions. Solomon encourages us to notice the condition of our resources so we can make informed choices.

Suppose one of you wants to build a tower. Won't you first sit down and estimate the cost to see if you have enough money to complete it? For if you lay the foundation and are not able to finish it, everyone who sees it will ridicule you, saying, "This person began to build and wasn't able to finish." . . . Salt is good, but if it loses its saltiness, how can it be made salty again? It is fit neither for the soil nor for the manure pile; it is thrown out. Whoever has ears to hear, let them hear.

Luke 14:28–30, 34–35

In this famous passage, Jesus instructs people to "count the cost" of their choices. This encouragement applies to every area of life, including our finances. In many cases people get into financial trouble because they bought things they didn't really need and they bought on impulse instead of sound reasoning. Like the man who wanted to build a tower, we need to think carefully about how we're going to pay for the things we buy, and even more, whether we need them in the first place.

PRAYER STARTER 7

Jesus, planning for the future begins with taking stock of where things are today. Help this person be honest about his current financial position so he can make informed choices. Thank you for your grace, your forgiveness, your wisdom, and the courage your Spirit gives when we walk with you . . .

8 RECOMMENDED RESOURCES

Munchbach, Jim. *Make Your Money Count: Connecting Your Resources to What Matters Most*. Baxter Press, 2007.

Palmer, Bethany, and Scott Palmer. *First Comes Love, Then Comes Money: A Couple's Guide to Financial Communication*. HarperOne, 2009.

http://www.ronblue.com/

http://www.mvelopes.com/focusonthefamily/

http://www.daveramsey.com/home/

http://www.crown.org/

Vacations

- Glen and Liz took their kids to the mountains every summer to be with Liz's parents, but this year money was a lot tighter than usual. As Liz made plans weeks ahead, Glen gave subtle hints that they might not be able to go. Finally, when Liz announced final preparations, Glen bluntly told her, "We're not able to go this year. I tried to tell you that we're broke, but you wouldn't listen." The next few weeks were painful in many ways.

- Juan and Veronica enjoyed nice vacations every summer, but their friends Rob and Janice had a ball going on several cruises and European vacations each year. They always had more pictures for Juan and Veronica to see. Veronica would like to be able to go on some of these exotic excursions too, and Rob and Janice had invited them to go along several times with them. When Veronica mentioned it again to Juan, he blew up and then growled, "We can't afford braces for one child, a violin for the other, and a new lawn mower—and on top of that drop ten grand on a vacation!" Veronica was deeply hurt. "I was only wishing we could go," she whimpered.

- Rudy and his buddy Allen competed in just about everything—at work, playing basketball, driving the nicest car, wearing trendy clothes, and other things. When Allen told Rudy he'd booked a ski trip for his family in Colorado, Rudy asked him how much he was paying. Allen proudly said, "I got the full package for $7,000." Rudy smiled and then told him, "I saw you looking at the site online, so I checked around. We'll be there with you—same place, same meals, same ski tickets, and same plane flights—but I got it all for $3,200!" Allen was not amused.

- Bryan and Angela have been going through tough times. He was laid off at his job and, after six months out of work, finally got a new job. Then Angela's job as an art teacher was eliminated at her school. They had taken family vacations to the beach every summer but this year they were on a much tighter budget. Bryan felt really bad about disappointing Angela and the kids, but she assured him, "We'll stay home this summer but we'll have the best vacation ever. We'll go to the museum, to parks, and play games. We'll have a blast!" And they did.

2 DEFINITIONS AND KEY THOUGHTS

- Americans have the fewest days of *paid vacation* of any industrialized nation. According to a 2011 survey by Expedia.com, Americans average thirteen days, Japanese workers are next at fifteen days, British employees have twenty-six days, and the French enjoy thirty-eight days of vacation each year.
- People take vacations for many different reasons. According to a survey, 69 percent planned ahead to celebrate a life event, but 31 percent took a vacation trip on the spur of the moment. In 48 percent of families, the children played an important role in planning vacations, and about 88 percent of adults went online to get travel information, plan a trip, and make reservations. About 23 percent of people visited blogs to see reviews of destinations or travel possibilities.
- In a culture that is "plugged in" and "always on," finding *down time* to reflect and rejuvenate is often difficult. Getting away is important to *relieve stress, reconnect with family members,* and *restore some creativity.*
- In some cases, however, *poor planning* for vacations increases the load of stress instead of enabling it to dissipate.
- Even the planning and preparation phase of a vacation can be stimulating. Many people pore over websites and brochures to get additional information so their time away is as meaningful as possible.
- Involving children in making vacation plans is an important part of building a strong, healthy family. Everyone can express his or her opinion, even if there's not enough time or money to meet everyone's expectations.
- *Financial limitations* may curtail some plans, but families can find ways to have fun together on a reduced budget.

3 ASSESSMENT INTERVIEW

People may come to counseling before or after conflicts related to vacations. It may seem odd to talk to people about a topic that should provide stress relief and fun, but often vacations produce lofty expectations that are easily shattered, leaving deep hurts and rifts in relationships. Explain the Money Personalities, and use these as a foundation for talking about expectations and communication.

1. How has a vacation caused stress for you?
2. What is your Money Personality? What is your spouse's? What are points at which you complement each other? What areas of finances seem to cause misunderstandings and conflict?
3. How have these misunderstandings and disagreements shown up in your vacation?
4. What are some creative solutions for funding a meaningful vacation or changing expectations?
5. How would showing love and respect to one another smooth the way to find a good solution?

6. How has the conflict and stress affected others in your family, particularly your kids but perhaps your parents and siblings too, if they are part of your vacation planning?
7. What will you do next time to avoid this additional stress in your relationship?
8. How can I help?

WISE COUNSEL 4

When money is tight, the first thing to get cut from the budget is fun—things like vacations, dates, and family outings. But those are the things that make life interesting! And what good is having a tight budget if people aren't enjoying the life they've worked so hard to build?

Even if money is tight, people should not automatically assume they can't take a vacation. Instead, they should take a good look at their budget and use these guidelines to decide the kind of outing they can afford.

- *Make it about memories and don't break the bank.* When it comes to family time, money shouldn't be your only consideration. As a family, talk about past vacations and experiences. What made them memorable? What kinds of memories would you like to make this year? Of course you want to be responsible and not blow the kids' college fund on a trip to Hawaii. Great websites for deals include www.travelzoo.com and www.bookit.com. You could always be a "tourist in your own town." Turn off your phone, don't worry about the mail, and tell all your friends you are on vacation. Then treat yourselves to the tourist activities in your area. You'll have special meals and fun memories that you usually get out of town and you'll save a ton of money while you're doing it. Make once-in-a-lifetime moments with your family without breaking the bank.

- *Start planning now.* Get your vacation on the calendar, make a reservation, arrange to take the time off from work, and start saving. We find that, if a vacation is on the calendar, we make it happen, one way or another. But if you wait until you have the money in hand to start planning, you'll never go. This can be especially true for Savers who are hesitant to spend money on anything. But by making your plans now and putting away a little money every week, your vacation will not only become more affordable, but more fun.

- *Do some homework.* Advance planning not only helps you save up for a vacation, it can give you time to really plan your vacation spending. For Savers, vacations become stressful when the little things—meals, souvenirs, taxis, tips, and so on—start adding to the cost of the trip. By budgeting a realistic amount of money for incidentals, everyone can relax. According to a 2007 survey by AAA, the average family of four spent $269 per day on food and lodging for their family vacation. Use that number as a guide for making plans.

- *Redefine vacation.* The most important part of a vacation isn't where you go but whom you're with. So if you can't afford a big trip to the ocean or family amusement park, don't go. Instead, go camping, do a bike tour, take a few day trips. Don't let the lack of money stop you from finding ways to have fun together. The whole point of healthy financial communication is making sure money doesn't rule your life. So as you look at your summer budget, provide for some fun. It will give you a great return on your investment.

5 ACTION STEPS

1. When a person comes for counseling and talks about stress and conflict related to a vacation, this problem is almost certainly only "the tip of the iceberg" of difficulties in her relationship with her spouse and family. Take time to explore her history to look for a broader pattern of hurt, disappointment, manipulation, and other difficulties.
2. Explain the Money Personalities, and invite her to identify herself and her spouse. Use this as the foundation for more discussions about perceptions, understanding, and conflict in her relationships.
3. Discuss principles of active listening, good communication, and conflict resolution. Encourage her to begin having regular Money Huddles with her husband, and give her an assignment of having one before the next counseling session.
4. Address difficulties related to the presenting problem of stress from a vacation (or stress because the family couldn't afford a vacation). Help her learn to communicate with love and respect, listening to her family and valuing them.
5. If possible, spend time helping the couple brainstorm creative alternatives for future vacations.

6 BIBLICAL INSIGHTS

Come to me, all you who are weary and burdened, and I will give you rest. Take my yoke upon you and learn from me, for I am gentle and humble in heart, and you will find rest for your souls. For my yoke is easy and my burden is light.

Matthew 11:28–30

God has given us many gifts to enjoy, including vacations, but ultimately, true rest comes only from a rich, vibrant, close relationship with him.

Peace I leave with you; my peace I give you. I do not give to you as the world gives. Do not let your hearts be troubled and do not be afraid.

John 14:27

Our culture says we must have more and go faster. We've tried that. It's exciting for a while, but we burn out and crash mentally, physically, relationally, and spiritually. When we get away, we need to remember to recharge our spiritual engines so we grow stronger in our faith in Christ.

So I say, walk by the Spirit, and you will not gratify the desires of the flesh. For the flesh desires what is contrary to the Spirit, and the Spirit what is contrary to the flesh. They are in conflict with each other, so that you are not to do whatever you want. . . . But the fruit of the Spirit is love, joy, peace, forbearance, kindness, goodness, faithfulness, gentleness and self-control. Against such things there is no law. Those who belong to Christ Jesus have crucified the flesh with its passions and desires. Since we live by the Spirit, let us keep in step with the Spirit. Let us not become conceited, provoking and envying each other.

Galatians 5:16–17, 22–26

If we have the wrong view of vacations, we actually produce more stress and conflict than if we didn't go on vacations at all. Instead, we should look at vacations as Jesus did—time with his men to rest and recharge so they could do the Father's will even more effectively.

My dear brothers and sisters, take note of this: Everyone should be quick to listen, slow to speak and slow to become angry, because human anger does not produce the righteousness that God desires.

James 1:19–20

In our relationships with our spouse, kids, and maybe others who are involved in vacation planning, we need to show love and respect. Even if we have different desires and expectations, we can love each other, listen carefully, and seek solutions that build the family instead of tearing it down.

PRAYER STARTER 7

Jesus, this person wants her family to have vacations the way you had them with your men. They want to get away to rest but also to know you and each other better. Help her not to demand her own way and give her family a spirit of love for each other—and a great time together . . .

RECOMMENDED RESOURCES 8

Munchbach, Jim. *Make Your Money Count: Connecting Your Resources to What Matters Most.* Baxter Press, 2007.

Palmer, Bethany, and Scott Palmer. *First Comes Love, Then Comes Money: A Couple's Guide to Financial Communication.* HarperOne, 2009.

http://www.ronblue.com/

http://www.mvelopes.com/focusonthefamily/

http://www.daveramsey.com/home/

http://www.crown.org/

Wedding Planning

1 PORTRAITS

- Mark and Lois's daughter Audrey was getting married, and everyone was thrilled. She had been dating Philip for two years, and they were genuinely in love. After they set the date and began talking about the details of the wedding, Mark announced proudly, "Nothing is too good for my angel!" Lois had seen this before. Mark had a history of grandiosity, which led to irresponsible behavior regarding money. The problem was that there was virtually no money in savings. At every point, Lois tried to put on the brakes and scale back the expectations and expenses, but Mark and Audrey were a powerful force that refused to be denied. Soon the battle lines were drawn. The struggle over money for the wedding became so fierce that Audrey thought about eloping. In the end, the wedding cost more than $50,000, saddling Mark and Lois with the debt. Lois felt abandoned and betrayed again.

- When Jennifer got engaged to Jon, she told her parents she wanted a simple wedding. Her parents had plenty of money in savings for a nice wedding, but Jennifer had been in many weddings where countless thousands had been spent. She met with her parents and decided on a budget. She found a dress on sale and asked friends to help with the music and food. She and Jon asked his friend William, a young pastor at their church, to marry them. Jennifer wanted to splurge in one area—she wanted a professional photographer. In the end the wedding cost less than $10,000. It was beautiful and meaningful, and it didn't break the bank.

- Tanya didn't want to talk to her parents about the finances for her wedding. At every point she insisted, "Don't worry. I'm looking after the budget. It'll be fine." Her dad told her to keep it "around $20,000," but by the time all the bills came in, the total was over $35,000. Her dad got the bills just before he walked Tanya down the aisle. He tried to smile but he was furious. It was financial infidelity, but this time it was his daughter who was unfaithful.

- By the time Barbara and Rick left the reception for their honeymoon, everyone in the family was angry. Rick's father is a respected and wealthy physician, but Barbara's parents aren't wealthy, so her father gave her a budget they could afford. Barbara and her mother just couldn't live within the budget but they didn't want to tell her father how much they were spending. Her mom told every vendor to give her the bills. "I'll take care of it," she almost whispered to each one. She knew there would be a day of reckoning when her husband learned the truth. She hoped she could put it off for a long time, but the week before the wedding, he made some calls and found out. He was livid. He blew up at his wife but tried to control his anger with Barbara. The wedding should have been a happy day in the family's life, but it was tense and bitter.

DEFINITIONS AND KEY THOUGHTS : 2

- A wedding is one of the most important events in the life of a family. It can be beautiful and full of meaning, but if the finances are handled irresponsibly, the day can be dreadful. Few moments in a family's existence produce more financial infidelity than a wedding. This creates confusion, hurt, and feelings of betrayal.
- Today the *average wedding* in America costs about $25,000. In many cases, some or all of this becomes debt incurred by the parents or the couple.
- The bride and her parents need to clarify expectations from the beginning of the planning process. If they don't agree on a *budget*, costs can spiral out of control, and even worse, each person can feel deeply hurt and angry.
- In the planning process, *creativity* and *flexibility* are helpful. For instance, the total dollar amount needs to be fixed, but the bride may want to make adjustments in spending on the individual elements. The flowers may be more important than pictures, or the quality of the food may be more important than anything else. A *fixed budget*, combined with creativity, good humor, and love, can make the bride and her parents partners instead of adversaries.
- In the process of budgeting, preparing, and carrying out the plans on the day of the wedding, working together can build the relationships instead of producing tension. In many cases emotional triangles can develop in which, for example, a bride and her mother are pitted against the dad, or the bride and dad against the mom, or the parents against their daughter. Of course, the groom and his parents are part of the mix too, so their expectations can support or explode the plans of the bride's family. Financial infidelity, based on overt demands or secrets, can cause years of heartache.
- Some parents offer financial choices to their daughter and her prospective husband. They may say, "We've saved $25,000 for your wedding. You can use it all for that day, or if you want to spend less, we'll give you the difference for a car, a down payment on a house, your honeymoon, or anything else. The difference is yours."
- The tools that work for couples—the Money Personalities, principles of good communication, conflict resolution, and Money Huddles—work beautifully in planning a wedding.

ASSESSMENT INTERVIEW : 3

Explain the Money Personalities. In many cases tension between the bride's parents is the precipitating factor that brings them to counseling. These questions are designed for the parents.

1. What are the expectations each of you has for the wedding?
2. How are these similar to or different from your daughter's expectations?
3. Do you have a budget for the wedding? Who thinks it's reasonable? Who thinks it isn't? How is the difference showing up in tension in your relationships?
4. What is your Money Personality? What is your spouse's? What is the Money Personality of your child and her fiancé?
5. What characteristics of these personalities work together well? What are some differing perceptions that are causing misunderstanding and conflict?
6. What would make this wedding a glorious event, one that fits into your financial limits but is full of love and hope for the future?
7. What conversations do you need to have to adjust expectations?
8. How can I help?

4 : WISE COUNSEL

The bride's parents need to talk openly and honestly, first with each other and then with their daughter, about the budget, expectations, and hopes for the wedding.

To create a workable budget, they should include every detail and every anticipated expense, perhaps with a category of "Other" for unexpected expenses. They should look at their savings and adjust expectations so that the event doesn't become a financial burden on the parents or the couple. They should consider asking for help from a financial advisor, getting advice about writing the budget and keeping expenses under control.

As parents talk with their daughter, they should try to make the planning process fun and meaningful, talking about the hopes and dreams of the couple getting married and the things that will be most meaningful. Parents' assumptions may be wrong, so they need to listen carefully to their daughter and prospective son-in-law's desires. To stay within the budget, they may need to be creative, set priorities, look for bargains, enlist friends, and make adjustments.

In planning for a wedding, hopes are high but emotions can be quite fragile. Watch for hurt feelings when expectations aren't met. Each person involved needs to listen carefully, avoid making assumptions, and be flexible in finding creative ways to stay within the budget while making the event very meaningful.

The principles and processes used to help couples communicate clearly and find common ground work beautifully for the bride and her parents. Use the Money Personalities, principles of good communication, and the Money Huddle.

5 : ACTION STEPS

1. Discuss the five Money Personalities, and help the couple identify themselves, their daughter, and perhaps the groom.
2. Explain the principles of active listening and conflict resolution and answer any questions.

3. Explain the significance of the Money Huddle. Help them use this process of communication to discuss the budget for the wedding, first between them and then with their daughter.

4. Discuss the budgeting process, the need to address and adjust expectations, and creativity and flexibility in planning.

5. As the parents gain confidence and reduce any chance of financial infidelity, their communication builds trust between them. Then they can enjoy the process of planning as well as the wedding itself. Encourage them to celebrate each step of the way.

6. The reason the couple came to counseling was to mend or support their relationship. Money and budgeting for the wedding was the precipitating factor, but they want to grow in trust and love. Continue to monitor their progress as they grow stronger together.

BIBLICAL INSIGHTS 6

The rich rule over the poor, and the borrower is slave to the lender.

Proverbs 22:7

In our culture, most people consider debt to be inevitable and a normal part of life, but the Bible indicates that we become slaves to those who lend to us. That means our lives, to some degree, become devoted to serve the lender. In planning for a wedding, parents and the couple need to avoid debt as much as possible.

And why do you worry about clothes? See how the flowers of the field grow. They do not labor or spin. Yet I tell you that not even Solomon in all his splendor was dressed like one of these. If that is how God clothes the grass of the field, which is here today and tomorrow is thrown into the fire, will he not much more clothe you—you of little faith? So do not worry, saying, "What shall we eat?" or "What shall we drink?" or "What shall we wear?" For the pagans run after all these things, and your heavenly Father knows that you need them. But seek first his kingdom and his righteousness, and all these things will be given to you as well. Therefore do not worry about tomorrow, for tomorrow will worry about itself. Each day has enough trouble of its own.

Matthew 6:28–34

In his most famous sermon, Jesus reminds us that loving and serving him is far more important than riches and pleasure, especially when we're spending considerable riches on pleasure that will last only a few hours. If our priorities line up with his, we can sleep well at night, enjoy relationships with those we love, and trust God to accomplish his purposes for the future.

Command those who are rich in this present world not to be arrogant nor to put their hope in wealth, which is so uncertain, but to put their hope in God, who richly provides us with everything for our enjoyment. Command them to do good, to be rich in good deeds, and to be generous and willing to share. In this way they will lay up treasure for themselves as a firm foundation for the coming age, so that they may take hold of the life that is truly life.

1 Timothy 6:17–19

Even for families with considerable resources, God still wants them to make financial decisions based on his values, not the world's. They can ask themselves why they want to spend lavishly on a wedding. Is it to honor God or to show off their wealth? Honest reflection is important all the time, but in weddings, our hidden motivations may surface more than at other points in our lives.

What causes fights and quarrels among you? Don't they come from your desires that battle within you? You desire but do not have, so you kill. You covet but you cannot get what you want, so you quarrel and fight. You do not have because you do not ask God. When you ask, you do not receive, because you ask with wrong motives, that you may spend what you get on your pleasures.

James 4:1–3

It's a tragedy when a potentially glorious day is poisoned by financial infidelity, deep hurt, and resentment. As the Spirit of God points out our sinful desires in the planning process, we have the opportunity to repent, to thank God for his forgiveness, and to change direction.

7 PRAYER STARTER

Lord, this couple needs your help. They want to honor you with their money and in this wedding, and they're not sure how to put the two together. Through the process of planning, they want to respect each other, listen carefully, and make good choices. They want all of this to build their family, not break it apart. Thank you for your wisdom and grace . . .

8 RECOMMENDED RESOURCES

Munchbach, Jim. *Make Your Money Count: Connecting Your Resources to What Matters Most.* Baxter Press, 2007.

Palmer, Bethany, and Scott Palmer. *First Comes Love, Then Comes Money: A Couple's Guide to Financial Communication.* HarperOne, 2009.

http://www.ronblue.com/

http://www.mvelopes.com/focusonthefamily/

http://www.daveramsey.com/home/

http://www.crown.org/

Workaholism

- For more than a year, Stella wondered if Gil was having an affair. He was, but not the kind she was thinking about. He left for work each day before the kids got out of bed and he seldom came home before 9:00 at night, and often later. She had confronted him several times, but he vehemently denied any sexual liaison. He always told her he had a lot of work to do, but the last time she tried to talk to him about it, he blurted out, "When I'm at work, I feel good about myself. I make a difference and I'm making money for our family. When I'm at home, I feel empty. What do you expect me to do?"

- Juliette graduated at the top of her business school and she rapidly advanced in her company. Her former friends saw very little of her, and when she finally agreed to have dinner with them, all she could talk about was her fat salary and extraordinary bonus. After the dinner when Juliette had left, two of her friends said they couldn't believe the change in her. "All she can talk about is money," one of them said, "but she thinks it's normal."

- Bart's boss loves him because he makes more money for the company than anyone else. For the last four years, he's been the top salesman and he's been richly rewarded for it. Recently he was promoted to VP of Sales and he struts around the office like Gordon Gekko in *Wall Street*. He has been losing touch with his wife, whom he now dismissively calls "the little woman at home." When she tried to talk to him about the distance in their relationship, he insisted, "Hey, my work is my life, and I love it. It puts plenty of food on the table and nice cars in the garage. Don't complain. You can buy anything you want!" She replied sadly, "But I want you."

- Tommy had always been fond of making money, but in his new career in sales, he had the opportunity to make a killing if he hit his quota each month. He was driven to be the best, but his work ethic almost killed him and his marriage. He spent long hours at work, often seeing clients after hours. He had been making a good living at his previous job, but it wasn't enough for him. He was making more money now, but he was losing his wife and kids in the process.

- *Workaholism* is a "process addiction" in which a person becomes addicted to particular behaviors (or processes) that change the chemistry of the brain, much

209

like substance addiction changes the same brain chemistry. The term *addiction* is any recurring obsession or compulsion experienced by an individual despite negative consequences in his life and relationships, coupled with the inability to cease the activity.

- A corollary symptom is *leisure illness*, a condition that occurs on weekends and vacations when the person ceases work and tries to relax but becomes physically sick.
- Typically the disorder includes *obsessive thoughts* and *compulsive behaviors*. The person can't stop thinking about work, making deals, and earning more money, and when he tries to disengage from these behaviors, he feels empty and tense.
- To these people, work has value only because it promises *status*, *power*, and *reputation*. They view money as a measuring stick to prove they are of value, so it is disproportionately important.
- In workaholism, like every other addiction, denial prevents the person from facing the consequences of his behavior. Another addictive factor, *tolerance*, causes him to desire ever-increasing amounts of success, money, and applause to fill the gaping hole in his heart.
- Often family members of addicts enable the person's destructive behavior, making excuses for him, minimizing the damage, or denying the problem altogether.

3 : ASSESSMENT INTERVIEW

Sometimes the workaholic comes for help, but more often, the spouse comes to counseling, either for personal help or to get advice about how to help the addict. These questions are designed for the spouse of a workaholic but can be tailored for use with the addict if necessary.

1. How are your spouse's work habits affecting him? How are they affecting you, your relationship, and the kids?
2. When you try to talk to him about his behavior, how does he respond?
3. When are some times when he's able to relax and enjoy you and the children?
4. Does he break promises that he will be there for you and the kids? What excuses does he give? How do you respond to them?
5. How have his emotional and spiritual health changed (if at all) since the problem began?
6. Is there anyone (such as friends, other relatives, or his boss) who applauds his obsessive-compulsive behavior about work?
7. How does he talk about money? Are you comfortable with the way he values money? Why or why not?
8. How can I help?

WISE COUNSEL 4

Workaholism is the most respected and affirmed type of addiction. Many spouses appreciate the effort and the income, and employers may richly reward it. In some companies the top management looks for people with this disorder to hire or promote them.

When the workaholic is working, his mind is obsessed with money, deals, customers, and products. When he's at home, he can't switch gears and focus on the family. He still thinks about those things and he feels guilty for not being at work.

This disorder is a form of financial infidelity, and like any addiction, the individual and the family both suffer. The workaholic misses family gatherings, is disinterested in the lives of family members, is distracted by thoughts about work and money, and is disconnected from the people he loves. The spouse and kids may make excuses for a long time, but sooner or later they feel betrayed, angry, and alone.

Workaholism, especially in its advanced stages, is an obsessive-compulsive disorder that requires clinical intervention, diagnosis, and treatment. It is a serious addiction with very destructive consequences, inflicting damage on the marriage and the family. Some studies claim that it kills more than a thousand people a year through stress-related heart attacks and strokes, but the damage to family relationships is far broader and deeper.

ACTION STEPS 5

1. When the addict is stabilized through professional care and is making progress, explain the Money Personalities so he understands himself better.
2. Explain the principles of active listening and conflict resolution, and help the client learn the Money Huddle to use with his spouse. Their first conversations might be explosive, so consider asking them to have the first one (or two or three) with you as the mediator. Address the secrets and feelings of abandonment and betrayal.
3. Continue to work with the addict to create a better lifestyle with new neural pathways based on medications and establishing new, healthy habits. Work with the spouse to assist in truth telling and setting boundaries.

BIBLICAL INSIGHTS 6

Do not wear yourself out to get rich; do not trust your own cleverness. Cast but a glance at riches, and they are gone, for they will surely sprout wings and fly off to the sky like an eagle.

Proverbs 23:4–5

The obsessive thoughts and compulsive behaviors of workaholism are seriously misplaced. They promise to fill our lives with joy and meaning if we gain status and wealth, but instead, they leave us empty, craving more, and they ruin our most cherished relationships.

One who oppresses the poor to increase his wealth and one who gives gifts to the rich—both come to poverty.

Proverbs 22:16

We may not think of our families as "the poor," but they become poor when workaholics don't value them, cherish them, and delight in them.

But seek first his kingdom and his righteousness, and all these things will be given to you as well. Therefore do not worry about tomorrow, for tomorrow will worry about itself. Each day has enough trouble of its own.

Matthew 6:33–34

Workaholics are chronic worriers. They worry about the next deal, the customers, their reputations, and the money they hope to earn, but all of this worry only short-circuits God's work in their hearts. God wants us to put him first and trust him with our future. In him are peace, joy, and true rest.

Submit to one another out of reverence for Christ. Wives, submit yourselves to your own husbands as you do to the Lord. . . . Husbands, love your wives, just as Christ loved the church and gave himself up for her.

Ephesians 5:21–22, 25

In marriage the husband and wife are to submit to one another out of love, which means putting the relationship above everything but Christ and being devoted to one another. Workaholics need to reorient their priorities.

7 PRAYER STARTER

Lord Jesus, this person has missed your best for too long. He's struggled with misplaced priorities and needs to correct that. Help him, Lord, to put you first and to value his marriage and family more than money, status, and promotions. Thank you for your forgiveness and strength. Help him trust you to lead him and change him . . .

8 RECOMMENDED RESOURCES

Munchbach, Jim. *Make Your Money Count: Connecting Your Resources to What Matters Most.* Baxter Press, 2007.

Palmer, Bethany, and Scott Palmer. *First Comes Love, Then Comes Money: A Couple's Guide to Financial Communication.* HarperOne, 2009.

Final Thoughts

Helping People in Crisis

As counselors, we have had the privilege of caring for countless hurting people over the years. They have come with histories of sadistic, chronic sexual abuse. They have come bruised and swollen because of the battering of people who were supposed to love them. They have come because spouses have left them. They have buried children and spouses. Some have lived with chronic illness—their own or another's. They have struck me dumb with the depths of their suffering. They have told stories of evil and pain that have been incomprehensible to me. They have highlighted in living color my own inadequacies and failures, and they've challenged me, frustrated me, frightened me, loved me, hated me, and enriched my life beyond words.

I assume that because you are reading this, you care about and desire to minister to people who are suffering or in crisis. A crisis is literally "a separating," something in life that is so significant that it becomes a marker—you think of life before and life after a crisis. A rape, the first time someone hits you, learning you have cancer, the loss of a child, the death of a spouse, financial ruin, and infidelity are all separating moments. Each is a turning point, a crucial time in a person's life. It is also a frightening time. The road map with which you are familiar no longer points the way. What was known is gone, what felt safe now feels unsafe, and what seemed predictable is totally uncertain. A crisis is essentially what we might call an alarm moment in a life.

Oswald Chambers talks about having "staying power in the alarm moments of others' lives." Think about those times when you have accidentally set off an alarm and you have a little flavor of what people are experiencing when they are in crisis. There is a lot of emotional noise in their lives; there is chaos. They cannot think what to do. They are afraid. They feel that they are in danger, something is wrong. They want someone to help. They want the noise to stop, the fear to subside. They want to feel safe and to be able to think.

If people seek you out during their alarm moments, one of the things they will bring you is their noise. They will walk into your life and bring anger, violence, sobbing, ranting, terror, panic, fear, and anxiety. You may even become the focus of their anger, accusations, or fear. How hard it is to have staying power at such times!

They will also bring you their silence. Pain brings silence, for often suffering is so great that there are no words. Trauma silences; death silences. The psalmist says, "I am shut up, and I cannot come forth" (Ps. 88:8 KJV). They will bring tears, sometimes wrenching sobs. We tend to respond by simply handing out tissues, which can be a subtle hint that the crying should be over by now. We prefer human beings with clean faces. We feel awkward with loud sobbing. We are uneasy in the face of unadulterated terror or pain. How are we to have staying power in alarm moments such as these?

When an alarm goes off, we want to turn it off. The noise bothers us; it disrupts our world. When an alarm goes off, it makes us want to flee—a normal response. Alarms mean things are not okay, and we want our world to be okay. Anytime a person in crisis walks into your world, you are facing an alarm moment. It is a separating time for that person. It is actually a separating time for you as well. The fact is that anytime someone brings you her crisis, the person is actually creating one for you as well. Will you enter in, and if so, how should you conduct yourself so that your presence is a help and support, not a contributor to the noise and chaos?

It is crucial that we understand something of what we encounter if we are to minister to people in crisis. There are characteristics that we need to grapple with if we are to really understand what it is we need to do. I fear we may think that helping people in crisis is simply about telling them good and true things; then they will listen and get better. But it is rarely as simple as that.

AMBIGUITY, CHANGE, AND REPETITION

One of the things you will encounter as you move in to help is ambiguity. Interactions between humans on a good day are often fuzzy and confusing. And while a life alarm is going off, interactions are frequently unclear. You think you understand an issue and then it shows up in someone's life and what you know does not seem to fit. Or someone brings you a problem, and then you realize it is not the real problem at all. People want to feel better. They want answers. You may quickly feel that you have no idea what to do or you may realize that what you thought was the right response ends up producing a more complicated mess.

Those in crisis want change—or do they? They do, oh how they do—but we forget that change makes human beings nervous. Change requires massive effort, and they are exhausted. Change is not something that usually occurs simply because someone told you the right answer. Not only that, when a person does decide to do the work of changing, he or she may make other people frightened and angry. They push back; that creates more crises! It feels as though things are going in the wrong direction!

Change is not just in the wings for the person who is suffering; it is there for you as well. Somebody in crisis walks into your life with a story yet untold. This person and their story *will* impact you. Suffering people will take you places you have never been and maybe do not want to go. You cannot let yourself down into another's life without being impacted. You cannot be present to abuse, violence, trafficking, deceit, brokenness, terminal illness, and darkness without being affected. You will find yourself thrown by the things humans do to one another. You will struggle with disbelief. You will want to say it could not be true.

Repetition is necessary for someone in crisis. You say something and then you say it again. You live it out in the flesh for him and he still questions its truth. You cannot confront the debilitating effects of chronic childhood abuse, domestic violence, oppression, or addiction without being repetitious. You speak truth and watch it devoured by a sea of lies. Over and over you rework the ground of trust, only to have someone say, "But can I trust you here too?" And so you must restate, rework, relive what you thought was so clear.

LEARNING TO WAIT

You will have to learn how to wait. You will wait for a thought to bubble to the surface of a confused mind. You will wait for truth to penetrate a dark mind. You will wait while an addict fails *again*, and old ground has to be covered again. You will wait while the Spirit of God works internally in a life with yet no outward sign of growth. You will wait because God's timetable is not yours, and he is teaching you about waiting as much as he is teaching the person you are caring for. He is teaching you how to think and love while the alarm is still going off.

You must never forget that you are dealing with a combination of suffering and sin when you work with people in crisis. Suffering silences people and scars lives. Silence and scars are not proof of sin in a life—you have only to look at the life of Christ to know that. You do not push someone to tell you how the alarm got set off while it is still screaming in their ears. At that moment they cannot think clearly.

ENCOUNTERING SIN

Sometimes we set off our own alarm moments; sometimes another has done so. Often, but not always, it is a combination. Many people suffer because of another's sin, not their own. David suffered because of what Saul did. His suffering was undeserved. Remember that when you sit across from suffering. Do not add to the burden of the suffering one by assuming the need to go on a sin hunt.

Sometimes we suffer because we live in a fallen world and no one's sin is involved. A person who lives with chronic illness is faced with never-ending grief and loss, pain and body chemicals that may result in unremitting depression, not due to sinful actions on anyone's part.

You will, of course, also encounter deep and habituated sin. Not necessarily in the person you are caring for but perhaps in others in the person's life. It is critical that we not be naive about the impact of such sin on a person's life. A woman who grew up with chronic sexual abuse has been shaped and trained by evil. A person who has endured someone else's control, rage, battering, or constant verbal abuse has been profoundly impacted in their thinking, emotions, spiritual life, and relationships. A person who has had a drug, sex, or gambling addiction has practiced self-deception for a long time and will be so wrapped up in it that truth will penetrate slowly and in very small doses. People who have been beaten down by sin for years, their own or another's, cannot stand up straight all of a sudden. People who have lived with habituated sin, their own or another's, are altered, or shaped, by that sin. Their spiritual hearing and seeing have been crippled.

We are careful about our children's diets because we know that the food they consume can affect everything, both now and in the future. We are careful about what they read or see for the same reasons. We become good at those things we habituate and we know that what is done frequently has profound consequences. If you practice silence and a blank mind to deal with battering over a period of twenty years, then you will not be able to think or articulate clearly just because someone has stepped in to help.

MINISTERING LIKE JESUS

So if simply speaking the truth is not sufficient on its own when responding to those in crisis, how can we respond so that they are helped and ultimately transformed? We can, of course, learn from our Lord. He stepped into the alarm moments of our lives. He entered the chaos and noise. He encountered the suffering and the sin of this world and had staying power. He has called us to be like him. Let us consider something of what that was like for him so that we might follow him into the lives of those he brings to us.

Leave Glory

The first thing one must do to enter into the alarm moments of others' lives is leave glory. The leaving must occur before the entering can happen. Jesus left his world, its beauty, its comfort, its safety, and its peace. He left what was rightfully his and entered what was foreign to him. He left perfect love for hatred, order for chaos, beauty for ugliness, and light for darkness. He left behind functioning as the self he is in heaven so that he might function as a self like us. He put on the cloak of humanity.

You must leave glory if you are to help those in crisis. You must leave that which is familiar, ordered, predictable, and comfortable for you. You must enter into foreign territory that you do not know, encountering what is unfamiliar. You will be forever changed by the sufferings and sin of others.

Become Little

Second, in leaving glory, Jesus became little. He is the Creator and Sustainer of the universe. He is eternal, immortal, and infinite. He became unlike himself. He reduced himself in size, power, impact, words, and potential to help. He became little for our sakes. He became like us so we could receive him. His becoming like us is a kind of listening unlike any the world has ever seen. He allowed himself, as it were, to be "taught" by us about what it is like to be human.

When you enter a life in crisis, you must become little. You will not help if you swoop in, tell people what to do, and take over. You need to leave glory and enter in, in small doses, so you can truly listen and understand and be touched by their infirmities.

If you have never been chronically sexually abused, you do not know what that kind of life is like. If you have been, you know only your experience, not theirs. Enter in, listen, live with, observe, and learn. Be little; it is about them, not you. You will put yourself into the mix by eye dropper amounts, just the way the Lord of the universe has done with you. If he poured everything in his mind into yours, yours would blow up. You could not hold it, organize it, understand it, or use it.

Enter the Darkness

Third, in leaving glory, Jesus entered darkness. He dwelt in the unfamiliar, and it had an impact on him. He, who is the beginning and the end, could not see tomorrow. He who is the light of the world was eclipsed. He who is the Word became silent. He who is perfection was scarred. His life was touched by many things that were utterly foreign to him, things that were an assault on him.

Typically, when we enter into another's suffering, we try to drag the person into our world. We want them to think what we think, choose what we would choose, understand what we see, and live more in the way we do. These are not necessarily bad goals, but you can get people to reach them only if you enter into their darkness. You must go in and get them so that you can bring them out. You cannot call people out of suffering. You must go in to them and sit with them and listen and understand, and then little by little you can begin to walk with them toward a new and different place. You cannot help if you do not enter the darkness.

Bring Christ's Character with You

Fourth, Jesus was not lost in the darkness. He brought the character of the Father with him when he became little and entered our darkness. He brought truth and love manifest in the flesh when he came and sat with us. When he came into the darkness and sat down, he was bearing the character of the Father, full of grace and truth. He lived out that character while he walked with us and ate with us and talked with us. Who he was when he was with us explained the Father to us. Light began to dawn for us because it was lived out in the flesh in front of us.

So often we think we need techniques, programs, plans—and these can all be very helpful. However, suffering and sinful humanity needs the character of God the Father manifest in the flesh before them. People do not need just knowledge about the character of God but the actual demonstration of it in the flesh, in you—his truth, his love, his mercy, and his grace. As we sit with them and live with them, they are greeted with evidence of him through us. Someone who has been abused has been saturated with evil, lies, manipulation, humiliation, and rage. Oh, how they need to sit with the loving and truthful character of the Father in you! They need more than hearing about it. They need to experience it (love, mercy, grace) in you, in the flesh.

Don't Abandon Them

Fifth, our Lord did not abandon us. He left glory and entered into our darkness and did not run, even when facing the cross. He felt like running. He was overwhelmed by what he faced but he did not abandon humanity. He did not leave us alone in our mess, our alarm moments. He does not leave us now. Had he abandoned us, we would not have ever found our way out. We could not see; we could not think; we could not walk upright. He stays and waits and calls us to come to him, to come with him.

You will want to run away but you cannot. Your client will make one phone call too many, one mistake too many, one bad choice too many. You will get weary and it will feel heavy. You will want a life free of crises and alarms. But the love of the Father does not abandon his own. Many times I see how we in the body of Christ start off well with a crisis but do not have staying power. We find it difficult to maintain connection with crises, especially chronic ones, and so we abandon those who have no choice about the presence of suffering in their lives. They are left to endure it alone. Our Friend, who entered in, never abandons us.

Maintain Spiritual Strength

Sixth, our Lord left glory and entered the darkness but he did not catch the disease from which we suffer. It is very easy when working with alarm moments to get caught up in the crisis and lose perspective. He did not. He did not sin, even when he suffered with our sufferings. He did not allow the chaos, darkness, evil, and noise to destroy him. He entered into the darkness but stayed light. He entered into frailty but did not get sick.

How can we work with people in crisis and not catch the soul diseases they bring with them? How can we have staying power in the alarm moments of others' lives? How do we maintain spiritual strength so we do not become twisted and crippled by an ongoing exposure to evil?

Staying power means having the ability to endure, holding out against discouragement, sustaining our involvement without impairment, bearing with patience the ups and downs of the relationship. If we are to help those in crisis, then clearly we need a place to stand. We will abandon them or end up impaired without that place. We will become cynical, bitter, or despairing.

Handley Moule, Bishop of Durham, said the following (slightly adapted): "If you would deal aright with the people in crisis, earnest Christian of the church, live at the Center. Dwell deep. From the person turn back evermore to Jesus Christ, that from Jesus Christ you may the better go back to the person, bringing the peace and power of the Lord Himself with you." In other words, it is only as we come to him and drink deeply that we can endure in the carrying of living water to dry and thirsty places.

THREE ESSENTIALS TO REMEMBER

I would have you remember three things if you are to minister to suffering people in the body of Christ. *First, you are doing God's work with him.* Do not make the mistake of thinking of this as your work. Yes, you are the one bringing down the character of God into flesh and blood, but it is not your work. It is a piece of the work of God in this world and he has given you the privilege of sharing in it. It is his work, the people are his people, and you are not your own. You are not the Redeemer, merely his servant.

If you remember that it is his work, you will continually run to him about the piece of that work he has for you to do. If it is his work, the results are in his hands, and you will not need to demand certain outcomes by a certain time, thereby pressuring hurting people to get better so that you feel successful.

It is not only His work to do *with* Him, but *it is his work done for him.* You are not working for the suffering; you are not working for anyone else looking for their approval or certain status in the church. You are Christ's worker, working for him. If you do the work as if it is for the suffering, then you will be governed by them. Their needs will be your ruler, and you will end up in their noise and chaos. They are central, they are considered, and they must be understood, but the work is done *in* their life and *for* your God. He says this, not that; these limits, not those; this response, not that one. The needs of others are not the call nor are they your governance. The call is from God, the governance is God's alone, and from *that* place you enter into the suffering of another.

Third, you can only do this work by God and through him. You cannot do the work of God in suffering lives, nor will you please God with your work, unless he works redemptively in and through you. The work of the Redeemer in this world is a difficult work. He was a Man of Sorrows and acquainted with grief. I prefer to be familiar with comfort. He was despised and rejected. I prefer to be honored and accepted. He took up our sickness, frailties, and disabilities. I prefer health, strength, and wholeness. He was pierced and crushed and oppressed. I prefer no injuries, no smashing, and no injustice.

I do not like alarm-moment work and I cannot do it. God has taught me through the lives of many suffering people that I cannot do his work. Yet he has called me to this work. The resolution of this dilemma has come as I have learned to bow to the work of redemption in me. I have had to allow God to alter me, fit me, for his work. If I would bend down to bear the burdens of my brothers and sisters, then I must first be made a fit burden-bearer. To be a fit burden-bearer is to be like Jesus and wherever I am not like him, I am not fit, for I will misrepresent him to those who suffer.

I can attest to the fact that working with suffering people, bending down to bear their burdens, will expose you to yourself. You can tell yourself you are very patient but unless that patience is tested, you will not know the truth of your belief. As I said early on, crises are separating, not just for the one in crisis but also for the one coming to his or her aid. You will have a time of "this is what I thought I was" and then a time of "this is who I turned out to be." God is always working both sides. He has not just called you to care for the person in crisis. He is also creating a crisis in you so that he might show you areas of yourself where you are in desperate need of his work. It is only as we bow to the work of his Spirit, exposing and calling us to repentance, that we will truly be able to go out to the circumferences and carry his grace to those in need. The call of God to care for those who suffer is ultimately a call to be made to look like Jesus Christ in this world.

THREE ESSENTIALS FOR DOING THIS WORK

One last set of things in closing. There are three essentials for doing this work. *First, you must know about people.* Read, please read. Read about trauma, sexual abuse, domestic abuse, grief, chronic illness, depression, addictions, cancer, or whatever God is bringing across your path. If you do not read and understand, you will make wrong judgments. You will expect change prematurely and you will give wrong answers. Study avidly. Listen acutely. You cannot appropriately care for people you do not understand.

Second, know God. Know his Word. Be an avid student of that Word. If we are going to serve as his representatives to others, we need to know him well. We need to be so permeated by his Word that we learn to think his thoughts. And we must remember that to know his Word, according to him, means it is woven into our lives and we are obedient to him. Where we do not live in accord with his Word, we do not truly know him.

Third, do not do this work without utter dependence on the Spirit of God. Where else will you find wisdom? How will you know when to speak and when to be silent? How will you discern the lies from the truth? How else will you love when you are weary or be patient when you are depleted? How can you know the mind of God apart from the Spirit of God? How can we possibly expect to demonstrate the character of God in the flesh apart from the indwelling power of his Spirit? How can we think that the life-giving power of Christ crucified will be released into other lives unless we have allowed the cross to do its work in our own lives? To work with crises is to work with lies, darkness, and evil. You cannot fight the litter that hell leaves in a life unless you walk dependent on the Spirit of God.

Such a work will change you; it will challenge you; it will force you to your knees, hungry for more of Christ. Frankly, whether a particular person you counsel ever changes or makes good choices or truly comes to grasp the grace of God in her life, *you* will be changed into his likeness by walking his way and learning of him.

Diane Langberg, director
Diane Langberg, Ph.D. & Associates

Dr. Tim Clinton is president of the American Association of Christian Counselors (AACC), executive director of the Center for Counseling and Family Studies, professor of counseling and pastoral care at Liberty University and Liberty Baptist Theological Seminary, and a licensed professional counselor.

Bethany and Scott Palmer, "The Money Couple," are financial communication experts and the authors of *Cents and Sensibility* and *First Comes Love, Then Comes Money.*

THE QUICK-REFERENCE GUIDES

The newest addition to the popular Quick-Reference Guide collection, *The Quick-Reference Guide to Counseling on Money, Finances & Relationships* focuses on the ever-growing need for sound counsel on financial issues. It is an A–Z guide for assisting people-helpers— pastors, professional counselors, and everyday believers—to easily access a full array of information to aid them in formal and informal counseling situations.

Women have unique needs and unique problems that require understanding, empathy, and direction from their pastors and counselors. For anyone who is called to counsel women, *The Quick-Reference Guide to Counseling Women* will be a welcome guide to bring hope, life, and freedom to women in need.

Youth culture changes rapidly, so those in the position to counsel and advise teens often find themselves ill-informed and ill-prepared to deal with the issues that youth routinely encounter today. *The Quick-Reference Guide to Counseling Teenagers* provides the answers, addressing the following issues: sexuality, stress, drugs and alcohol, parent-adolescent relationships, and culture and media influence.